The Changing of Organizational Behavior Patterns

*Classics in Organization
and Management Series*

Robert T. Golembiewski, Series Editor

The Changing of Organizational Behavior Patterns,
Paul R. Lawrence

The Costs of Federalism, Robert T. Golembiewski
and Aaron Wildavsky.

The Human Group, George C. Homans, with new introductions by
A. Paul Hare and Richard Brian Polley

Integrating the Individual and the Organization, Chris Argyris

Ironies in Organizational Development,
Robert T. Golembiewski

Men, Management, and Morality, Robert T. Golembiewski,
with a new introduction by the author.

Organization Development, Robert T. Golembiewski.

The Changing of Organizational Behavior Patterns

A Case Study of Decentralization

PAUL R. LAWRENCE

With a New Introduction by the Author

Transaction Publishers
New Brunswick (U.S.A.) and London (U.K.)

New material this edition copyright © 1991 by Transaction Publishers, New Brunswick, New Jersey 08903.

Originally published in 1958 by Division of Research, Harvard Business School. Copyright © 1958 by the President and Fellows of Harvard College.

All rights reserved under International and Pan-American Copyright Conventions. No part of this book may be reproduced or transmitted in any form or by any means, electronic or mechanical, including photocopy, recording, or any information storage and retrieval system, without prior permission in writing from the publisher. All inquiries should be addressed to Transaction Publishers, Rutgers–The State University, New Brunswick, New Jersey 08903.

Library of Congress Catalog Number: 90-23238
ISBN: 0-88738-894-9
Printed in the United States of America

Library of Congress Cataloging-in-Publication Data

Lawrence, Paul R.
    The changing of organizational behavior patterns: a case study of decentralization / Paul R. Lawrence.
       p.   cm.
    Originally published: Boston: Division of Research, Harvard Business School, 1958.
    Includes bibliographical references.
    ISBN: 0-88738-894-9
    1. Organizational change–Management–Case studies. 2. Organizational behavior–Case studies.   3. Decentralization in management–Case studies. I. Title.
HD58.8.L38   1991   90–23238
658.4'063–dc20   CIP

Contents

	INTRODUCTION TO THE TRANSACTION EDITION	ix
I	INTRODUCTION TO THE ORIGINAL EDITION	1
II	TRADITIONAL ORGANIZATIONAL BEHAVIOR	7

History of the Industry . . . Food World—1935: *Physical Arrangements; Organizational Behavior Patterns* . . . Food World—1954: *Physical Plant and Work Procedures; Top Management Behavior; District Manager Behavior; Assistant District Management Behavior; Store 20; Department Manager Behavior; Store Clerk Behavior (Requirements of the Job; Attitudes Toward Company, Future, Job, Supervisors, Other Departments, Customers, Cashiering, Part-Timers; Work Activities and Interactions; Summary); Organizational Behavior—1954*

III	PLANS FOR CHANGING ORGANIZATIONAL BEHAVIOR	45

Management Appraisal—1954: *Industry Trends; Internal Organizational Problems* . . . Reorganization Plans in Management Terms: *General Objectives; Top Management Structural Change; Store Manager Plan; Middle Management Changes, New Control Procedures; New Communication Procedures; Summary* . . . Reorganization Plans in Researcher's Terms: *New Required Role—Store Manager (Activities, Interactions, Sentiments); New Required Role—District Manager (Activities, Interactions, Sentiments); Management Change Methods*

IV	A CHANGED SUPERVISORY PATTERN	69

Behavior Pattern, DM1 and SM1: *Initial Indoctrination; Routine Supervision, DM1–SM1;*

Routine Supervision, SM1—Store Personnel; Relations with Merchandisers; Comments on DM1–SM1 Relationship; Summary

V A CHANGING SUPERVISORY PATTERN 97
Behavior Pattern, DM2 and SM2: *Initial Indoctrination; Routine Supervision, DM2–SM2; Relations with Merchandisers; Routine Supervision, SM2—Store Personnel; Summary*

VI AN UNCHANGED SUPERVISORY PATTERN . . . 115
Behavior Pattern, DM3 and SM3: *Initial Indoctrination; Routine Supervision, DM3–SM3; Routine Supervision, SM3—Store Personnel; Relations with Merchandisers; Comments on DM3–SM3 Relationship; Summary; Conclusion*

VII INTERACTION PATTERNS—THREE DISTRICT MANAGERS 130
The Research Method . . . Results: *Summary*

VIII SELF-CONCEPTS—THREE DISTRICT MANAGERS . 142
Self-Concept, DM1: *As a District Manager; As a Superior; As a Subordinate; Summary of DM1; Attitude Toward Reorganization* . . . Self-Concept, DM2: *As a District Manager; As a Superior; As a Subordinate; Summary of DM2; Attitude Toward Reorganization* . . . Self-Concept, DM3: *As a District Manager; As a Superior; As a Subordinate; Summary of DM3; Attitude Toward Reorganization* . . . Conclusions

IX TWO YEARS LATER—RESULTS AND INTERPRETATION 174
Evidence of Changed Behavior: *District Managers—Changes in Behavior; Store Managers—Changes in Behavior; Summary* . . . Influencing Behavior Patterns: *Direct Influence on Interac-*

tions; Influence by Prior Consultation; Influence by Changes in Personnel and Structure; Influence by the Behavior Patterns of Superiors; Influence by the Peer Group; Influence by Subordinates; Influence by Organized Training Programs; Summary

X CONCLUSIONS 206
Achievement of Organizational Purpose . . . Achievement of Self Maintenance and Growth . . . Achievement of Social Satisfactions . . . Multi-Functional Approach to Changing Behavior . . . Ethical and Societal Considerations . . . The Adminstrator's Role in Changing Organizational Behavior

Appendix: Methodology of the Measurement of Interaction Patterns 229

Bibliography 235

List of Exhibits

1	Partial Organization Chart, 1935	12
2	Partial Organization Chart, 1954	16
3	Floor Plan, Store 20	25
4	Organization Chart, Store 20	27
5	Partial Organization Chart, 1955	70
6	Prevailing Conditions During Observation of DM Interaction Patterns	133
7	Percentage of DM and SM Talking Time by Categories	134
8	Percentage of DM–SM Talking Time by Topics	137
9	Percentage of New Topics Initiated by DMs and SMs	138
10	Average Duration of a Single Comment	139
11	Comparison of DM–SM Talking Time in 1955 and 1957	176
12	Comparison of Average Duration of a Single Comment in 1955 and 1957	178
13	Interactions and Activities of Store Managers Six Months and Two Years After Reorganization	181
14	Initiation of Interactions by Store Managers Six Months and Two Years After Reorganization	182
15	Percentage of SOM and DM Talking Time by Categories in One-to-One Conversations	196
16	Percentage of SOM and DM Talking Time By Categories in Meetings with all District Managers	196
17	Sample Interaction Scoring Sheet	231

Introduction to the Transaction Edition

The republication of this book prompted me to read it from cover to cover for the first time since it was written over thirty years ago. As the reader can imagine, it was quite a trip down memory lane for me. The leading characters came back to mind in sharp focus. My many days visiting supermarkets with district managers were again vivid. Prompted by these memories I got in touch with the person who had been the most senior executive in the study. Identified in the text only as the Vice President of Sales, he is, of course, now retired as are all the other principals who are still living. He kindly authorized me to make public in this introduction the rather poorly kept secret that "Food World" has actually been a rather thin disguise for Stop and Shop Inc., the well-known regional supermarket and discount store chain. He is Irving W. Rabb, widely known in the industry for his long and distinguished career in retailing.

In our conversation Irving made an intriguing observation. He commented that organizational issues and people do not really change. "You know, Paul, the book is as relevant today as it was in 1958." That remark prompted me to focus this introduction on testing his observation.

The central theme of this book is the management of organizational change. Even an incomplete listing of the books that have been published on this theme since 1958 indicates the continuing importance of the theme. (See Bibliography, p. xi). Publication dates suggest an even increasing interest. In the business community generally organizational change is now seen as a survival issue. The vocabulary for talking about it is sometimes different: today we might talk about organizational transformation rather than organizational change, and the change toward decentralization might be labeled a move toward employee involvement or employee commitment. But the basic ingredients of organization change remain the same. The levels of change we would think about today are all discussed to some degree in this study: goal clarification, structural change, executive replacement, educational programs, evaluation and feedback systems, reward systems, modeling desired behavior, and coaching. As would be considered desirable today, the study addresses change at both the individual (micro) level and at the system (macro) level. It connects personal meanings and self-concepts to the overt behavior expressed in superior/subordinate interactions. Its ties change at this day-to-day behavioral level to the strategic vision of the entire firm. It identifies and describes the stickiness that makes behavioral change difficult. It is the type of longitudinal and dynamic study currently recommended.[1] It combines the rigor of quantitative data with the clarity of a descriptive qualitative story.

Even the choice of the specific industry (retailing) and the specific issue (the role of store personnel in decision making) seems pertinent. Many industries in the United States have come under severe competitive challenge from overseas. During the seventies it was the steel and auto industries that were in the spotlight for losing the competitive battle. The eighties brought little respite for these industries even as machine tools, electronics, and consumer products generally were slipping on the global scene. Now the service industries such as retailing, long considered invulnerable, are under severe competitive pressure. Within the field of retailing probably the hottest competitive issue is the shifting of merchandise ordering decisions to store personnel so that these decisions can be responsible to local customer tastes as well as to more general economic trends. This was the same competitive challenge that the Stop and Shop change effort was addressing.

Having rather immodestly said all of the above, I must confess that this book reads today as a somewhat naive account. Its chief fault probably is that it makes organizational change seem too easy. Research and experience in the intervening years have clarified that such changes involve shifts in power that tend to be resisted and fought in subtle but effective ways. Managers can find many excuses for not sharing power with subordinates. Being a "bossy" boss was undoubtedly a source of personal pleasure to DM3. So role structures have self-perpetuating mechanisms that often prevail even in the face of strong economic pressures. Given these new insights, the considerable success of the change effort carried out by the top management team at Stop and Shop is even more instructive today than it was in the fifties.

The issue of organizational change clearly poses a complex and difficult leadership challenge. It is my hope that the republication of this book will renew its contribution to meeting this challenge.

Paul R. Lawrence
Boston, Mass.

Note

[1] Organizational Science, Vol. 1, No. 3, 1990; Special Issue; Longitudinal Field Research Methods of Studying Processes of Organizational Change.

Bibliography

Beckhard, R., and Harris, R.T., *Organizational Transitions: Managing Complex Changes*, (2nd ed.) Reading, Addison-Wesley, 1977.

Beer, Michael; Eisenstat, Russel; and Spector, Bert, *The Critical Path to Corporate Renewal*, Boston, HBS Press, 1991.

Beer, M., *Organization Change and Development: A Systems View*, Glenview, Scott, Foresman, 1980.

Bennis, W.G., *Changing Organizations*, New York, McGraw-Hill, 1966.

Golembiewski, R., and Keipper, Alan, *High Performance and Human Costs*, New York, Praeger, 1988.

Goodman, P.S. and Associates, *Change in Organizations*, San Francisco, Jossey-Bass, 1982.

Huse, E.F. and Cummings, T.G., *Organization Development and Change*, St. Paul, West, 1980.

Kanter, R.M.; *The Changemasters: Innovation and Entrepreneurship in the American Corporation*, New York, Simon and Schuster, 1981.

Killman, R.H., Covin, T.J. Associates (Eds); *Corporate Transformation*, San Francisco, Jossey-Bass, 1987.

Kimberly, J.R. and Quinn, R.W., *New Futures: The Challenge of Managing Corporate Transitions*, Homewood, Dow Jones-Irwin, 1984.

Lawrence, P. and Dyer, D., *Renewing American Industry*, New York, Free Press, 1983.

Mohrman, Allan M., Jr., Mohrman, Susan Albers, et. al., *Large-Scale Organizational Change*, San Francisco, Jossey-Bass, Inc., 1989.

Nadler, D.A., and Tushman, M., *Managing Strategic Organizational Change*, New York, Delta Consulting Group, 1986.

Quinn, J.B., *Strategies for Change: Logical Incrementalism*, Homewood, Irwin, 1980.

Tichy, N., *Managing Strategic Change*, New York, Wiley, 1983.

Tichy, N.M., and Devanna, M.A., *The Transformational Leader*, New York, Wiley, 1986.

Zaltman, G., and Duncan, R., *Strategies for Planned Change*, New York, Wiley-Interscience, 1977.

Foreword

In 1952 the Division of Research published a volume by Professor Lawrence and Miss Harriet Ronken entitled *Administering Changes: A Case Study of Human Relations in a Factory*. That study dealt with the human effects of technological change in the day-to-day operations in a factory, the resultant social dislocations, the effects on the attitudes and relationships of the people involved, and the supervisory problems involved in the assimilation of and adjustment to technological change. The authors found that the stickiness encountered in assimilating technological change stemmed primarily from the required changes in the activities of people and from the new types of behavior and interactions being introduced into a theretofore relatively stable social system.

This study also deals with the administration of change, not technological change affecting workers and supervisors but organizational change affecting personnel at management levels. The setting of the study is a medium-sized supermarket chain in which several important management functions were being shifted from the home office to newly created store managers. The origin and reasoning behind these organizational changes, the methods of introducing the changes, the process of shifting the organizational roles of key individuals, and the consequences of the changes on the organization are considered by Professor Lawrence.

The study draws heavily for concepts and research methods on the numerous earlier studies in the field of organizational behavior which have been made at this School and elsewhere, as well as on the related literature of the behavioral sciences which underlies this broad field. The study breaks new ground, however, in devising techniques to measure changes in the behavior patterns of individuals, in focusing attention on the behavior of persons at the management levels of an organization, and in clarifying the stubborn facts of human behavior involved in changing administrative patterns.

This study was financed from a broad grant of the Ford Foundation in support of the research program of the School. We are indebted to the Foundation for this continuing support of our research.

BERTRAND FOX
Director of Research

Soldiers Field
Boston, Massachusetts
June 1958

Acknowledgments

The researcher of organizational behavior asks a great deal of the companies and the individuals he studies. This was especially true in this study. The time, patience, and friendliness the people of Food World generously extended to me were only the lesser of their contributions. Their biggest gift was their willingness to share their personal thoughts and feelings, their innermost worries and aspirations, with a researcher they knew was committed to making a published report. This was particularly true of the three district managers around whom this study concentrates. These men read the parts of the manuscript pertaining to themselves, and approved them for transmittal to their supervisors without requesting a single significant change. The sales vice president, in turn, released the entire manuscript for publication without suggesting a single change. In this fashion these men demonstrated their willingness to sacrifice some of their rights to privacy to make a contribution to our understanding of business organizations. It is to these men, who must remain anonymous, that I feel most deeply indebted.

It is a pleasure to acknowledge my grateful indebtedness to the following additional people for their help on this study:

To Professor James V. Clark for his perceptive assistance in the field work and his helpful ideas on the form of the research report.

To Professors F. J. Roethlisberger, R. A. Bauer, J. C. Bailey, and A. F. Kindall for reading the manuscript and pinpointing places that needed improvement.

To Professors C. R. Christensen, J. D. Glover, R. L. Katz, E. P. Learned, G. F. F. Lombard, H. Raiffa, J. R. Surface, and A. Zaleznik for their timely advice and encouragement.

To Mary Fuller Bailey for her skill and patience in typing all the drafts of the manuscript.

To Ruth Norton for her expert and rapid guidance of the manuscript into published form.

To Professor Bertrand Fox, Director of Research, for his helpful comments on early drafts of the manuscript, and his steady support of the entire study.

To Dean Stanley F. Teele for making this study possible.

Although this study would have been impossible without the assistance of many people, I, of course, assume full responsibility for the data and the conclusions.

PAUL R. LAWRENCE

Soldiers Field
Boston, Massachusetts
June 1958

*The Changing of Organizational
Behavior Patterns*

CHAPTER I

Introduction

THIS BOOK presents the study of a systematic attempt by management to change some basic behavior patterns in a large organization. Since man first began to use complex formal organizations to serve his purposes, there has been thinking, talking, and writing going on about the nature of organizations. Only recently, however, has come a fresh burst of interest in making the organization the focal point of systematic research and theory building. This new interest is reflected in many recent books.[1] The interest undoubtedly springs from many reasons but four are especially important.

One reason is the increasing importance in our society of the large business organization. Big business is not new but it has had such an increasing influence on our culture in the last few decades that the need to understand its significance for our times needs no demonstration. Many critics of large-scale business organizations have centered their comments on the influence big organizations have on the individual. They see and fear excessive conformity to organizational codes. They are afraid that individuals lose their capacity for independent thought in these organizations. One of the themes of this study will be the impact of organizational change on the individual and the question of conformity.

The second source of this new interest comes from the rapid development of the behavioral sciences. There has emerged only recently many new conceptual tools and research methods for man's study of his own behavior. The early efforts in this field have focused primarily on the study of individual behavior and the study of entire cultures. More

[1] See the Bibliography for references to some of these books.

recently there has been increased interest in using similar methods for the study of intermediary social levels—the small group and the formal organization. This present study centers on organizational behavior while drawing on methods and insights that have come from the entire field of the behavioral sciences.

Another source of the increased research interest in large organizations stems from the observation that these organizations are strategically in a position to greatly influence human behavior—for better or worse. Large organizations, more than any other social units, have been the center for deliberate and conscious efforts to plan and control man's behavior, and with good reason. Organizations are big enough to justify the costs of careful planning of behavior, and yet small enough to encourage man in the belief he can see some results from his own efforts. And it has also long been believed that those who would change man's behavior are wise to work on his basic institutions as the strategic leverage point. This study focuses on such an effort to change the behavior patterns of people by organizational influences, and addresses the question of the nature of organizations as change agents.

A final source of interest stems from the practical administrator's increasing tendency to look to systematic research for help in handling his "how to do it" questions about organizations. This study is also concerned with the problems of organizational change from the point of view of the responsible business administrator. The researcher first became intrigued in making this study by talking with a small group of executives who were determined to effect some basic changes in the traditional behavior patterns within their organization. To these men understanding the nature of their organization and determining how it might be changed were not academic issues. And from the beginning of this study, at the risk of losing his own objectivity, the researcher has also been concerned with the practical questions of change methods and their results.

The situation described to the researcher by these executives was ready-made for study. The researcher, as a student of organization, was bound to be interested in the opportunity to study on a firsthand basis a systematic attempt at changing organizational behavior. But the project took on added interest because of the particular kind of change that was being planned. The executives involved were planning a concerted effort to "decentralize" their chain of supermarket stores. (The term "decentralization" inadequately describes their organizational plans but it must serve for the moment.) Their motivation for this change came from two principal sources. First, they believed that the company needed to move in this direction to compete more effectively in its industry. Secondly, they believed that such a move would make their organization a better place to live and work. This dual motivation added to the attractiveness of the project. Furthermore, the planning for the changes was nearly complete and the researcher could be present at their inception. The company was big enough to provide an example of the reorganizational problems of a large-scale enterprise and small enough so that the researcher would not get lost. The top management group was highly articulate and highly cooperative. The researcher was intrigued, and the project was undertaken.

Upon undertaking the study, the researcher's first problem was to state and clarify the research questions that were to be answered and the research methods to be used in securing these answers. The researcher finally settled on two major sets of questions which in turn required the use of two quite different types of research methods. The early part of the research effort was concerned with the questions: What is the nature of the basic behavior patterns in this organization? What are the key factors involved in changing these patterns? These questions called for the use of the dual research methods of direct observation of behavior and interviews. The researcher spent many days talking to people at all levels in many parts of the organization and observing them going about their work. He kept voluminous field notes of what they said and did. His research interviews were open-ended—he was interested in what the individual thought was important to describe about his job and his work relationships. He observed what people did, with whom they dealt, and the way they handled themselves in these relationships. Out of this part of the study grew the researcher's answers to the first set of questions that are reported in Chapters II through VI.

Chapter II presents a description of the supermarket industry and of the Food World [2] organization as it existed in 1935, and again as of 1954. This chapter is designed to give perspective on the organizational changes to come. Top management's conception of where it wanted to lead the organization, and how it started to do it, will be presented in Chapter III. Chapters IV, V, and VI present a description of some of the experiences the company had in implementing its reorganization plans. These three chapters focus on the experience of three district managers, key middle-management people who each supervised a group of supermarkets. As the story unfolds, it will become clear why these district managers were selected for an intensive study of the problems of implementing the company's plans. The chapters describe these three men going about their work of breaking in some new store managers in three different supermarkets. This description gives a "feel" for the day-to-day problems that these people experienced in implementing top management plans and their contrasting ways of handling these problems. It also reveals the key factors that were controlling the implementation of the reorganizational change and thereby provides the basic groundwork for proceeding to the second major set of research questions.

The second set of questions this study addresses was: Did a significant measurable change occur in the behavior patterns of people? If so, how was it accomplished? To answer

[2] This name and all other names of persons and places have been changed to disguise the source.

these questions the researcher had to adopt some quite different research methods. He had to find ways of measuring the key behavior factors that constituted the desired changes and then get a "before" and "after" measure of these variables. The "before" measures were taken during the initial stages of the reorganization effort and are reported in Chapters VII and VIII. The "after" picture was taken two years later and it is reported and interpreted in Chapter IX. Chapter X states the conclusions that can be drawn from this study and its general implications for administration of organizational change.

Now for a word on presentation. Throughout this study the researcher will be switching back and forth between two different levels of description of behavior. This is done to handle a dilemma that is posed as soon as one starts to study human behavior. On the one hand, there is the risk of getting buried in a welter of detailed observations of behavior that would not lend themselves to systematic presentation or to drawing useful conclusions. On the other, there is the risk of dealing only in highly abstract statements about behavior that are apt to lose a clear relation to everyday life. To try and avoid these risks, the researcher will give the reader a rich enough description of the experiences of this company so that the reader can appreciate the intimate day-to-day problems that the people of this company had in striving to change the patterns of their daily work behavior. It is our hope that the people involved in this story will "come alive" for the reader as they were for the researcher. On the other hand, the writer will also be presenting a description that will lend itself to making certain generalizations from this company's experiences. From time to time in the book the reader will be asked, in effect, to step back ten paces to take a more abstract and generalized look at the situation. At these stages, we shall be using more "high level" terminology and drawing on concepts of our own definition and others that have proved useful in the fields of psychology, anthropology, and sociology to help us conceive in more transferable terms the significance and meaning of the experiences of the company. The writer is mentioning this aspect of the book now to try to get the reader's willingness to make these jumps from one type of description to the other. And as a first test of this willingness we need now to define some of the terms that will be used in the succeeding chapters.

While there is a rich everyday language for talking about organizations, there does not exist a very adequate language for talking about an organization with precision and, in places, we shall need some fairly precise terms. I have just used the term "organization." This requires our first definition.

In this study we shall be conceiving of a formal organization as a social system that is formed to serve certain purposes, and to which individuals and small groups act as contributors.[3] Each organization exists in an environment that determines certain required behavior that the organization must perform if it is to survive. Each organization, with its required behavior as a starting point, evolves behavioral characteristics that are unique to it and tend to persist over time in certain patterns. For the purposes of this study we shall treat the elements of behavior as activities (what people do—walk, sit, talk, etc.), interactions (verbal and nonverbal contacts between people), and sentiments (what people feel and think—likes and dislikes, attitudes, beliefs, etc.).[4] We shall be using this conceptual framework to talk about what happened at Food World when we want to make a more general statement, but in the next chapter we shall be using more everyday language to describe the traditional characteristics of the Food World organization and its industry.

[3] Chester I. Barnard, *The Functions of the Executive* (Cambridge, Harvard University Press, 1946). See especially Chapter VI.
[4] George C. Homans, *The Human Group* (New York, Harcourt, Brace and Company, 1950). See especially Chapter II.

CHAPTER II

Traditional Organizational Behavior

THE YEAR 1954 was in many ways a crucial year of decision for the Food World Company. The time was ripe for a change. The company operated a chain of slightly over one hundred supermarkets in parts of three states. Its sales and profits had been growing, but slowly, during the previous five-year period. Some top management reassignments had cleared the way for change. The vice president of sales characterized the need for change:

> These stores on our extremities are sick. I must have key people in my organization out there in the field, and these people must have a breadth of vision. We must have a *decentralization* of thought, action, and authority, or we will kill our circulation in the extremities.... Sixteen of our stores are now doing over $2 million in sales each year, and we're going to be opening stores of that size at the rate of one per month. It is inconceivable that these stores are operating with *no one over-all store manager*. How can we build a $200 million business unless we have wide-awake businessmen running our stores?

These few words summarized Food World's problem and top management's answer to that problem.

But there were still many questions to be answered. The vice president of sales recalled the most crucial question he was asked by one of the top executives:

> How can we get a different outlook in the stores when they are being supervised by our old line managers? How can you expect to introduce change down the line through a manager like Mr. X?

In response the vice president of sales asked a question of his own:

> Would you like to fire Mr. X and our other old-timers like him?
> No, I wouldn't.
> Then we have no choice but to get busy and train them.

So in 1954 the commitment was made to introduce some drastic changes in the organizational behavior patterns of Food World. The commitment was made to introduce the change without replacing the existing management personnel. The problems would be many. The risks were high. But we are getting ahead of our story. To understand the nature of the organizational changes at Food World, it is necessary to look backward as well as forward.

Organizational behavior patterns change slowly, and future patterns must of necessity be evolved from the historical patterns of the company and the industry. In this chapter we shall be looking at the recent history of the supermarket industry and more particularly at the traditional behavior patterns of the Food World organization. This look will provide our base line, the reference point from which we can analyze the organizational changes that are the focus of this study. What kind of an organization was it that top management planned to change?

History of the Industry

One indication of the rapid change that has come in food distribution in the last two decades is that twenty years ago the "supermarket industry" was nonexistent. Of course, there was a food distribution industry two decades ago and we are well aware of the changes in the American culture that contributed to transforming it into the supermarket industry. We are probably not so aware of the magnitude of changes within the industry. A brief look at these historical changes will give perspective to changes within the Food World organization itself.

The most obvious change has been in the size of stores. In 1935, only 3.9% of the food sales of the country were handled through stores that did a business of $300,000 or more per year and there were only 479 such stores in the country. In 1955, 59.7% of all food sales were handled through store units that had a sales volume of $375,000 a year or more per year.[1] Another way of stating the phenomenal growth of the large supermarkets is to look at the change in opinion as to what constituted the optimum size store. In January 1937 the trade journal *The Progressive Grocer,* stated in an article: "Under average conditions, *maximum* operating efficiency is reached when a store has from $100,000 to $150,000 volume [per year] and any more volume sometimes impairs its efficiency."[2] In 1955 virtually all the 2,260 new stores that were built were supermarkets, and most of these were built to do a volume of more than $1,000,000 per year. In the same year, 1955, 11,000 small stores ceased operation.[3]

Along with the trend to larger stores was a similar trend from service to self-service markets. The trend toward self-service operations in grocery stores started first with the dry grocery items and has more recently been adopted in meat departments and in fresh produce departments. The exact amount of this change is difficult to measure, but *The Progressive Grocer* estimated that in 1955, 35% of all meat was sold on a self-service basis and of course a much higher percentage of groceries was handled in that fashion.

It is estimated that in the middle thirties a good grocery store handled somewhere around 1,000 different items. By 1955 this had grown to a point where a well-stocked super-

[1] *The Progressive Grocer,* "Self-service Stores, and Supermarkets," (undated supplement).
[2] *The Progressive Grocer,* "Facts in Food and Grocer Distribution," January 1937.
[3] *The Progressive Grocer,* March 1956.

market was carrying some 5,000 items. This growth reflected the addition of completely new product lines like frozen foods, bakery mixes, drug items, and other nonfood items, and also the addition of a much larger variety of items in all staple lines. And not only was the number of items growing by leaps and bounds, but there was also a continuing trend toward prepackaging of all items handled.

The past two decades had also seen a drastic revision of the merchandising methods used in this industry. During this time it had become essential to provide adequate parking space as a part of the usual service to customers of a supermarket. There had developed a widespread use of promotion premiums, stamp plans, and give-aways. There had been increased emphasis of both newspaper advertising and point-of-sale merchandising.

During this same period of time there had been a continuing trend toward reducing the gross profit margins in supermarkets. This meant that the industry had been putting increasing emphasis on cost reduction and controlled payroll and had been working under a severe and constant competitive price pressure.

This brief summary of the more important changes that have come to this industry in the last twenty years gives a picture of revolutionary change, but the figures alone do not adequately portray what these changes meant to the people working in the industry. We shall get a better look at this by taking a look at what was happening to the Food World organization during this period of time.

Food World—1935

Physical Arrangements

In 1935 the Food World Company was a medium-sized chain of small neighborhood grocery stores that were scattered throughout a large metropolitan area. At this time the company owned and operated 600 of these stores and the average store had an annual sales volume of $30,000. The typical store put its emphasis on the sale of dry groceries. This merchandise was arranged around the store on shelves and on table counters. These were service stores. A customer was taken care of by a clerk who walked around to pick up the different items of merchandise that the customer wanted. Each of these stores was typically manned by a head clerk with two or three assistant clerks. These stores had no parking lots and some of them offered a delivery service to their customers. By present-day standards they offered a very limited selection of merchandise. The company put a heavy emphasis on giving personalized attention and service to their customers. In these small stores the problems were relatively simple and the work that had to be done was obvious. Employees were expected to work hard and become proficient in all aspects of store operations.

Organizational Behavior Patterns

The people who worked for Food World in 1935 attributed the growth and development of this chain of small grocery stores almost entirely to the drive and leadership of one man, the president of the company. This man had, at a very early age, taken over the management of the Food World organization and had made most of the decisions as the company grew to be a medium-sized chain. Most of the employees in the chain felt they knew him personally and spoke of occasions when he would drop in on the different stores for a quick visit. The old-timers at Food World who remembered these days were not nostalgic for the long hours of hard work at low pay, but they spoke with pride to the researcher about "the old days" when they worked for "that great guy [the president]." The president, in turn, believed in looking out for his employees and strong bonds of loyalty were built up on this paternalistic basis.

The formal structure of the company in 1935 was a simple one. As Exhibit 1 indicates, the supervision of the stores

EXHIBIT 1

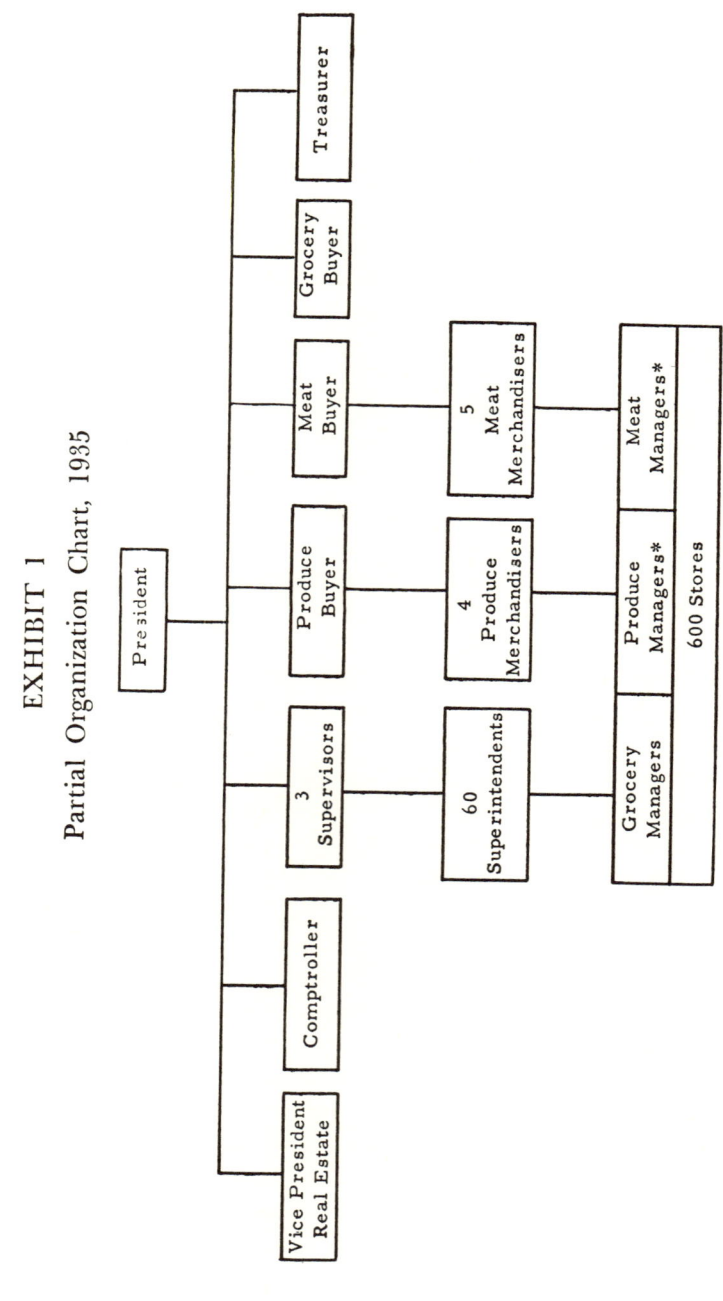

Partial Organization Chart, 1935

* These positions existed in relatively few stores.

was principally carried out by 60 field superintendents, each of whom supervised around 10 grocery stores. These 10 stores constituted a relatively small "territory" and as one executive put it, "in those days, a superintendent could practically cover his territory on a bicycle." This allowed the superintendents to make the decisions on even the details of store operations and to become intimately acquainted with the store people and their problems. In its larger stores the company was just beginning to sell meats and fresh produce, and the sale of these items was supervised from the home office by the men who were buying them. This meant that in these larger stores, there were three supervisors coming into the stores from the home office to supervise the three major product lines.

In comparison with the relatively simple problems at the store level, the problems of the company's home office were complex. The emphasis at the home office was on the intricate problems of buying, promoting, warehousing, and distributing products to the many store units. Given the nature of the business, it is not surprising that Food World followed the industry in running a highly centralized operation with close authoritarian supervision of store personnel mollified by a paternalistic interest in their well-being.

Food World—1954

Physical Plant and Work Procedures

The physical plant of the Food World Company in 1954 bore very little resemblance to what it had been in 1935. While the sales of the company had more than tripled, its number of store units had declined to a little over 100. The typical store in the chain now, along with its parking lot, covered nearly half a city block. It employed (counting both full-time and part-time workers), upwards of 50 people in the store. The work of these people had become much more specialized, and the emphasis had shifted from waiting on customers to such basic functions as materials handling, packaging, shelf-stocking, record keeping, and cashiering. The store sold its products on a completely self-service prepackaged basis including meats and fresh produce. It relied on many different kinds of merchandising methods—huge island displays, large-scale newspaper advertising, raffles and give-aways, special sales of premium merchandise, and trading stamps. Of course, in all these changes Food World had been following and sometimes leading the trends of the entire food distribution industry. But to the people within the Food World organization who had seen these changes and worked to bring them about, the magnitude of the changes often struck them as being something akin to a miracle. One of the executives put it this way:

> I remember in the first store I ever went into we did a meat volume that first week of $126. We thought we were doing very well. Nowadays we open up a store and we're unhappy if it doesn't do $10,000 in meat the first week. If it doesn't do $10,000, we've flopped. Now we have a chain of 100 supermarkets of that kind. I could never have visualized this a few years ago.

The physical plant of the company and its work procedures had been revolutionized during these years.

Top Management Behavior

In 1954 the same man was still the chief executive officer of the company. By 1954 he was playing a somewhat less active and obvious role in the supervision of the entire organization, but, nevertheless, he was still the dominant figure in the business and was making most of the key decisions in the conduct of the business. He was a man with tremendous personal energy and a very quick mind. He had a facility for speaking to people in a personal way and for doing favors for people that built up strong personal loyalties to himself. He was receptive to new ideas but probably generated more ideas and instructions than he received from others. He had a tendency to give instructions to people without regard for organizational channels. He gave close personal attention to the pay system and the promotion and demotion of his management people.

The president had surrounded himself with key top management people who are most important to our understanding of the organizational behavior patterns in effect in 1954. (See Exhibit 2 for a chart of the formal organizational structure in 1954.) This group was composed of people who had come into the business at the higher management level from other companies and of a smaller group that had worked their way up through the ranks of store supervision with Food World. A minority of them had had a college education. All of them had had extensive experience in the food distribution field.

Most of these men could best be characterized as shrewd merchants and hard-driving bosses. This was particularly true of the vice president of merchandising and the senior buyers who reported directly to him. Different executives in the organization characterized the vice president of merchandising in the following terms:

> He likes to go for big promotions and big merchandising stunts in order to get high volume business. He is frequently jumping around from one thing to another in order to promote volume.
>
> * * * * *
>
> He's a man who comes up with a lot of ideas, but he isn't always willing to work through regular organizational channels to get things done.
>
> * * * * *
>
> He tends to want perfection in the way things are carried out, and sometimes he blows up when he doesn't get it.

The senior buyers who worked immediately under this

EXHIBIT 2
Partial Organization Chart, 1954

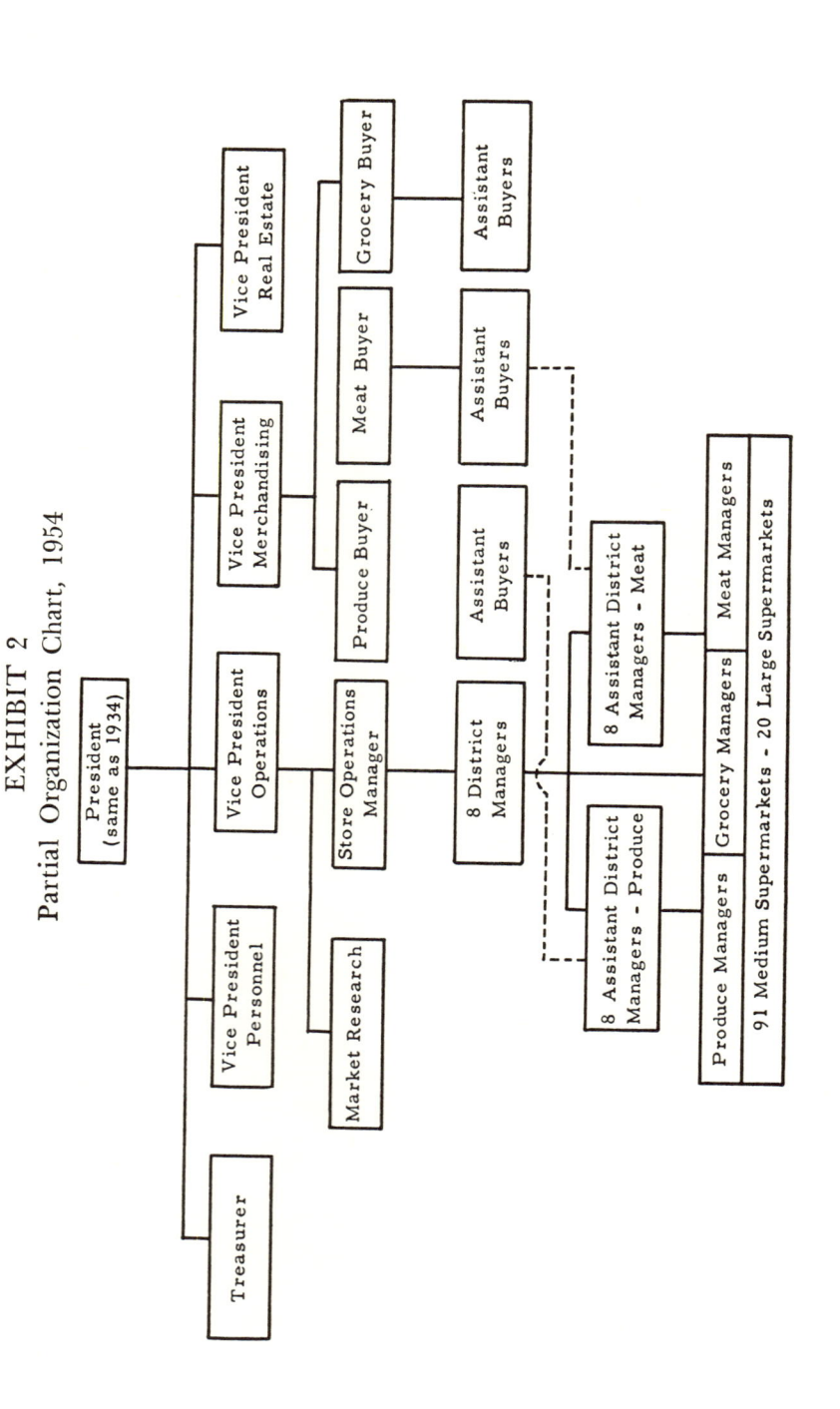

- President (same as 1934)
  - Treasurer
  - Vice President Personnel
  - Vice President Operations
    - Market Research
    - Store Operations Manager
      - 8 District Managers
        - 8 Assistant District Managers - Produce
        - 8 Assistant District Managers - Meat
        - Produce Managers | Grocery Managers | Meat Managers
        - 91 Medium Supermarkets - 20 Large Supermarkets
  - Vice President Merchandising
    - Produce Buyer
      - Assistant Buyers
    - Meat Buyer
      - Assistant Buyers
    - Grocery Buyer
      - Assistant Buyers
  - Vice President Real Estate

man were very influential with the president and were considered by others as "having a lot of weight" in the organization. A subordinate of one of these men said:

> My boss is a shrewd gambler, a man who does a lot of worrying and thinking about his job and is very uneasy about the different big purchases he has to make, in terms of whether or not he's going to be able to get his money out of it. He prides himself on being able to predict what's going to happen in the market and in making good buys.

In speaking of his job, this man said:

> It's not uncommon for us to pay $6,000 for a carload of perishable stuff knowing that the best we can do is to get our money back. We gamble that money to make an impression on the customer.

Another key man was in charge of store operations and the immediate boss of the district managers. He was spoken of as a "driver" by other members of the organization. As one executive put it:

> He saw his job as putting the heat on the district managers to get what top management wanted. He would call them into regular meetings and spend all the time criticizing their performance and telling them what he wanted them to accomplish. He didn't consider it part of his job to represent their point of view in the deliberations of top management.

This top management group was oriented toward keeping up with and, if possible, keeping ahead of the competition in the industry. They were striving to introduce the changes into their organization that they saw as necessary in order to keep ahead competitively. This involved a heavy emphasis on keeping their physical plant and their store procedures up to date. They put a heavy emphasis on introducing new merchandising methods and on making shrewd purchases. They were constantly initiating new ideas within the organization and gaining satisfaction from this activity. They spent most of their time at the home office working out their plans and problems with one another. They saw themselves as competing with one another for the recognition of the president to whom they felt a personal loyalty. They spent relatively little of their time and energy in trying to keep in touch with what was actually going on in the stores. They were, however, issuing orders and pushing to introduce their ideas into these stores. They primarily relied on the district managers to see that their instructions were carried out in the stores.

These top management people were not the only members of top management. Another group of executives with somewhat different ideas and methods will be described in the next chapter. The men described above, however, and their way of running the business, had had a strong influence throughout the organization and this was still true in 1954. Their philosophy and their way of dealing with their subordinates were reflected in the behavior of the district managers who in turn supervised the stores.

District Manager Behavior

The district managers were responsible for the field supervision of the company stores. While the stores were much larger, the job of supervising them was comparable to the jobs of the superintendents twenty years earlier. The district managers spent almost their entire work time making regular supervisory visits to each of the stores in their territory. The researcher spent a great deal of time traveling with these district managers as they called on their stores. The account that follows presents a summary of one such visit by a district manager to a store. This particular visit has been selected because it seems to the researcher to typify the pattern that the district managers were using in supervising their stores in 1954. The district manager who was involved in this instance was one of the more senior district managers in the company. The store he was calling on was a medium-sized store in the chain that had been opened shortly after World War II. It did an average weekly business of about $35,000.

The district manager entered the store at about 10:30 in the morning and spent an hour and a half making his supervisory tour. When the district manager first entered the store, he was approached by the grocery manager who stayed with him the rest of the time he was in the store. The district manager first asked the grocery manager if the store had sufficient food carriages for its customers. They discussed whether or not a shortage of carriages had caused a jam-up of customers on the previous weekend. The district manager raised a question about the arrangements for personnel assignments in the meat department, and the two men were joined in this conversation by the meat assistant district manager.

The district manager led the grocery manager to the store's one small office, took a notebook out of his brief case, and began to go over a long list of figures. This operation lasted for about 20 minutes and consisted primarily of the district manager's reading off to the grocery manager the figures he had received from the home office on the recent operating results of the store, while the grocery manager wrote the figures into his own records.

The district manager then asked the grocery manager what his recent experience had been with bad checks. The grocery manager spoke of the difficulty he was having in teaching his cashiers to distribute trading stamps properly. The district manager asked what the grocery manager was doing to keep the right kinds and amounts of grocery bags on hand. He then asked about the sales of cakes and made a suggestion on how it might be improved. The district manager told the grocery manager about a new form he was to fill out as a check on the store's housekeeping procedures.

The district manager then suggested that the two men take a tour of the basement. As they walked along, the district manager pointed out damaged goods that ought to be cleaned up. He gave the grocery manager some suggestions for rearranging some of the merchandise. He initiated a discussion of how to handle some extra coffee that the grocery manager had in stock. He discovered some damaged carriages in the basement and told the grocery manager to put in a request that these be repaired. He discussed with the grocery manager the handling of a question involving who should have the keys to certain areas of the basement.

The two men then went out into the parking lot area outside the store. The district manager pointed out some broken bottles that should be cleaned up. He pointed out some light bulbs that had been broken. The grocery manager complained that some of the boys in the neighborhood were breaking the bulbs as fast as they could put them in. The district manager expressed his sympathy with the problem. This ended the district manager's visit to this particular store, and he moved on to the next one.

As we were leaving this store, the reseacher asked the district manager whether or not he thought the grocery manager would be able to get all the things done that he had called to his attention.

DM: Well, that's a good question. I don't think he really will be able to do it all. He's just going to forget some of it. Of course, most of the things I gave him are routine stuff that any good grocer would do as a matter of course. And, in time, he'll get most of it done. Now I know for a fact that those signs in the window haven't been fixed since I mentioned them to him last week and they may not be fixed in another week, and I'll mention them again. You can't expect him to get everything done, but you do expect him to keep moving along on these jobs and taking them as fast as he can and fix up his store. Of course some of these things I'm telling him about, I'll forget myself. But most of the things, I'll try to follow through on and check on them again.

In this account of a district manager's supervising the

store personnel, we see him spending most of his time and effort in giving the store people instructions from the headquarters of the company on the kind of performance they wanted in their stores. We see him going into many details in trying to get the stores to measure up to these standards. He saw his job somewhat as a combination of passing on instructions, inspecting the store, and following up to see that instructions were carried out. In doing this he often felt squeezed between what top management was asking him to accomplish and what he saw as the problems and limitations on what could be done in the stores. He resolved this conflict partly by worrying and working harder, partly by pushing the conflict down onto store supervision, and partly by condoning a certain amount of sub rosa slippage between what was expected and what was done. He had found from experience that he could allow some slippage without getting in trouble because of inconsistent follow-up on orders from top management. In most matters he tended to identify more with the problems of the store people where he spent most of his time than with the problems of the home office people. Note that the district manager described above offered his sympathy with the difficulties of carrying out his instructions. But he knew his sympathies along these lines must not get in the way of his continuing to push to achieve the desired results.

This gives a rather unattractive picture of the district manager's job, but it was not without its satisfactions. The district manager worked out his own daily schedule. He saw his boss at home office meetings every two weeks and between these meetings he received instructions by mail. Occasionally some "brass" would make the rounds of his stores with him, but this happened rather infrequently. He enjoyed this mobility and relative freedom from close daily supervision. He did not feel free to initiate new ideas, but he did feel some freedom in choosing how he would get the results that were expected of him. His job as a "traveling supervisor" gave him considerable prestige in the organization. When he walked into a store, he was treated as "the big boss." So his job had its satisfactions even though he was not given much chance to participate in decision-making and even though most of the district managers knew they were not being considered for any further promotion within the company.

Assistant District Manager Behavior

In 1954 each store was still broken into three separate organizational compartments: grocery, meat, and produce. The district manager was the boss of all three, but he was given two assistant district managers to handle the detailed supervision of the perishable departments. The only significant change between the Food World organization charts of 1934 and 1954 (see Exhibits 1 and 2) involved the new position of these assistant district managers for meat and produce. In 1934 these perishable supervisors had been working directly under the meat and produce buyers. In the early fifties they had been shifted to report to the district managers, but in 1954 they still received many of their instructions from the buyers.

The researcher had a number of opportunities to observe the meat and produce assistant district managers as they supervised the work of the perishable departments in the stores. The incident described below was selected as highlighting the way these men traditionally supervised a perishable department.

> The researcher was in the store when the assistant district manager entered. He proceeded to walk around in the produce department and look at the appearance of the tables. At this time, the produce manager of the store was out of the store for the customary coffee break. When the manager returned, the assistant district manager walked with him into the produce back room and started reading down a list of items that he had noted that he didn't like about the store setup.

ADM: I don't see why you've got some of your potatoes up there on the end rack. They shouldn't be there. They should all be in the stack of regular potatoes. You could put turnips up at that spot. You've got them down below now. Another thing I notice, you're practically out of the cider business out there. Haven't you got some cider you can put out there and sell?

The above comments were typical of six of the different directions he gave. Meanwhile, the produce manager said nothing and continued to work packaging merchandise in the back room. As soon as the assistant district manager stopped reading off his list, the produce manager walked out to the selling part of the produce department and began immediately executing the six suggestions. During this entire exchange, the produce manager had said nothing.

The assistant district manager commented to the researcher about this particular produce manager: "You know, this fellow here is a very bright guy and he knows a lot about this business. He's had a lot of experience in it, but something is wrong in his store every time you come in. Anybody you talk to in the business will tell you the same thing. He never quite seems to produce."

A little later the produce manager gave the researcher his reaction to the assistant district manager's supervision: "Well, you can see what he had me do and you know it really doesn't make any sense. The front table is practically empty of oranges and what I ought to be doing right now is getting that table filled up so that we can have something to sell the customers. But I've learned the hard way that what I have to do is what he says. Get the potatoes out of there and put the turnips up. I don't see that it makes any difference but I don't question it. I used to question things like this but not any more. I've learned that what they want in this business is yes men, so I yes them. If I had learned that when I was younger, I would have been an assistant district manager myself by now and long before this fellow made it."

In this incident we see a somewhat extreme but not unusual example of how the perishable departments in the stores were supervised. It clearly fits with the pattern we saw with the district manager. The assistant district managers were thought of as a combination of understudy to a district manager and "pusher" for the ideas and instructions of the perishable buyers. They took their instructions from different home office people but tended to model their supervisory methods to those of the district manager with whom they often traveled in making their supervisory rounds. It was common for the district managers to see their two assistants as protégés, and they shared their problems of dealing with the home office and getting results in the stores. The assistant district managers aspired to be promoted to the job of district manager or, if they were very fortunate, to a job as a buyer in their specialty.

The incident described above also gives us our first look at a store employee's reaction to the supervision he was given. In this instance, we see his silent compliance with orders and his later expression of resentment at his treatment. This glimpse needs a more complete description of behavior at the store level before it can be correctly interpreted.

Store 20

In order to round out the picture of how the Food World organization did its business around 1954, the researcher decided to spend some time in a store that he selected to be typical of the units the company was operating at this point of time. Once this store had been selected (which we shall call store 20), the researcher spent several days in the store talking to the personnel and observing them as they went about their daily routine.

Store 20 had been built by the company very shortly after World War II. In the mid-1950's, this store was doing an annual sales volume of $1.25 million. This was more than the chain average but less than the company's newest stores that normally did a business of over $2 million a year. Store

TRADITIONAL ORGANIZATIONAL BEHAVIOR 25

EXHIBIT 3
Floor Plan—Store 20

Customer Parking Area

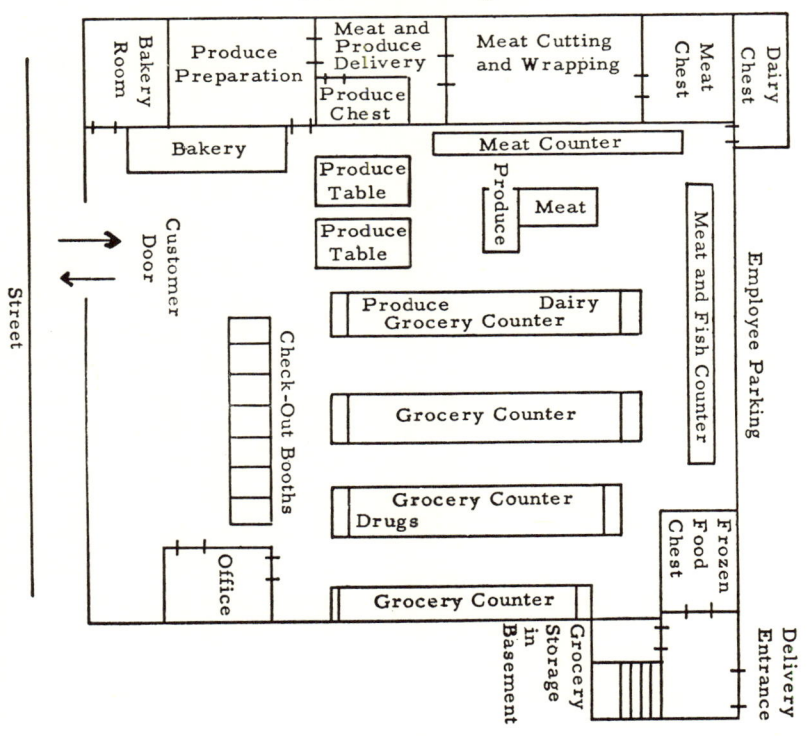

[Floor plan diagram showing: Bakery Room, Produce Preparation, Meat and Produce Delivery, Produce Chest, Meat Cutting and Wrapping, Meat Chest, Dairy Chest, Bakery, Meat Counter, Produce Table, Produce, Meat, Produce Table, Customer Door, Check-Out Booths, Produce Dairy Grocery Counter, Grocery Counter, Meat and Fish Counter, Employee Parking, Grocery Counter Drugs, Frozen Food Chest, Office, Grocery Counter, Grocery Storage in Basement, Delivery Entrance, Street]

20 was in all respects a full-fledged supermarket. It had a good-sized parking lot and had a complete line of merchandise for sale on a completely self-service basis. This included prepackaging of meats and prepackaging of many of the fresh produce items. The physical layout of the store is indicated in Exhibit 3.

Store 20 employed 16 people on a full-time basis including the 3 departmental managers in the store. It also employed 17 people on a part-time basis. Each of these people was assigned to one of the store's three separate departments and reported to the departmental manager. The way in which these people were formally organized is indicated by the organization chart of the store, Exhibit 4. Almost all the full-time men in the store had completed their high school education. Two men in the store had finished one year of college. Most of the personnel of the store were young. The grocery manager was 36; the produce manager, 40; the meat manager, 23; the full-time grocery clerks ranged in age from 21 to 29. In terms of years of service in the Food World organization, the grocery manager and the produce manager had the longest service—each having 18 years. The full-time grocery clerks had an average of three years in service with the organization. In terms of ethnic background, the group was a mixture primarily of Irish, Italian, Polish, and Jewish.

Like all the clerks within the Food World organization, these clerks were members of one of two unions: the meat cutters' union or the grocery clerks' union. These unions had negotiated a rather elaborate pay schedule that governed the pay of these people. Through a man's third year with the company, seniority governed his pay rate, but as he received promotions to and above the job of head clerk, his job classification and the size of his store determined his pay.

Department Manager Behavior

The researcher observed that the grocery manager of store 20 spent more than half his time in the store office. In this office he kept the store's records which included cash records, payroll records, and a variety of other company records. He also spent an appreciable amount of time cashing checks for customers. Aside from working in the office, he spent about one-fourth of his time around the front end or, in other words, around the check-out booths. He did some supervision of the cashiers at that position and did some talking to customers in the handling of customer complaints. He divided the rest of his time among the various back rooms, in the bakery area, and on the grocery floor working with the grocery clerks directly.

EXHIBIT 4
Organization Chart—Store 20

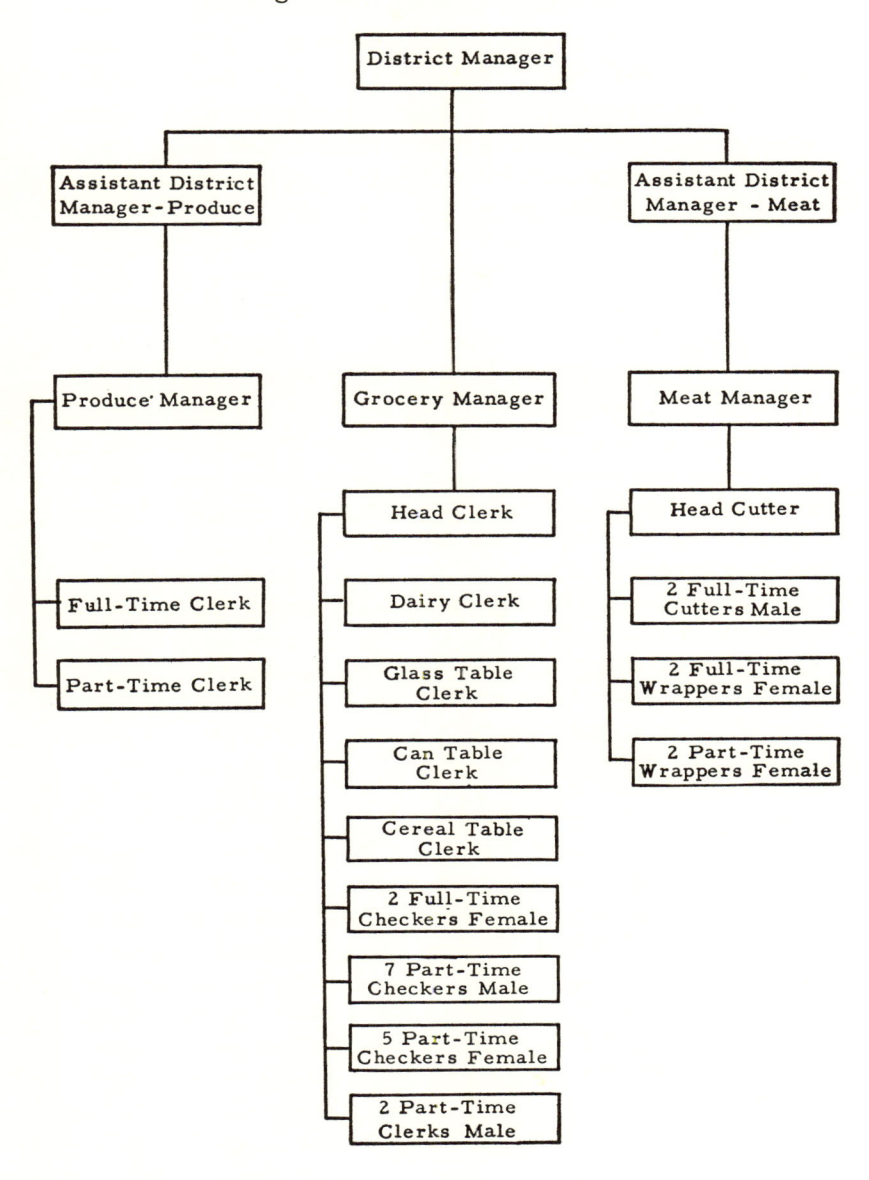

- **District Manager**
  - **Assistant District Manager - Produce**
    - **Produce Manager**
      - Full-Time Clerk
      - Part-Time Clerk
  - **Grocery Manager**
    - **Head Clerk**
      - Dairy Clerk
      - Glass Table Clerk
      - Can Table Clerk
      - Cereal Table Clerk
      - 2 Full-Time Checkers Female
      - 7 Part-Time Checkers Male
      - 5 Part-Time Checkers Female
      - 2 Part-Time Clerks Male
  - **Assistant District Manager - Meat**
    - **Meat Manager**
      - **Head Cutter**
        - 2 Full-Time Cutters Male
        - 2 Full-Time Wrappers Female
        - 2 Part-Time Wrappers Female

In contrast to the grocery manager, both the produce manager and the meat manager spent almost all their time working directly with the merchandise. The produce manager split his time between the produce back room and the area around the produce selling tables. He was observed as being busy during almost the entire day either preparing produce in the back room or putting it on the display tables. Likewise, the meat manager split his time between his back room and his selling counters. He spent more time than the produce manager discussing the work with his meat cutters and meat wrappers, but most of his time was spent in personally doing a variety of jobs in all parts of his department.

During the course of a number of conversations with the researcher, these managers told how they thought about their jobs, their company, and the people they worked with. Without exception, these three managers spoke highly of their jobs and of the company they were working for, but they had some reservations. They all wished they were allowed to have more discretion in the way they ran their store. Many of the instructions they received from district supervisors did not make sense to them in terms of their view of what would be best for the store. They quite often felt pressured to get certain results that they thought were virtually impossible. For example, they could not see sometimes how to meet simultaneously the demand for cleaner stores and the demand for a reduced payroll. One of them complained:

> My district manager never really takes a look at the things I am doing. I don't think he really knows what is going on in my store.

But they had learned to expect to be criticized and given detailed instructions when the district supervisors made their visits to the store once or twice a week. They saw these visits as a necessary evil. The meat manager who was new to his assignment found there were still many details of his job that he was having to work hard to learn. The other two managers felt confident about knowing all the requirements of their jobs and seemed to be learning little that was new. Nevertheless, they spoke with enthusiasm of their enjoyment of the work itself.

All three men were hoping to progress further in the organization. Two of the managers felt that they should have progressed faster in the past and believed that promotions were somewhat a matter of luck. As one of them said:

> As I told you before, I've been held back three years in the company because I got on somebody's black list. I'm getting older and smarter about a lot of things. I always used to say exactly what I felt was the thing to say. But now I figure that the company wants some other things from me so I'll play it their way. I don't want to get pushed back again.

Both the grocery manager and the produce manager felt that the most important part of their job was in their handling of their subordinates. The grocery manager put it:

> If you handle your people right and get the work out of them, the rest of the job will take care of itself.

The meat manager felt that the most important part of his job was being an expert on his merchandise and knowing how to handle it properly. All three of the managers seemed to be judging their subordinates by two things: by the amount of work they did, and by "the way they used their brains." The grocery manager explained that he could tell pretty well how a clerk was doing by whether the man was able to keep his grocery display counters well-loaded and neat. The grocery manager believed in being very frank with all his employees and told the researcher of several incidents where he had made it very clear to his subordinates what he expected of them and he reported that he was getting good results from his people by doing this.

The three department managers spent very little time talking or working with one another. Even though management encouraged temporary exchanges of help between departments, it was done rarely and only observed twice in store 20. As one of the managers stated:

> There is good feeling between departments in this store, but each manager here pretty much runs his own end of the business.

The department manager's efforts were focused on the immediate day's work that he was responsible for completing. He supervised the work of the clerks but often by the example he himself set of working hard and steadily on the job at hand.

To round out our picture of the Food World organization in 1954 we shall look at the behavior of the store clerks—or more precisely, the full-time grocery clerks of store 20. We shall look first at the requirements of the job, and then the actual attitudes and activities of the clerks.

Store Clerk Behavior

Requirements of the Job: The jobs of the grocery clerk were many and varied. Each of the full-time male grocery clerks had been assigned a section of the grocery counters as his personal responsibility to keep clean and loaded with merchandise. The clerks spent more than half of their time at this assignment and this tended to be a somewhat solitary job. These men spent approximately a quarter of their time in the back rooms of the grocery department. While they were in the back rooms, they were engaged more in group work. At this time, they were unloading the trucks that were delivering merchandise to the store or loading up their own hand wagons with the merchandise they would subsequently put on their shelves. In addition to these primary jobs of keeping their shelves loaded with merchandise, the clerks were asked to do a wide variety of work around the store. A

TRADITIONAL ORGANIZATIONAL BEHAVIOR

listing of these jobs will give an idea of the nature of this work and its great variety. The list helps to explain why no one expressed boredom about his work.

> Grocery area: Change price marks, straighten up merchandise, clean the shelves, sweep the floor, order merchandise, take inventory, answer customers' questions, plan displays, put up island displays, allocate shelf space, talk with direct vendors.
> Front end: Ring the cash registers, bundle groceries into grocery bags, bring in carriages from outside the store, arrange carriages inside the store, carry bundles out to customers' cars, pick up the cash from the cash register, balance the register, talk with the customers, clean the parking lot, clean the cash register booths.
> Bakery: Make up the order, put the merchandise on the shelves, change prices, check the order, straighten up the merchandise, tie up the bakery boxes.
> Back Room: Straighten up the bottle returns, clean up, unload trucks, stack cartons, take inventory, fill out forms, allocate space.

At one time or another the grocery clerks were expected to work on all these assignments. The reasons why each of these jobs needed to be performed were usually very obvious to all. To coin a phrase, the jobs had a high visibility of purpose. The jobs ranged from unskilled work that any raw recruit could do to fairly skilled operations. Probably the most skilled operation they were expected to perform was the filling out of the grocery order to be sent to the company's warehouse for future delivery to the store. This required the exercise of judgment in forecasting future sales.

The full-time girls in the grocery department were expected to spend almost all their time in the check-out booths ringing the cash registers. They spent a small portion of their time putting merchandise on the drug counter and cleaning up around the front end. The part-time male clerks spent most of their time around the front end of the store ringing cash registers, bundling groceries, and cleaning up. As they became more experienced they were given opportunities to help in the main body of the grocery floor.

Attitude Toward Company: Without exception, the grocery clerks felt that Food World was a good organization to work for. One man commented:

> We just got a new contract signed today and it is a really good one. The fellows over at the X stores were crowing about theirs, but ours is much better. I've been in this store three months. During the last three years I've been at fifteen stores altogether. It's really a great idea to move around to all of those different places because there's no other way I could get the training I need. Nowadays the grocery business is a science and the only way we can learn that science is to get training in a lot of different places. It's really a very good idea.

One of the clerks expressed some reservations about this generally favorable attitude toward the company in the following terms:

> Sure, this business is O.K. The company's only fair though. The majority of the people do get a fair shake and I suppose if you don't get one you can always ask for a transfer to another store in another district or just get out.

Attitude Toward Future: All the men the researcher talked to wanted to "get ahead" in the company and felt reasonably optimistic about their chances. They all expressed interest in the expansion program of the company and this seemed to encourage them as to their prospects. One man commented:

> I guess I'm due to move out of this store any time now. Usually a year in one spot is about the length of time you

stay in any place in this company. You know they move us all over the place. I really think that that is a wonderful idea because there is no other way in which we have the opportunity to get the experience that we need to get ahead.

One man expressed the apparently general attitude that it took time to get promotions.

When I first came with the company, I figured I would work a few years and then get my promotion. Well, that's the wrong idea. It just doesn't happen that way. You just can't expect to go up overnight. I figure if I get a promotion in another year, which will give me four years with the company, I'll be really lucky. I'm not really expecting anything. Not that quick. You got to put in your time.

Attitude Toward Job: The male grocery clerks saw their jobs as centering around the stocking of their grocery shelves and keeping them in good shape. They spoke with pride of their responsibility for doing this. As one of them commented:

I have the responsibility for this whole aisle and do all the ordering and everything else. This kind of setup is different from store to store, but most of the bigger stores are doing this nowadays and I think it's a good idea because it gives us a chance for experience all up and down the line.

These men took pride in their jobs even though they knew that many people outside the business did not think highly of the job of grocery clerking. As one man said:

You know, you tell someone on the outside that you are in the grocery business or that you want to stay in the grocery business and they look at you like you were a jerk or something. I think this job is interesting and takes a lot of experience to really get to know how to do it right.

Another man, in speaking of his reason for liking store 20, said:

> It's like going to school. That's why I think being in this store is such a wonderful experience because if I make some kind of a mistake and I've got complete responsibility for it, it gives the assistant or the manager a chance to come up to me and say, "Well, I think you were a little heavy on canned soup this week and why don't you try to lay off a little bit next week and maybe it will work out better." I've got the feeling now that if I get promoted out of here to a bigger store, I'll have confidence and ability to handle any kind of a grocery table.

Attitude Toward Supervisors: The clerks made a variety of comments about their local supervision, but in general they seemed to respect their grocery manager and their head clerk. One commented, after being told by the head clerk to change some of his merchandise:

> What are you going to do. He is the boss. What the hell! All that because he just wants the tomato juice together. I was only going to put it about five feet away. Now he's got me moving everything. Well, he's the boss; that's the way things go, you know.

Another clerk spoke of one of the few instances where the researcher was aware of the clerks engaging in anything that could be classified as horseplay. The clerk commented:

> You know, the only time I've ever seen the grocery manager really mad at us was the day when we were goofing around down in the basement and we took four hours to unload a load that really should have only taken us an hour. We were really going at it. Yelling at each other. The grocery manager really got sore. I've never seen him so mad before or since. We were unpacking Mickey Mouse hats. They sent a couple of guys down to help us and we wouldn't let

anybody down in the basement unless they wore a Mickey Mouse hat. When the head clerk came down, we told him we wouldn't let him in unless he put on a Mickey Mouse hat. I thought he was going to blow his cork. Then we took the Mickey Mouse hats up in the front end and gave them to all the girls to wear. We told them it was a new big promotion the company was having.

These clerks had some of the same reservations that the grocery manager did about the district manager. They felt that he was inclined not to give a clerk who was in trouble a second chance, and they felt that he made more promises than he could deliver on. These men also tended to join the department managers in resenting some of the recommendations for change that were relayed to the store from headquarters. When their department managers permitted it, they were glad to engage in sub rosa avoidance of these instructions. One controversial subject in the company was a new procedure for ordering groceries that many of the clerks resented since they saw it as reducing the discretion they could exercise in the groceries they ordered. One of the clerks commented on this:

> Yeh, we're going on the new ordering system now. The stock takers were in here yesterday and I guess they really raised hell with us so we've got to go under the system. It will never work in here but they don't know that. We don't have enough room in our basement. I'm going to put a lot of my items on shelf stock so I won't have to worry about the new ordering system. I can order as I please.

Attitude Toward Other Departments: The grocery clerks had very little to do with the personnel in the perishable departments in the store and that is the way they seemed to want it. One of the clerks worked on an aisle that was immediately adjacent to the meat department, and, although he worked alongside some of the people in the meat department, the researcher never saw them speak to each other. The researcher asked one of the clerks whether he ever had coffee with the people in the meat department who made their own coffee in their back room. He replied:

> Hell, no. You start eating with them meat bastards and they'll start acting like you're *obligated* to them or something.

Attitude Toward Customers: The grocery clerks spent relatively little time talking to customers on their average work day. Most of these were occasions when customers would ask for help in finding some item. The clerks saw these customer contacts as nuisances that interrupted their primary job of loading their shelves. The clerk who put it in the following strong terms was not exceptional:

> Oh, God; I must spend an hour during the day with those customers. I tell you, so many times I'm standing right in front of some can and some damn dumb customer comes up and asks for it. Oh I tell you, I feel like telling those people, "Look, lady, why don't you use your eyes instead of your mouth." They really give you a pain.

This attitude of the clerks toward the customers was a contrast to that of the department managers who spent a fair amount of their time talking to customers and handling their complaints. The managers saw the customers as being crucial to their achieving the volume of sales they wanted and they tried to keep the customers happy. The grocery manager put it:

> Well you know the manager's biggest concern is customer relations. You have to do everything you can to please your customers. When you first start in this business, you don't always recognize how important that is.

Attitude Toward Cashiering: Grocery clerks were called to help at the check-out booths when long lines of customers formed there. The clerks' attitude toward being called to the front end was similar to that held toward the customers. They saw it as an interruption in the important part of their work. When the researcher asked a clerk if he ever went to the front end to help out on a cash register voluntarily, the clerk replied:

> No, we'd never come up here if we had our way. The head clerk tells us to. You know if you come up here for an hour or two, particularly over the weekends, you're completely dead at your shelves. You get behind, and you never catch up again. No, this is work for them damn part-timers.

The grocery manager and head clerk recognized this attitude on the part of the clerks, and by and large were sympathetic toward it. They called clerks to help out at the front end only when there was no other way of handling a jam-up of customers. They also were careful not to give any one man more than his fair share of this assignment. The grocery manager stated:

> You know some of these kids have a real pride in their work, and it just breaks their hearts to be taken off a table to come up and do something like this cashiering. It's really the best kids, the ones who are really hard workers and proud of their aisles, who don't like to ring the cash register and I would agree with them. The front end job is the toughest job in the store. You've got to be dealing with customers all the time; you can't leave for a smoke and stuff like that, so that they naturally feel that the part-timers should take the front end because they are lower, you might say, than the full-timers.

Attitude Toward Part-Timers: The reference to "part-timers" in the above paragraph gives us a clue to the attitude of the full-time clerks toward these people. By and large they felt that they were a rather irresponsible group who should be given the more undesirable jobs in the store. The full-time clerks were not very happy if these part-timers were assigned to help them in their work of loading shelves.

Work Activities and Interactions: The researcher noted that, like the department managers, the full-time personnel of the store seemed to be busy working at one job or another almost all the time. The group seemed to have a self-enforced code of expecting each man to put in a solid day's work. They expressed a dislike for a clerk who had been in the store temporarily on the following grounds:

> He was really awfully slow, never did any work. Didn't catch on. Was never around when his direct shipments came in. He wasn't worth a damn.

Most of the clerks' jobs such as stocking shelves restricted their opportunity to talk to one another. However, on most jobs where they worked together such as unloading the trucks, they engaged in a great deal of conversation and banter. While much of this conversation was general small talk, a fair amount of it was about work topics, such as estimating how the different kinds of merchandise would sell and making minor bets on these estimates.

On occasions when the clerks worked as a team, they went about these jobs with considerable gusto and divided up the work without any supervisory instructions. While they were handling cases and passing them from one man to the next, they worked very rapidly, occasionally throwing the cases at one another and kidding one another in the process. When the head clerk worked with the clerks on these group jobs, as he often did, he gave only a few minor instructions. Wherever a job had to be done, someone did it as the men shifted back and forth doing the various tasks. When the researcher asked the head clerk about this, he commented:

> I don't need to tell any of these guys to do anything. This is a very good group of guys that way. If there's a job to be done, they will all pitch in and do it.

While the above observations indicate that the full-time grocery clerks would meet a sociologist's definition of a small work group, these men did not have an elaborate set of nonwork activities and interactions. Their mild horseplay and informal games were centered around the work itself. They apparently did not get together as a group outside the store. They did develop special friendships by pairs and these special friends had coffee and lunch together.

Summary: The required work of the grocery clerks provided variety, mobility, and a mixture of solitary and group work. The need for the performance of each task was as obvious as a customer standing in front of an empty counter. The jobs varied in the skills required and provided opportunities for on-the-job training and job up-grading. The full-time clerks, being noncollege men from lower to middle socio-economic backgrounds, came to these basic job requirements with relatively modest expectations. The satisfactions of the work in the store usually exceeded their expectations. In fact the full-time clerks expressed an astonishing degree of positive sentiments about their work, the company, and their fellow employees. As we summarize this picture, however, we should remember that we are speaking only of full-timers, and there was some evidence that the part-time employees, who were not interviewed, held more negative sentiments.

Almost all the clerical people in store 20 seemed to derive considerable satisfaction from the work itself. They felt that they were constantly learning new job skills. They enjoyed the responsibility they felt for looking after their own section of the grocery shelves. They enjoyed the variety of work and the mobility that this variety gave them. They enjoyed the occasional team projects and the opportunity to organize spontaneously their own methods of doing this work. They enjoyed their frequent contacts with their immediate bosses in the store, and both parties to this relationship seemed to have an accurate and intimate acquaintance with the point of view of the other party, which they took account of in working with one another. There was no big gap between management and the worker in the store.

The people in the store looked forward optimistically to their prospects with the company. They were all interested and highly motivated toward getting ahead in the organization. They saw themselves moving up a fairly clear-cut promotional ladder, one little step at a time. They saw themselves as learning their current jobs to prepare themselves for ever-increasing responsibilities in bigger stores on a continuing basis. This view of their future prospects was probably closely related to their favorable general attitude toward the company. They seemed to indicate a sense of indebtedness to the company for the opportunities provided for advancement. This was true in spite of the fact that they sometimes felt promotions were somewhat a matter of luck and in any event would take considerable time to achieve.

In return for what they saw the company offering them, they seemed willing to comply with the quite rigorous expectations that the company and management generally had as regards their work. They accepted as their own the standard that a clerk should work hard. They put pressure on clerks who did not meet this standard. They expected to receive orders from their boss and they generally complied with those orders even though they might not agree with them. Most of them believed that it was not wise to raise objections to management's wishes, particularly those of higher management. The men identified with their merchandise, with their immediate boss, with their own particular department within the store (not with the entire store unit), and with the company as a whole. They looked down on part-timers who did not seem to share their values. Since there was a fairly high turnover rate among part-timers and a fairly low rate among full-timers, there was probably a self-selection process at work. Those part-timers who found that they could obtain satisfaction from this work environment and could willingly and easily accept the codes of the store stayed on and were selected to become full-time clerks.

Organizational Behavior—1954

In our review of the Food World organization from top to bottom as it existed around 1954, we have seen that in many ways this organization was well equipped to compete successfully in the supermarket industry. We saw that top management was oriented toward keeping up with the competition of the industry, initiating ideas for change in merchandising methods, and pushing these ideas into practice in their organization. We saw that the middle-management group and particularly the district managers saw their jobs as primarily carrying out the instructions of top management and keeping pressure on the stores to achieve the expectations of top management. We have seen in the stores a group of employees who felt a loyalty and an obligation to the organization. We saw that they were deriving satisfaction from their work itself and were willingly accepting and, with some exceptions, carrying out the instructions that were passed on to them from higher management.

In many ways, as a student of organization, the researcher was highly impressed with the relative effectiveness of this organization. The organizational system of Food World in 1954 was not principally a product of conscious and deliberate organizational planning. Of course, a great deal of conscious logical thinking had gone into the development of its work procedures but there were very few signs of conscious attention being given to the other aspects of the organization, the formal structure, the communication pattern in the line hierarchy, the relation between work routines and clerk attitudes, and so on. Instead, the company's organizational practices had evolved over the years by a process of unconscious adjustment into quite a workable system. The major strength of the over-all system from the standpoint of achieving the organizational purpose were (1) that it permitted the fairly rapid and relatively painless introduction of the many changes in the physical plant and work procedures that had come in the last few years, and (2) that people at all levels were working diligently on the jobs that had to be done to run the stores. This was no mean feat for any organizational system to achieve.

Our review of the organization has revealed some things that the top management in almost any organization would hope not to find—for example, the attitude of the store clerks toward customers and the slippage between top management instructions and the actual practices in the stores. Yet a closer look at these practices suggests that they also fit into the pattern in a useful functional manner. As for the attitude toward customers, it must be recognized that it was to the organization's benefit that the clerks were primarily oriented toward the task of attending to their shelves, if the alternative was a primary interest in chatting with customers and avoiding the work on the merchandise. It might be desirable to have both, but this probably was not in the cards. And in spite of their attitudes the clerks were outwardly civil to customers, if not friendly. Perhaps the customers in our supermarkets have been trained not to expect to find a warm, personal friendship in their grocery buying.

As regards the slippage, it should be noted that this was a matter of degree. The store people did, by and large, follow the code of doing what they were told without talking back. And the orders they evaded in practice were probably those that were least useful even from an over-all organizational standpoint. This was true because the store people were interested in running good stores. And there is no reason to think that top management was infallible, when we see the extent to which they were out of touch with the realities in the stores. Furthermore, it was around this sub rosa discretion that the middle management people gained some small sense of choice in their work, a feeling that undoubtedly contributed to their job satisfaction and willingness to work hard. So, while the signs of slippage might hurt the pride of top management, it was in many ways functional, a blessing in disguise.

This brings us to our final point in summing up the organizational system of 1954. In the paragraph above we were talking about the interdependence of one mode of behavior, slippage, with others, morale and productivity at the middle management level. This interdependence of the parts of the organizational system needs fresh emphasis. The researcher has not tried to spell out explicitly all the ways that the parts of the system were interdependent. To do so would be most complicated and difficult to substantiate. But he hopes that the reader has acquired at least a feel for the interdependence of the parts which the researcher was highly aware of as he studied this organization. For example, the researcher believes that there was a relationship of interdependence between (1) the management practice of giving clerks individual responsibility for shelves plus an opportunity to organize spontaneously their group tasks, (2) the clerical job characteristics of mobility, variety, and visibility of purpose, and (3) the fact that the clerks had accepted and internalized the organizational code of hard work and obedience. Similar sets of interdependent factors could be spelled out at great length. The point is that there appears to be an inner wisdom in the way the parts of the organizational behavior system had worked out over the years into an interdependent whole. Some kind of trial-and-error, "survival-of-the-fittest" process of social innovation had clearly been at work. The resulting wisdom of the system should give pause to those who would rush in with elaborate, highly logicized plans for reorganizing such a system. This is not to say that the researcher is against conscious, careful organizational planning. To the contrary he is professionally committed to the assumption that, by improved understanding of organizations, we can build organizations that will more adequately serve our varied human purposes. We must, however, proceed with caution and a humble recognition of the limits of our present knowledge in these matters, if we are to do a better job than the kind of unconscious, intuitive, adjustive wisdom that put the Food World organizational system together.

While this seems in many ways an ideal picture from the standpoint of a smoothly functioning organization, there were several problems that were beginning to arise. There were several members of top management who were becoming concerned as to whether this type of organization was so well designed to meet not only the competitive pressures of 1954, but of the years that would come. The story of the problems that these men saw, and their plans for changing some very basic characteristics of the organization to meet these problems, will be presented in the next chapter.

CHAPTER III

Plans for Changing Organizational Behavior

IN THE PRECEDING chapter we have been looking at the traditional behavior patterns in the Food World organization. By many standards this was a picture of a successful organization. It was growing, it was making money, and to some extent it was providing satisfaction to its employees at all levels. But we also saw certain potential trouble spots in this organization. In this chapter our focus will be more on these trouble spots, and more particularly on the way these problems were diagnosed by a group of five executives who, in 1953 and 1954, were making an intensive review of the organization and its competitive environment, and working out plans for introducing some sweeping organizational changes.

In 1953 these five men had various top management assignments, but to simplify matters we shall refer to them by the titles they assumed under the 1955 reorganization; namely, vice president of sales, merchandising manager, store operations manager, personnel manager, and a fifth who had left the company by 1955. This small group of five executives had worked closely with one another for many years. They had found as they worked with one another that they tended to have a common view of the organization's problems, as well as common aspirations for its future. The senior man in the group and its leader in these planning functions was the vice president of sales. While these were not the only men involved, they were the prime movers in assessing the organization, in developing plans, in getting these plans approved by others, and in implementing them.

The description of these events that follows will be presented in a fairly logical sequence in order to keep the matters clarified, but the reader should remember that these men did not work out these ideas in this particular sequence or in such a systematic fashion. For example, the vice president of sales recalled that he had originally got the idea for the central part of the plan in 1938. Other parts of the plan also had a long history of thought behind them. In 1955 these men had still not formalized on paper all the aspects of their plan, even though it was well formulated in their minds.

Management Appraisal—1954

Industry Trends

In order to gain perspective on the strengths and weaknesses of their own organization, these executives were doing a great deal of thinking about the trends of the entire supermarket industry and what this meant for the company's future competition. In addition to their general knowledge of the industry, these men made visits to some of the leading but noncompeting firms in the industry to learn of their appraisal of the industry's future and of their long-range organizational plans. Out of this review grew several conclusions. They concluded that, while the industry would continue to expand, the explosive growth of the large supermarkets which had come largely at the expense of the small grocery stores was beginning to run its course. While they expected to continue changing their marketing methods, they did not foresee in the near future any revolution in methods comparable to the changes of the past two decades. They predicted that the most crucial competition of the future would be with other modern supermarkets and more particularly those run by strong, local independents.

> Our toughest competition is from local independents. Chains don't bother us too much, but when a fellow is

right there on the spot and can battle with local conditions, he's got an edge on us if we can't move quickly enough. What we've got to do is to be sure that we're always in a good competitive position relative to the other people in this business. We think the important thing in doing this for the next few years is to be a little more flexible and a little more aggressive in our stores, and in order to do that, we have to have a clean-cut organization behind those stores. We want the advantages of the independent in being able to take quick, appropriate action on the local scene combined with the advantages of big business—merchandising specialists, high-volume purchasing, area-wide advertising, well-known names, and that sort of thing.

They saw the local independent as having a potential advantage in being able to tailor his store to any unique merchandise needs of his customer, to build his own employee team, and to watch personally over expense control. They believed that the final advantage would go to the company that could successfully build an organization that would combine the advantages of both size and flexibility. This size-up of the competitive future of the industry was critical to all the subsequent organizational planning. By reaching the conclusions they did, these executives were in effect gambling that the competitive edge of the future in the industry would go to the company that put its emphasis on building a well-coordinated organization that was, in addition, highly adaptive at the local store level. This meant not putting emphasis on other possibilities—radical new designs for stores, radical new food-handling methods, building a high-powered promotional system, or even building a more tightly regimented organization. This policy decision to emphasize the building of a strong decentralized organization was based on, not only the review of the competitive picture, but also the appraisal these executives made of the internal problems the company was having in achieving its potential effectiveness.

Internal Organizational Problems

As these executives looked around them in their own organization, they saw several major problem areas. Their diagnosis of these problem areas grew out of a special study of the organization that the group carried out on their own initiative in 1953. At that time this group decided that they were out of touch with what was going on in the stores and, more particularly, with how the district management was supervising the stores. They set up a series of questions that they wanted to have answered concerning district supervision. They then undertook to spend at least one day visiting stores with each of the district managers and assistant district managers to observe what went on. The informal report of this survey as well as direct quotations from these executives will be used to describe their final analysis of the organization's major problems.

One of the chief problems these men saw in the organization resulted from what they characterized as "one man leadership." One of them said:

> Our business has grown to the point where the stimulation that has been provided for the organization by the top people in this business, and in the past this has been mostly by [the president], just isn't felt much any more down at the bottom of the organization. We're getting too big for that style of management to carry the whole load.

Another one stated:

> Back in the old days [the president] used to go into a store and radiate a lot of enthusiasm. He would cheer everybody up and make them excited about the organization and give them about a dozen ideas and then walk out. The people would try out those ideas, but, when nobody expressed any continued interest in them, they would slide back to their old habits.

This last quotation hints at another major organizational problem seen by these executives. They were concerned with the inconsistency of leadership from the top. They attributed this not only to a lack of consistent follow-up on programs that were initiated by top management, but also to the fact there was, in effect, a split command at the top. The stores were receiving directions both from the store operations hierarchy and from the merchandising hierarchy. The latter group not only did the buying and pricing, but also, through its strong ties to the assistant district managers, got into the handling and displaying of merchandise in the stores.

> The pattern has been that merchandising people from the home office go out to the store and give the store people instructions on how to display their merchandise and how to price it and how to set up their racks, etc. In the past this has been done in such a way that it undercuts the district manager and the local manager. He doesn't always know what instructions are whose and who has been told to do what.

The vice president of sales stated:

> As you know [the former vice president of merchandising] really went in big for a lot of flashy promotions. I simply don't agree with that whole approach. As far as I'm concerned, I think we should be in a position to compete over the long pull on sound merchandising policy. I believe in stressing the fundamentals of good merchandising, and not jumping around from one promotion stunt to another.

On another occasion he said:

> It has been very difficult to get things done with the split command between store operations and merchandising. There were counter orders, conflicting orders, and a lack of consistent direction. We were following a zig-zag course. The men were getting one thing one day and another the

next. The people in the field soon caught on and got by by directing themselves to the things the top was interested in for the moment.

A third major organizational problem seen by these men was overcentralization and a related lack of responsible decision-making at the middle and lower levels of supervision. As one man put it:

> The byword of the day has been, "If you have a problem, call somebody at headquarters and they will fix it up." Our top managers have been excellent fire fighters, but there has been very little organized planning. Our thinking at the supervisory levels has simply atrophied.

These men saw little evidence of supervision at the district or store level taking the initiative in finding ways of improving their stores. They saw instead an almost complete dependence on the thinking and ideas of top management.

> There is too much reliance on general office thinking and decisions. Supervisors have been stymied by general office pressure. They take "no" for an answer too readily and do not fight for their beliefs. Supervisors are fighting fires, not solving basic problems in line with an organized program.

These comments were made on the basis of observing these men in action even though the group also concluded:

> As a group, the company's district management are fine men, sincere, hard-working, interested in their own growth and that of the company.

Another closely related concern was with what these executives saw as a communication gap between top management and the store personnel. They were worried about the slippage between what top management wanted and what actually happened in the stores. One of them stated:

We don't kid ourselves that what we at headquarters want to see happen in the stores and what actually does happen out there, are the same thing. Top management has not been keeping themselves very well informed about what the real problems are in the stores.

They saw the communications as being pretty much one way and felt that as a result top management was apt to be unrealistic in its planning and the lower level supervisors felt left out of things.

The people in the stores got to feeling that they had no representatives at headquarters who would really go to bat for them.

To summarize these problem areas, this group of executives were worried about organizational problems at every level of management. At the top they were concerned with too much one-man leadership, a lack of consistent leadership, and too much emergency "fire-fighting" instead of steady effort toward planned objectives. At the district management and store management level they saw a lack of creative thinking and initiative, a lack of a two-way communication link between the top and the bottom, and too much of a "fire-fighting" approach to store supervision. Given this appraisal of their problems, the group of executives proceeded to lay out their ideas for reorganization, in terms both of general objectives and of specific action steps.

Reorganization Plans in Management Terms

General Objectives

The executives, in expressing their objectives for the reorganization, used such terms as "decentralization" and "systematic management procedures." While different executives used different terms, they all seemed to have a basic agreement on what they wanted. The researcher heard such statements as:

We're very interested in setting up a straightforward organizational basis in this company. I believe we need to have a certain amount of structure and some sense of objectives and goals in order to get good results. We're going to operate by giving a man responsibility to go ahead and do his job.

* * * * *

There are two important aspects of our plans. One, we need a few key people who must be able to think through problems, and must be able to direct groups toward their solution; and two, we must have a decentralization of thought, action, and authority. The purpose of this whole thing, this whole program, is to bring our action as close as possible to the arena of battle.

The vice president of sales summed it up:

I'm in favor of setting a systematic administrative framework whereby we're running our business with something other than a one-man approach.

These executives had some quite specific plans on how they wanted to go about reaching these general objectives.

Top Management Structural Change

The first specific step in the plans of these executives was to make certain structural and personnel changes in top management that would enable these men to proceed to make changes further down the line. This step involved combining the jobs of vice president of operations and vice president of merchandising into the single job of vice president of sales. This move gave the group the singleness of top command that they felt was necessary to avoid the inconsistencies of leadership of the past. The former vice president of merchandising was transferred to quite a different post in the business. The former store operations manager left the company and was replaced by one of the group of five key executives, and the newly created job of merchandising manager was filled by another from the group. These moves at the top level put the key executives who initiated the reorganization plan in a position to exercise the formal authority to implement the plan. These top management moves had required careful planning and considerable time and effort, but our story will not include a detailed analysis of them. Exhibit 5 is an organization chart indicating these moves and the other shifts in supervision.

Store Manager Plan

These executives believed that the most important part of their reorganization plan was the development of a new position in the organization, the store manager. They believed that if they could develop the right kind of over-all manager in each one of their larger supermarkets, they could go a long way toward achieving their general objectives. The most important thing they wanted from the store manager was to provide the store with unified administrative leadership. They wanted the store managers to build up a spirit of unity among all the store employees and a store-wide approach to problems that was lacking in the three-headed leadership of the existing stores.

> I think the number one thing we want from [the store manager] is capable administrative leadership. We need a man in the store who can provide dynamic and stimulating leadership. If we've got a good man, it can make an awful lot of difference in our business. You see we operate on a margin of only 1½% profit on our sales. Our payroll runs to about ten times our profit margin. If we have good administrative leadership, it allows us to get all the more productivity in our stores and it's going to make a tremendous difference in our ability to compete.

They were secondly interested in store managers as a way of improving communications between the stores and the general office.

We want our store managers to provide a better link between our stores and our district and top management. He can be the one who receives the general directions that come down from the top and interpret them intelligently for the local situation. He can also be the one to keep the top informed about what the problems are in the store. We particularly need that second point.

A third objective was to provide through the store manager for better local merchandising methods.

We want him to provide some judgment as to good merchandising methods that are sort of tailor-made for the local needs. In every one of our stores we sell basically about the same merchandise but there are some variations between different stores and different neighborhoods. We think that variation, while it isn't much in terms of volume, is very important in terms of running a good store. We want to have specialties in our stores that appeal to the local people. That small difference can be very important in terms of customer appeal.

Finally, they were convinced that there was a need for an over-all supervisor in the store who would have the time and ability to do some advance planning and systematically work toward planned objectives. They wanted a store manager who would also generate ideas and take a great deal more initiative in the conduct of the entire business.

I want to see businessmen running my stores. I want a store manager to come into my office and say: "My store is going to hell. I've made a study of the town. I think we should build a store over here. Traffic count is high; competition just built on the other side of town. It's a good solid, middle-class neighborhood. Just our type. I recommend you build." I haven't got people in this business talking that way yet, but that's what I want.

In summary, they saw the new store managers as the key to combining the advantages of a chain operation with the advantages of the strong independent.

Middle Management Changes

Closely related to the idea of introducing a strong store manager were certain changes in the supervisory link between the home office and the stores. The principal feature of the plan at this level was to shift the assistant district managers from the line function of directly supervising the perishable departments in each store to the staff job of acting as merchandisers. Where these men had been reporting to the district managers, they were now to report to their respective merchandising managers (formerly called buyers). The objective of this change was to build a single unified chain of command from the store operations manager through the district managers directly to the new store managers, while still providing the perishable departments with some staff merchandising help through the new merchandisers.

The new store operations manager stated his objective of how he would like to see the merchandisers work with the new store managers in the following terms:

> I want the merchandiser to be a technical adviser to the store manager on the perishable departments. This can be a two-way deal because the store manager is the merchandiser's agent for following up on the merchandiser's ideas in the store.

New Control Procedures

As an additional part of their plan, these executives were introducing a number of new control procedures in the company. The principal one of these was a new procedure for budgeting sales volume and payroll in each of the stores. Prior to the start of each three-month period, each district manager was expected to work out with his store managers or department managers a target for sales volume and payroll. In turn, the store operations manager worked out his own targets for each one of these stores. These two sets of targets, which were independently developed, were then reconciled by a discussion between the store operations manager and his district managers. Once these targets were agreed upon, they could then be used to compare against the actual operating results which were reported to the stores by four-week and again by three-month periods.

The store operations manager stated the objectives of this program in these terms:

> Our whole objective in putting in this new budget system was so that the men on the road and the fellows in the stores would not feel that these targets had been imposed on them. What we're trying to achieve here is to have a realistic budget that everyone has participated in arriving at so that the fellows will feel that they've got an attainable target to shoot at.

As another part of the budgetary procedure, the new merchandising manager worked out sales targets by product classification (grocery, meat, and produce) with his different managers. The executives did not worry about completely reconciling these figures with those prepared by the stores. As the new store operations manager put it:

> My figures may or may not be the same as the merchandising manager submits, but these are the figures I use with my men and if he wants to submit a different figure to management, I told him that's his business. This doesn't seem to be causing any trouble, however, because the figures I come up with and the figures he comes up with and uses have been turning out to be very close to each other.

As an additional part of their new control procedure, these executives were introducing a more systematic way of evaluating the field personnel. They looked to the new budgeting procedures for considerable help in making better evaluations of their personnel, but they also were adopting more systematic forms for the periodic review of the performance of each of the men in the organization. The store operations manager commented on his reasons for this program:

> Of course, you'll see this form we're using here is nothing new or startling. It's a pretty standard setup. What we're really interested in is getting our people out in the stores to think more about the fact that their performance is being judged by their immediate superiors in the store and the district managers. We, in turn, want to rely more on these reports from these field supervisors in making our selections for advancement. We hope this will tend to minimize any feeling that these promotions are based on luck or the chance opinion of somebody at headquarters.

A third aspect of the new control procedures was a program to write up more complete and accurate job descriptions for all the jobs in the organization. The executives felt that the discussions that would have to precede reaching an agreement on job descriptions would help the people in the organization to clarify in their own minds just what was expected of them. They thought that the resulting descriptions would also be useful in the training of personnel that were new in the organization or moving to new assignments. They wanted the descriptions to arise out of meetings that would be held at different levels to get greater agreement on the content and nature of the different jobs.

A fourth program the executives introduced to secure better control procedures was a new system for ordering merchandise in the stores. The procedure centered around a mathematical formula that had been developed to use the previous week's sales for each item in the store as the basis for determining the next week's order for that item. This system was designed to keep the store's inventory at a minimum, while still providing safeguards that the store would not run out of any item. As a part of this same program, a new procedure was developed for allocating space on the store display shelves for the many items carried.

New Communication Procedures

As a final part of their plan for reorganizing the company, these executives developed some new routine communication procedures, designed, not only to help the organization conduct its normal day-to-day business, but also to help implement the changes that have been outlined above.

Every other week all the district managers were called to a meeting at headquarters that consisted of two parts. The first part was a session with the merchandising manager and some of his key people to discuss future merchandising plans. The second part of this meeting was conducted by the store operations manager to discuss with his district manager group some of their current problems. On alternate weeks it was planned to call all the store managers into a meeting at headquarters to have a discussion on their common problems with the store operations manager. The new merchandising manager also conducted weekly meetings at headquarters with each of his major merchandising groups.

Not all these meetings were new to the organization but in every case the purpose of the meetings had changed. Where formerly these meetings had provided a place for instructions to be handed out to field people, the new plan involved using these meetings more as a place to provide two-way communication. They were therefore organized as discussion meetings with opportunity provided for field people to raise their problems with headquarters people and to participate in making decisions and plans.

In addition to this schedule of meetings these executives were planning on keeping in touch with their field organization more systematically on an individual basis. For instance, the store operations manager scheduled three days of every week to travel with his district managers as they made their supervisory tours of their stores. The other top people also scheduled a considerable number of days to travel with the district managers to keep in touch with store operations.

Summary

The organization of Food World in the mid-50's was one that had evolved through the years essentially on a trial-and-error basis. It was an organization which had grown as a result of the thousands of day-to-day pressures on the business to conduct itself in a healthy and competitive way. The last chapter demonstrated that the organization that had evolved through the years had many inherent strengths. In 1954 the company had good stores and good central warehousing equipment, but its primary assets were still its people. These people were, by and large, loyal to the organization, hardworking, and highly skilled in the diverse operations of buying, transporting, displaying, advertising, accounting, and housekeeping that were the essential functions of their business. They were also highly skilled at perpetuating their own organizational arrangements for doing work. By this we mean that they were good at indoctrinating new members of the organization into the customary codes and practices of the organization. We saw a quick glimpse of grocery clerks indoctrinating new clerks in the codes of the organization, and the researcher saw the same process going on at all levels of the organization. So the company had an organization that knew its business and knew how to perpetuate itself.

Onto this scene came a small group of key executives who felt dissatisfied with the existing organization even while recognizing many of its strengths. Fundamentally they felt that what was making the company competitive in the mid fifties would not be good enough to make them competitive in the mid sixties. What they believed the company needed to lead in their industry was not something that you could buy like a new warehouse or a new group of larger stores— not that these items were not also in the thinking of these executives as essential ingredients. But they felt that the most critical ingredient that the company needed was a new and different internal system for getting work done. They believed that they needed a new kind of organizational system for coordinating the work of the people toward achieving the organizational purposes.

The thing that makes these plans particularly significant for study was the fact that they were the product of a deliberate and conscious effort to draw up a model for an optimum organization. It would be false to give the impression that top management's plans were a highly detailed blueprint, but they were certainly a great deal more systematic than "a seat of the pants" hunch. The men who had evolved these plans had accumulated many years of experience in the industry and the company. They had held many discussions among themselves as to what were the strengths and weaknesses of their own company. They had made systematic studies of what was going on in their own organization. They had gone on trips to leading competitors throughout the country to observe their organizational methods and to discuss their ideas with the chief executives of these companies. So it is accurate to say that their plans constituted a deliberate long-range planning of organizational behavior. This kind of planning effort was a new experience for Food World. While such long-range planning of organizational behavior is, of course, not unique in business generally, it is probably less common than is usually thought.

The reader at this point might have a number of doubts and questions about the reorganization plans as worked out by the top management of Food World. Was management's thinking too utopian? Were they seeking a magic cure-all? This management group did not think of their plan as foolproof or fixed. The president commented:

> No organization plan is static. It will always be necessary for us to make changes to improve the plan. I know of no perfect organizational plan.

The reader may also have noticed some ways in which the

company's plan was not completely consistent. For example, the objective of decentralizing some of the decision-making might well find itself working at cross purposes with another aspect of the plan, namely, the grocery ordering system which, in effect, would diminish the amount of judgment that store people would use in ordering their merchandise. The management was aware of these inconsistencies and even had a phrase for them, "retailing doubletalk." They felt that these inconsistencies were an inevitable part of achieving the objectives they desired.

The reader might also be wondering if the plans were not much too comprehensive and ambitious to be implemented at one time. The Food World management did not naively think that all the changes that they had in mind could be introduced at one time or even over a fairly short time period. They had in mind a time schedule that involved introducing these changes over a fairly long period of time. The changes have been described in this chapter in terms of being one plan because they were one plan in conception, but not in the sense of being installed at one point of time. The details of management's timetable are not important here but, suffice it to say, that a very few experimental store managers had been trained and installed in 1954, the new budget system was started in early 1954, most of the formal organizational changes were made in January 1955, and during 1955 the program of introducing store managers was speeded up as were the introduction of the other new control and communication procedures. One key executive commented in 1955:

> The whole store manager program is like a weak new sapling. It will take years of constant care and attention to get it to grow into a strong, self-sufficient tree.

So as of late 1954 the executives concerned had built a systematic model in their minds of how they wanted the organizational system to operate in the future. They had gained the approval of their executive colleagues. They were starting to take the initial formal steps to implement the plans that are outlined above.

Thus far we have looked at these plans exclusively in management's terms. Now, before proceeding, we need to sharpen the focus of our study and restate management's objectives in concrete terms that would allow an outside researcher to measure whether or not the objectives were achieved. We also shall restate the reorganizational plans in terms of our conception of the organization as a social system, in order to make our findings more useful for understanding other organizations.

REORGANIZATION PLANS IN RESEARCHER'S TERMS

The top management executives, in their roles as leaders of the Food World social system, wished to change some of the critical behavior patterns of the system. They were motivated to do this as a result of their observation of anticipated external pressures on the system and as a result of their perception of certain malfunctioning in the system itself that threatened its health and survival. They wanted their plans to have a significant effect on behavior throughout the entire organization. The researcher, however, could not hope to observe and measure all the effects of the reorganization. He chose, therefore, to concentrate his observations on two strategically critical positions; the store manager and the district manager. This choice was made on the assumption that the men in these positions would have to make the most changes in their behavior, and the desired results further down the line would be dependent upon their making these changes. We shall therefore be focusing our intensive study on the behavior of the people in these two strategic positions.

Members of top management stated their ideas about the desired behavior changes in terms of "decentralization" and "clear-cut administrative framework." They were not completely happy with these terms because they knew that they were subject to differing definitions, but regardless of the words they had a pretty clear idea of what they wanted. For our research purposes, however, we need to define these desired behavioral changes in more concrete and measurable terms. To do this we shall take the two key positions, the store manager and the district manager, and see in what specific ways management desired them to change their behavior. In other words, what were management's new requirements for the roles of these positions?

New Required Role—Store Manager

Earlier in this chapter we saw some general statements of top management concerning its objectives for the new role of the store manager. These statements specified the model of the new role requirements that we must now translate into terms of concrete behavior. For convenience and clarity we shall subdivide the role requirements into the three elements of behavior—the kind of *activities* the store manager was to engage in, the kind of *interaction* he was to have with others, and the kind of *sentiments* he was to hold.

Activities: Management expected the new store manager to spend considerable time in all departments of the store observing what was going on (in contrast to doing physical work). It expected him to analyze past performance and work out future plans and objectives.

Interactions: Management expected the new store manager to interact down the line primarily with his three department heads (in contrast to working directly with clerks). These interactions were to be two-way, problem-solving conversations in which the subordinate participated in choosing departmental objectives and merchandising methods, and in making personnel decisions. It expected the store manager to initiate interactions with the staff merchandisers to seek their technical assistance in the perishable department but not to let themselves or their department managers be dominated by these merchandisers. As regards his superior, the district manager, he was expected not only to receive and interpret instructions from above but also to pass on ideas and problems.

Sentiments: Management expected the store manager to conceive of himself as a businessman concerned with the over-all well-being of his store for the future as well as the present. He was to be loyal to the organization but feel more self-sufficient rather than dependent on his superiors. He was to have an enthusiasm for the possibilities of the store that would be reflected in his subordinates' attitudes. He was to think of himself as a leader and developer of his subordinates rather than as a dominator of them.

In considering the required role described above, we need to remember that the organization plans called for recruiting most of the new store managers from positions as grocery managers or other departmental managers in stores. From what we saw in Chapter II it is evident that the new store manager role requirements are by no means the same thing as the existing pattern of activities, interactions, and sentiments practiced by departmental managers. In fact, it might be predicted that these changes are so great that they could not be successfully made without the intelligent and active support of his immediate supervisor, the district manager.

New Required Role—District Manager

We saw in Chapter II that the district managers had traditionally been a strong link between top management and the store organization. They were traditionally giving their store personnel frequent and detailed supervision on the way top management wanted the work of the stores conducted. These were the men who were accustomed to making hundreds of detailed decisions about how the stores were to operate. They were giving instructions on how they wanted merchandise displayed, how they wanted work schedules handled, how they wanted the store plant maintained, and the hundreds of other detailed items involved in good store operation. We have seen that the whole system worked so that the store people had been trained to be loyal and hard-working order takers, and, so far as they were concerned, these orders were emanating from the district manager who to them had always been their personal "big boss," who would have the dominant voice in determining their own personal future with the organization. Under the new organizational plan, these district managers were being asked to change drastically their traditional role. Top management's new role requirements for the district managers are spelled out below in terms of concrete behavior.

Activities: The district manager was still expected to spend most of his time going from store to store in his territory observing and talking with his subordinates. He was, however, expected to spend more time looking over the perishable departments because of his loss of the assistant district managers. He was also expected to spend more time on planning functions and less on "fire fighting" current problems.

Interactions: The district managers were expected to provide opportunities for their subordinate store managers to assume more decision-making functions. They would have to converse with their fledgling store managers so that these men would assume greater responsibilities and discharge them adequately. This meant that in their interactions with their subordinates they were expected to make a fundamental change toward adopting a more problem-solving, two-way type of communication. They would have to strike a relatively even balance between the amount of time they spent talking to their subordinates and the time their subordinates spent doing the talking to them. It was expected that the district managers would still be in frequent contact with the staff merchandisers (their former assistant district managers), but instead of the traditional boss-subordinate pattern it was to be a relationship of a line-staff nature with the district manager calling on the merchandiser for advice and staff assistance and, in turn, teaching the store manager to use this staff assistance intelligently. The district manager was also to be expected to adopt different interaction practices with his superiors in the organization. This was most apparent in the way the plan called for conducting different types of headquarters meetings with the district manager group. These meetings were no longer to be primarily briefings where the district managers were told what top management orders they were to carry out, but rather they were now expected to do a more systematic job of keeping top management informed on the problems arising in the field and on the suggestions for improvement that were coming from the field. What is more, they were expected to participate more in making the plans and decisions that affected operations.

Sentiments: Like the store managers, the district managers were expected to conceive of themselves as more independent, self-sufficient businessmen who were concerned with the long-range well-being of their districts. They were even to think of their role as superiors, as being more that of teachers and developers of the capacities of their store managers.

These new role requirements were in considerable contrast to the customary ways of thinking and behaving that prevailed among these men. The district managers were, then, expected to change their role in the organization drastically—to change their behavior in every one of their key relationships, up, down, and sideways, that made up their daily work existence. These changes were strategically critical to the success of the entire reorganization plans since they were an essential prerequisite to changing the daily working practices of the people in the stores. It is for this reason that we shall be focusing in the succeeding chapters on the problems of change in the behavior of district managers in their relations with the new store managers, and certainly not because the individual district managers "ought" (in a moral sense) to change their behavior any more than anyone else.

Management Change Methods

The top management of Food World adopted a number of specific methods to clarify the new role requirements for store managers and district managers. The executives worked out new job definitions with the people concerned, gave speeches on what they expected of the new setup, wrote up various descriptions of what they wanted in the company's house organ, and redrew the company's official organization chart. They knew, however, that these customary steps to establish the new required roles had to be supplemented by other change methods—new work procedures and new incentives.

The new control procedures that required sales and expense goals to be agreed on at the store manager and district manager level were designed to foster the required interaction pattern. The same was true of the new procedure for having these supervisors participate in the systematic evaluation of their employees. Likewise the new type of management meetings were designed to give these supervisors a chance to practice filling the required roles.

Finally top executives gave their supervisors some explicit and implied incentives for behaving in terms of the new roles. They offered store departmental managers the incentive of a higher status title, "store manager," and increased pay for demonstrating that they could adequately meet the role requirements for store manager. With the district manager they implied that the larger, more desirable districts or even higher management jobs would go to those who could meet the new role requirements, while there was an implicit threat that failure to meet the requirements could result in demotion.

These, then, were the formal steps that management could and did make to translate the new required roles from the planning stage into the actual day-to-day behavior of the key supervisors. It remained to be seen if these formal steps were successful in making the plans a reality.

In early 1955 the observer heard a newly appointed store manager ask a kidding question of another store manager:

> Have you heard the new definition of a store manager?
> It's a grocery manager with a raise in pay.

This comment epitomized the question that was on the minds of many in the organization. Could management's plan get beyond the overt changes they could effect directly—the changes in title, in pay, and in job descriptions? Could it be transformed from a paper change into a basic change in the daily work habits of many people? Could it be a change of substance as well as of form?

In the next chapter we shall be looking at the problems the company, and more particularly certain district and store managers, had in living with their new role requirements. We shall also see to what degree they were initially successful in bringing their actual behavior into coincidence with these role requirements. We shall be using the new role requirements on a yardstick to measure change, not because the researcher believes that they should automatically be considered "right" or "best" as goals, but because, for the time being, they provide a convenient way of highlighting the problems of changing organizational behavior patterns.

CHAPTER IV

A Changed Supervisory Pattern

THE PLAN for reorganizing Food World described in the last chapter was not installed all at one point of time. However, the one event that most dramatically symbolized the introduction of this new plan into the company took place in the middle of December 1954. The occasion was a meeting of all the management personnel and supervisors of the company including the district managers and the assistant district managers. At this traditional pre-Christmas meeting the president of Food World announced all the changes of the organization structure as they are depicted in the organization chart shown in Exhibit 5. He also announced that the company planned in 1955 on training people for positions as store managers and assigning them their stores as rapidly as possible. All these related moves meant that, while 1954 was the year in which top management had concentrated on working out its plans and taking the initial steps, 1955 was the year in which the full impact of the change was to hit the organization.

In this chapter and the next two we shall present the story of the process by which the changes were introduced into the company and the problems that were encountered. We shall be focusing on the behavior of people at the two levels of the organization where the greatest change in the traditional pattern of the organization had to be made if the new plans were to be fulfilled. We shall look at some district managers and some new store managers as these people went about their work and their efforts to implement the new plans. More particularly we shall look at three district managers as

EXHIBIT 5
Partial Organization Chart, 1955

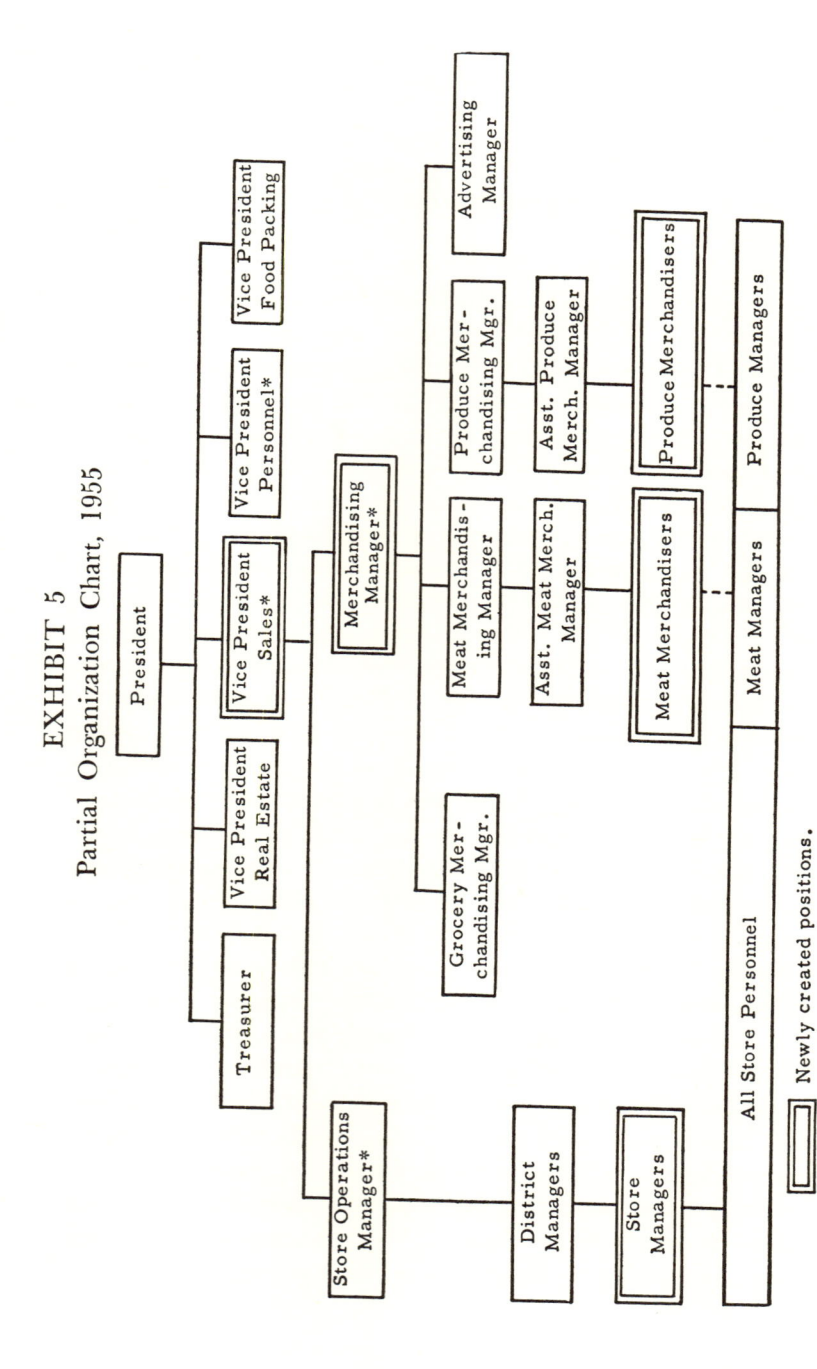

President
- Treasurer
- Vice President Real Estate
- Vice President Sales*
- Vice President Personnel*
- Vice President Food Packing

Vice President Sales*
- Store Operations Manager*
- Merchandising Manager*

Store Operations Manager*
- District Managers
  - Store Managers
    - All Store Personnel

Merchandising Manager*
- Grocery Merchandising Mgr.
- Meat Merchandising Manager
  - Asst. Meat Merch. Manager
  - Meat Merchandisers — Meat Managers
- Produce Merchandising Mgr.
  - Asst. Produce Merch. Manager
  - Produce Merchandisers — Produce Managers
- Advertising Manager

☐ Newly created positions.

▭ Men with major roles in planning organization.

*Men with major roles in planning organization.

A CHANGED SUPERVISORY PATTERN   71

they "broke in" three new store managers in their new duties.

In many superficial ways the three district managers we shall be observing were very similar to one another as were also the store managers. The three district managers were all long-service employees of the company. They were all in their fifties. The three of them had for some time been the district managers of three of the largest and most important districts in the company. All three had grown accustomed through the years to performing their duties in a way that was compatible with the traditional pattern described in Chapter II. All three of them had built up a substantial reputation in the business for being experts in their field and all three had a good reputation with top management because of the quality of their past performance.

Likewise, the three store managers had all been long-service employees of the company. All three of these men were in their forties. They were being promoted to store managers from being grocery department managers in large stores. All three had been picked for the promotion because of their good record with the company, and in every instance their respective district managers had had a major voice in the selection of these men for their promotion.

All three had been put through the company's initial training program for store managers. This training program consisted of a six-week period in which the men were relieved of all operating responsibilities and were moved from assignment to assignment to observe and learn more about their new duties as store manager. Specifically the six-week training program was broken down into a period of three weeks in which these men worked in a meat department, a week's work in a produce department, followed by a week of observing another newly installed store manager going about his duties, and a final week traveling with an experienced district manager. This training program was designed to acquaint these people with the store departments in which they had not had firsthand experience and to give them some of the know-how they could pick up from experienced district managers and store managers. So the stage had been properly set for the new store managers and their district managers to start performing their new organizational roles.

In the pages that follow we shall be providing some firsthand glimpses of the three district managers working with their store managers. As these descriptions are presented, the reader should be observing the extent to which these people are learning to work within the new organizational framework. The questions to be kept in mind are: Is the new store manager assuming the kind of leadership and initiative in the store that top management desires? Is he gaining the respect and loyalty of the people in the meat and produce departments as well as the grocery departments? Is he creating a "one-store" atmosphere? Is he improving the productivity in the store? Is he improving the merchandising appeal in the store by tailoring his store to the particular needs of the community he is serving? In short, is he performing in accordance with the newly required organizational role for store managers?

As regards the district manager we shall be asking: Is he learning to work with and through the store manager instead of through the three separate department heads? Is he succeeding in helping the store manager assume more active responsibility and leadership in the store? Is he helping the store manager establish the desired type of working relationship with the merchandisers who are coming into the store in a staff capacity? Is he giving the store manager more decision-making functions while still giving him adequate support? In short, is he acting in line with his new role requirements? With these questions in mind let us turn to our descriptions of these men at work under the new organizational arrangements.

Behavior Pattern, DM1 and SM1

The reorganization plans of Food World called for SM1 to be transferred from a job as department grocery manager to his new position as store manager of store 45, under the supervision of DM1, in late April 1955. Store 45 was one of the newer ones in the company, having been opened in the middle of 1954. It had always been considered a very successful store. During several months prior to the time that SM1 took over as store manager, the store had been under the supervision of one of the store managers in the first group of five experimental store managers who were given these appointments in late 1954. The store was a completely modern supermarket with all the usual physical facilities.

Initial Indoctrination

For the first week that SM1 worked in store 45, the store still remained under the nominal supervision of the outgoing store manager. The excerpt that follows is a portion of what took place that week on the one occasion when DM1 made a supervisory call on the store.

> When DM1 first entered the store he was greeted by the outgoing store manager and before SM1 joined the group, DM1 mentioned that he didn't like the looks of the pie display.

Outgoing SM: Well it doesn't bother me to hear you say that because it so happens that my successor put that display up. You'll have to talk to him. But of course the chief trouble is it hasn't been straightened out lately. (He stepped up and started straightening out the pie display.)

> SM1 joined the group and DM1 kidded him about the appearance of the pies, after which the three men stepped into the store office to continue their discussion.

DM1: Do you want to place an order for some new display steps with a formica top? Here's the story on them and this is what it would cost you to order them.

Outgoing SM: Let's see what that would figure out to be. It sounds like it would run to $400 or $500.

DM1: Well, how many two and three basket displays do you have now?

Outgoing SM: I've got three of the three basket and two of the two basket, so you see it would be a lot of money. I can't see spending that much.

DM1: That's what I feel, too. That's an awful lot of money. You've got to sell a lot of canned goods to make $500. O.K., so much for that. Have you figured out how much the wage rate changes are going to affect your weekly payroll?

Outgoing SM: I don't think it's going to be very much.

DM1: Well, I think you'd better figure it out. I think you don't realize how much it's going to be. It turns out to be more in some of these stores than they think. It could easily be $100 a week.

Outgoing SM: I don't think so. Last week we had a man out but we also had some overtime, and the payroll figures didn't go up at all. I think it ought to go up at the most about $50.

DM1: Well, maybe that's right. You may be that lucky but I thought you might want to figure that out. Did you see this new sheet they've got out on produce and how to keep it fresh?

Outgoing SM: Yes, I did.

DM1: How about you, SM1?

SM1: Yes, I read it over.

DM1: Well, I think you ought to do more than read it over. You know you're new at this sort of thing and this gives you a good excuse to really be fussy about using a piece of paper like this. The oldtimers think they don't need this sort of thing, but you've got a good excuse to use it and I've never seen anything before that did such a good job of stating the basic elements of keeping produce fresh. Why don't you make a note of that?

SM1: O.K. I have made a note of it, a big note, and I will follow through on that.

DM1: Have you showed SM1 how to fill out those forms on direct vendor purchasing?

A CHANGED SUPERVISORY PATTERN 75

Outgoing SM: Yeah, I showed him how. He can do that all right. (to SM1) You know, he isn't really as tough as he sounds.

DM1: Here is an item on whether or not we want to put in a garbage disposal unit. This thing's pretty expensive, $1,200, but it certainly would be a big help in the produce room.

Outgoing SM: Yeah, I saw one of those working at another store and boy, they certainly do a job.

DM1: Well, I think it would save a lot of time and it would keep the back room a lot neater and cleaner.

SM1: And it would eliminate those smells, too.

DM1: Do you have to pay anything for your garbage disposal?

SM1: No, we don't have to pay to have it hauled away, but we do have to spend time cleaning out the cans and that's an awful job. It does clog things up.

DM1: Well, I think this thing might well be worth doing. I think it would be a real improvement. You can just drop the trimmings into the machine as you work and it all disappears out of the way. . . .

DM1: We are going to schedule a meeting this coming Wednesday, SM1, for our territory people here—the department heads and store managers. You may have to refigure your day off for something like that.

SM1: Well, that will mean I'll have to reschedule the day off but I can work that out all right.

DM1: Well, we're going to have to have this on a regular basis and you'd better figure out how you want to handle it.

SM1: I'll figure something out on how I want to handle it.

After completing their business, the group proceeded to take a fast trip around the store, stopping first at the produce department. DM1 stopped the produce manager.

DM1: Say, I was just telling your new boss, SM1, that I wanted him to come out here and check up on you regularly and make sure you're keeping our produce fresh. I gave him a list of things to check, and I told him to get right after you and come out here and go right down that list and make sure you're doing it right.

> Produce Manager: Oh, sure, we keep things fresh. Everything's fresh around here. Just look up at the sign, see, it says right there we have fresh produce. Everything's fresh, even I am fresh.

> In the meat department DM1 picked up a dark looking piece of flank steak and commented to SM1 that it looked too dark to sell.

SM1: But that's still good meat, you know.
DM1: I know it is, but it's pretty dark.

> The meat manager walked up at this point. DM1 pointed out the dark meat to him and he tucked it under another piece of meat.

Meat Manager: Yeah, yeah, we'll get that taken care of all right, don't worry about that. But, doesn't the whole counter look nice, doesn't it look filled up nice?
DM1: Yes, it does look nice.

> Just before DM1 left the store he was alone for a moment with the outgoing store manager.

DM1: Tell me, how do you think SM1 is going to make out in running the store?
Outgoing SM: Well, he won't have any trouble at all. He won't have any trouble.
DM1: That's what I think, too. I think it ought to go smoothly.

Later on DM1 commented to the researcher:

> That outgoing SM is really a good manager. He's done a fine job down here. He's built this store up until we're quite consistently selling up around $50,000 worth a week and that's a very good business for a store of this size. He's always using his head and has a lot of ideas for selling things. He set up a record out here that's going to be a tough one for SM1 to keep up with and beat. But, that's the way it ought to be and I think SM1 will do a good job.

In this initial exchange involving DM1 and SM1 three points are of special interest: the apparent relaxed and informal nature of the relationship between the men, the fact that DM1 on two or three topics raised questions with the store managers for them to make decisions about, and the fact that DM1 used an instruction sheet on the produce department to coach SM1 on building a supervisory relationship with the produce manager. DM1 from this first contact seems to be treating SM1 as a store manager and coaching him in how to establish his leadership in all parts of the store.

Routine Supervision, DM1—SM1

During the weeks that followed SM1's assumption of his duties at store 45, DM1 made weekly or sometimes twice weekly supervisory visits to the store. The following incidents are illustrative of these supervisory calls.

DM1: (glancing at a large display of blueberry pies) Say, are you and Laurie (the bakery girl) going to eat blueberry pies over the weekend?

SM1: Oh, that'll all be gone by tomorrow. You wait and see. (Calling to bakery girl.) Say, Laurie, go get those figures and shut this guy up.

DM1: Did she go over $1,500?

SM1: Now, you just wait and see. She'll bring the figures in a minute.

The bakery girl came out, carrying a piece of paper behind her and presented it to DM1.

DM1: Sixteen hundred and fifty-four dollars! Laurie, I think that is simply tremendous. You are to be congratulated. That's a magnificent job.

Bakery girl: Well, thank you very much, DM1, but I don't do it all myself, you know.

DM1: Well, you've got the main responsibility for it and I think this is a superb job and you're really to be congratulated.

Bakery girl: Well, thank you very much. (Leaves)

Notice that SM1 took the initiative in setting up, not himself, but the bakery girl for a compliment from DM1. Here he was using his district manager to give a reward for a good sales performance and strengthening his own relations with the bakery girl in the process. DM1 followed through on the lead.

DM1: Say, don't you have a new clerk on this week?
SM1: That's right. He's from Denver, and I think he's gonna work out fine. I was talking to him a little bit the other day in the coffee room and he said that he's been around a meat department out there and explained to me how they cut out there. He said that they all used saws—they don't use any knives.
DM1: Yes, that's right. That's the way they do it there. I'd like to meet him. Is he around?
SM1: Sure, let's go back there. (They walked back to the meat department.) Jack, I'd like you to meet DM1. He's your boss and mine.
Meat Clerk: (looking embarrassed) Glad to meet you.
DM1: Jack, I want to welcome you to Food World and tell you that if you've got any problems at any time, that I want you to bring them to SM1 or me. I'm in the store quite frequently and I want you to let us know if anything's on your mind. Are you married, son?
Meat Clerk: Yes, sir.
DM1: How old are you?
Meat Clerk: Twenty-one, sir.
DM1: Do you have any children?
Meat Clerk: Yes, sir. One girl, four months.
DM1: Boy, you really started early. Well, we're glad to have you aboard, and if you do what the fellows tell you to, keep your eyes open and ask questions, you'll make a good Food World employee.

Here DM1 took the initiative in establishing a relationship with a new clerk. It's clear that SM1 has already done some of this because of his awareness of the new man's background. Notice DM1's statement of the traditional code of the organization, "If you do what the fellows tell you to, . . ." and his adoption of a somewhat paternalistic air toward the young man.

SM1: Say, DM1, the bakery girl is pretty disappointed. I think she feels that she should have gotten that Park Ridge job. You know she wanted to be over there because it's closer to home so she could go home at lunch time and look in on her grandmother and what not, and I think she feels pretty disappointed that she didn't get it. You know she's going on her vacation next week.

DM1: Well, that is a shame. It's certainly my fault. I should have talked to her about it a long time ago. Although I can't understand where she got the idea, except that I may have said something to her when I was bringing her over here one day. I may have mentioned that we were building a store in Park Ridge, and that we might have a place for her there. I don't know. I'm sorry, but let's talk to her now.

SM1: O.K. (He left and, in a moment, the bakery girl returned alone.)

DM1: SM1 tells me that you're worried about this Park Ridge thing.

Bakery girl: Yes, that's right, DM1.

DM1: Well, Laurie, you're not going to Park Ridge, and there's two reasons for it. One, you're doing a terrific job here. You know, you're doing the highest bakery volume in any of my stores.

Bakery girl: Am I?

DM1: Yes, you are, and that's really a tremendous job. And the other reason is that the other girl I'm moving in there—you know her—really needs a change. She's been in her store a long time, and she can get stagnant in there unless she gets a change. So, that's the decision that we made, and I think it's the best thing for the company.

Bakery girl: Well, that's right. I guess she does need a change. I appreciate your telling me about this because I'm going on my vacation next week.

DM1: Yes, I know, SM1 told me.

80   THE CHANGING OF ORGANIZATIONAL BEHAVIOR PATTERNS

Bakery girl: And I certainly would rather know about it now than worry about it. I love working in this store. There isn't anything like that. It's just that—well, it's a lot closer to my home and I'd sort of been led to expect that I was going to get that job.

DM1: Well, I don't know where you got that idea, Laurie, but I may have given it to you one day, and if I did, I'm sorry.

Bakery girl: No, it wasn't you, DM1. In all honesty, you never said one thing to me about it.

At this point SM1 re-entered the room.

Bakery girl: (accusingly) SM1.

SM1: Honest, Laurie, I didn't have anything to do with it. I'd love to keep you here, you know that, but I wouldn't stand in your way. I didn't have anything to do with it.

DM1: No, that's right, Laurie. He didn't have anything to do with this. He just mentioned to me that you were a little worried about it.

Bakery girl: SM1, you shouldn't have done that.

DM1: Well, he did, and I'm glad he did, Laurie. Now, in the future if anything bothers you at all, I just want you to bring it up, because that's what I'm here for; that's my job. And if you've got anything on your mind, I want to hear about it. O.K.?

Bakery girl: O.K., DM1, thank you very much.

Notice that SM1 took the initiative in asking for DM1's help on a problem which involved an interstore transfer issue. DM1 completely relied on SM1's diagnosis of the complaint and proceeded to act on that basis. DM1 tried to make sure that Laurie understood why it was appropriate for SM1 to bring him into the matter. He handled the question in a rather paternalistic "I'll look out for you" way but with the one difference that he emphasized that this was simply doing his job—not a personal favor. At the end he seemed to forget SM1 in encouraging Laurie to bring her problems directly to him.

A CHANGED SUPERVISORY PATTERN   81

    The produce manager came up and greeted DM1 and SM1.

DM1: There's the ugliest produce manager in the whole business.
Produce Manager: Well, that's O.K.; I sell the fruit, though.
DM1: Yeah, you sure do, you ugly Russian.
Produce Manager: Say, DM1, I want to talk with you.
DM1: Alone?
Produce Manager: Yeah.

    The two men stepped to one side for a moment. Later the researcher learned that the produce manager wanted to ask DM1 to talk to the assistant produce manager who was concerned about his future in the company and was looking for a transfer to a bigger job. DM1 called this man in to tell him about his prospects and had this discussion with SM1 present.

    In this incident the produce manager was following the traditional pattern of going directly (and privately) to his district manager with an important personnel situation. DM1 personally handled the problem so that he did not completely rebuff the produce manager's desire for a direct contact with the district manager, but he did get SM1 into the act to some extent.

DM1: Will you be here when your perishable department heads are out on vacation?
SM1: Oh, sure. I wouldn't leave when they're gone.
DM1: Well, that's good, because it'll really give you a chance to get in there and pitch in those two departments, and really learn more about that part of the business! Now, I don't mean that you should cut meat, or trim lettuce, or anything, but I really want you to get well acquainted with the kinds of problems they are up against in those two departments.
SM1: O.K., I will.

Here DM1 is again getting SM1 to think about establishing his leadership in the perishable departments and giving him a suggestion on how to do it.

    DM1 and SM1 were walking past the meat counter when the meat manager called to DM1.

Meat manager: Say, DM1, I have a question for you. Would it be all right if I worked two hours overtime this week? We're going to be a little short-handed and I think I can squeeze by without bringing in any extra help if I have a couple of extra hours.
DM1: Knowing what your schedule is and the way business is going this week, I'd say it is all right. You go ahead on that.
SM1: (after he was alone with DM1) You shouldn't have done that, DM1.
DM1: What do you mean?
SM1: Spoken to the meat manager like that. I'm the one who should have answered his question.
DM1: (pause) I think you're right. And thanks for reminding me.

Here we see SM1 putting pressure on his boss to act in accordance with their new organizational roles. And the correction was accepted graciously enough by DM1 so that SM1 will probably feel all right about doing it again if the need arises.

    DM1, SM1, and the grocery manager were inspecting the grocery storage area in the basement.

DM1: You fellows are on pre-marking [1] here, aren't you?
Grocery manager: That's right.
DM1: Well, have you ever thought about going to demand marking?

---

[1] Pre-marking refers to a system of price marking merchandise upon arrival at the store in contrast to demand marking which is doing the price marking just before the merchandise is placed on display.

A CHANGED SUPERVISORY PATTERN 83

Grocery manager: It's no good here. If you can show me the store that can unload, mark, and put their stuff up on the shelves in two days, that's on a demand system, then I'll buy it.

DM1: Well, that's right. (Shaking head)

DM1 and SM1 continued this discussion while the grocery manager took the researcher aside and pointed out that as far as he was concerned, this was the nicest looking basement in the whole chain—the cleanest and the least inventory. He said the inventory was down to less than two times the weekly grocery sales and they were not using the new inventory control system. He explained that he did it by memory. (Pointing to his forehead.)

DM1: Well, I think you fellows have a point; but when our methods consultant sends in a report that demand marking is better, I've got to listen to him, because I'm not a technician and I don't know about these things. So, my only point is let's not close our minds to this thing, because when a fellow like that comes up with a recommendation, I think we've got to consider it.

Grocery manager: What about the payroll in those stores? Is it the same?

DM1: Yes, it is. Doesn't cost any more the other way, and as a matter of fact, it costs a little bit less and they cut down the inventory.

SM1: Well, our problem here is, our load comes in on Thursday. On Friday everybody in the store is upstairs, waiting on customers, and you can't concentrate on the basement. You simply couldn't handle a demand marking system here, because our part-timers come in Thursday at 3:00 and they're here for three hours. Well, if those fellows had to stamp the merchandise, they simply wouldn't be able to get it on the shelves by 6:00, they just couldn't do it.

DM1: Well, I can certainly see that, and it's obvious that each store is not the same. But you fellows don't have shelf allocation here, and when you do get the shelf allocation system, you can go through the week on all but a few items with just putting them up once. Your shelves won't look as good—I know that, I won't argue that fact. The shelves look lousy, and I don't like it, but it costs you a lot less to stack on Monday, Tuesday, and Wednesday, than on Thursday, Friday, and Saturday, when your aisles are packed. You know for yourself that if you could come in here and stack merchandise on Sunday morning, you'd get through in half the time. I think if you had that system, you might find that your labor on stacking merchandise was a lot less. I think you're completely right, though, that when you don't have the grocery ordering formula system,[2] you can't go to demand marking. You've certainly done a tremendous job here in this store, and I have no complaint at all about it.

Grocery manager: Well, yes, but it's all guesswork, though.

DM1: That's right. And we've found, in the other stores, that you can cut your labor way down if you're on the grocery ordering formula, no matter how good guesses you've made in the past about the kind of stuff you need and when you need it.

SM1: Well, when they put us over on a formula system, I'll consider it.

DM1: Well, you're right. I think that's the time to consider it. And you've certainly done a hell of a job here and I think it's tremendous.

Grocery manager: Well, it's not just me, it's the guys here, like Dizzy. (Points to a young fellow who is opening a carton.)

Later DM1 brought up the formula system again.

DM1: Now, don't forget, you fellows. I agree fully that when we've got this formula system in, our shelves look like hell, and there's no getting around that, but I do think it can save us some money, and we want to consider it.

Grocery manager: Well, DM1, are they resigned to not keeping neat shelves now?

DM1: Well, I don't think they mean not keeping them neat. The point is they're not full. Now, us old-time storekeepers just don't like it, and I know that you feel the same way I do. But the point is that I think we can save some money on it.

[2] This is a reference to the company's new grocery ordering system that was beginning to be installed in a few stores.

A CHANGED SUPERVISORY PATTERN

Grocery manager: Well, you're probably right. I'm an old-time storekeeper, but I'm not so old that I can't keep up with things.

DM1 explained to the observer later that he was trying to "break the ice" on the idea of changing the ordering and price marking systems in the store. Notice that all three men were very active in discussing this topic. The subject was finally dropped when SM1 commented that he would consider the idea again when the store was put on a formula system. He seemed to take it for granted that it was his decision to make, and neither of the other two men questioned this. DM1 had got the two men to thinking about the utility of the new methods, while recognizing the local conditions and leaving the initiative with the store manager. The researcher was also interested in the pride and enthusiasm displayed by the grocery manager. This spirit was apparently not damaged by this conversation as it easily could have been.

DM1 held a store meeting with SM1 and his three department heads for the purpose of discussing the most recent figures on the store. After going over these figures, which were excellent by chain standards, DM1 turned to the meat manager.

DM1: How's your head cutter coming along?
Meat manager: Well, he's coming along fine, I think he's really doing well.
DM1: Do you think he'd do as well if he were under a new manager all of a sudden?
Meat manager: Well, I don't know, I think so.
DM1: Do you think he's ready to go out on his own yet?
Meat manager: Well, I don't think he is yet. But I think if you give him six months he will. He's certainly got all the brains that anybody needs to do this, and I think about six months' more experience and he'll be in good shape.
DM1: Well, that's the way to do it. After all, you know, you've turned out an awful lot of good fellows in this department

and they're all doing very well now. That's a real feather in your cap. You know, that's the real satisfaction in this business, fellows. When you've been in it as long as I have, you can look back and see the fellows that you've brought along and really have them develop. Say, SM1, I can even remember when you were a little squirt. Seriously, fellows, that is what really means a lot in this business, a lot more than money or anything else when you get to my age. Well, that's about it for today.

In this incident we see DM1 reviewing operating results in the store and then shifting the topic to put his influence behind the development of subordinates in the stores.

> DM1 and SM1 were going over their projections on sales volume and payroll for the next quarter.

DM1: (to researcher) Well, as you probably know, the store operations manager comes up with figures for each one of these stores on his mathematical basis, taking into account trends and all that kind of stuff. Well, he gives the figures to me and I revise them with my store managers in the light of our own feeling about the store, which of course is anybody's guess. Most of the stores in my territory I revised down which is an unusual situation, but that's the way it happened this time. On the other hand, in this particular store we revised it up $1,000 because we felt it's a pretty healthy store right now.

Researcher: Whose idea was it to revise it up?

> DM1 and SM1 just smiled at each other, but did not really answer the question. DM1 was busy copying down SM1's payroll estimates for each department. At no point did he question any of SM1's figures.

DM1: Well, there they are. You set the goals, my boy. Don't complain to me if you don't make them.

SM1: Well, we set them, we'll try to make them. (DM1 left the room for a minute.)

Researcher: Seriously, whose idea was it to raise the sales volume $1,000 in here?

A CHANGED SUPERVISORY PATTERN

SM1: It was mine. I figured out how much we were running ahead of last year as a percentage. Then I went back to last year's volume at this time, and simply added to it this percentage that we were running ahead of last year. That's the way I came up with it. It's anybody's guess, but I think we'll make it. I didn't make any correction for the Brookford opening,[3] which is going to be in effect during the whole last month of this period, because you just don't know what effect something like that is going to have, so I didn't put it in at all.

There's a lot of things going on around here which might just balance out. Now we're going to have a bank put up across from our parking lot and a big life insurance office is going up down the other way. Those are all plus factors. On the other side, out here on Route 16 there's a big sign that says a Blank Store is going to go up, but that sign's been there a year, and they haven't done any building. Not very far from there though, a big market is going up, and they're really building that thing fast. But again over on the other side of the fence, there's almost 1,000 homes going up around here in two new developments that are going to be selling somewhere in the $19,000–$21,500 bracket, which means that we're going to get a nice class of trade from those homes.

So you really can't tell what effect all this is going to have, so you just leave it out. It's quite possible that we might take a little slip in September, after Brookford opens up, but what you do in a case like that is just operate to make a profit on whatever volume you get, and hope to get back into the game and beat Brookford's volume someday.

In this situation DM1 has clearly given SM1 the primary responsibility for selecting his own projections on sales and payroll. The description SM1 gives of how he made his estimates indicates that he was doing much more than giving lip service to his responsibility for both the projections and the final results. He was doing a careful job of thinking through all the factors that could effect his volume and then

---

[3] Reference is to the opening of another Food World market in a nearby community.

deciding that his target be *raised*. And this was the kind of thinking and the kind of attitude that DM1 apparently wanted.

In all these incidents involving DM1 and SM1 the remarkable fact is how well they meet the new organizational model. While DM1 occasionally reverts to the traditional district manager role, as a rule he is not only delegating more responsibilities to SM1, but he is also actively helping him establish a strong leadership position in the store. There is also evidence here that SM1, for his part, is willingly accepting responsibilities for running the store and even pressuring DM1 from below when he needs reminding about the store manager's new role. To further check the validity of these observations, we shall now look at a few episodes involving SM1 at work with his department heads.

Routine Supervision, SM1—Store Personnel

On one of his early visits to the store the researcher greeted SM1 and said he did not want to interrupt the business of the store, but simply wished to observe what went on.

SM1: Oh, you're not interrupting anything. You've probably found out by now that you can learn a lot more in the stores on Monday, Tuesday, and Wednesday, because by Thursday everything is all set up for business and all I do around here from Thursday on is just kind of keep an eye on things. Everything is all organized now. (Looking around the store.) We've got a good store here and I've got good boys. I'll stack this store up against any other in the chain for gross profit and I can do that because I've got meat gross and produce gross that are really tops.

My meat manager is a very careful cutter. His trimming is right on the line—not too much, not too little. Other stores have waste, too, but not him. He's developed a little group of restaurant people and women with large freezers that call on him every Saturday. He gives them good buys on unsold merchandise. That's better than throwing it away, and everybody's happy.

A CHANGED SUPERVISORY PATTERN

My produce man is darn good, too. He always gets a couple of dozen 25-cent melons out of every load of 19 centers. He grades everything that comes in. It's that kind of stuff that up's your gross.

Researcher: Do you spend much time working with the perishable men?

SM1: Oh, yes, I work with the meat and produce men on display, for example. They do their own planning usually, but then they come to me with their ideas on Wednesday afternoon and I either say "O.K., that looks fine" or I suggest that they change this or the other thing.

Researcher: Did you find your training program helped you in being able to work with the perishable departments?

SM1: Well, I've always kept an eye on the produce department, all during my 20 years as a grocery manager. I don't mean anything by this but I think the produce department head is the lowest technician in the store. He must be because he's the lowest paid. So I always kept an eye on fruit and vegetables but that training program helped a lot on meat. I don't mean I can cut meat or anything like that, but I got a lot of ideas about what their problems are and I picked up some good ideas, too.

SM1 got up and started walking slowly around the store. Whenever he would see a can or anything else that was out of line, he would straighten it up and the same procedure held true as he walked by the produce department—straightening up grapefruit, relining boxes of plums, peaches, etc. When he came to the pears, which didn't look so good, he stopped for a moment shaking his head. The produce manager came up with an empty cart and started pulling the pears off the display and putting them on the cart.

Produce manager: Oh, these are really awful, really awful, look at them.

SM1: Well, like I said, you'd better start selling them six for 29 (they were selling six for 39) so we can get rid of them.

Produce manager: Yeah, I'll take a dime off, I'll take a dime off.

SM1: Well, I think we'd better do something with them so we don't have to throw them all out.

Produce manager: I'll take a dime off if they want, I'll take it off. (He left for the back room with the pears.)
SM1: (To researcher.) You know these pears came in just yesterday and they really weren't any good. I told him that we'd be better off selling them six for 29 or even six for 25, so we could get a few quarters out of it, but now he's taking them out in the back room and he's just going to dump them.

In this glimpse of SM1 at work, he seems to express complete confidence in being on top of his job. He expresses confidence in his men and the store organization. In a very easy manner he chides his produce manager for trying to get too much for some poor pears.

SM1 was in the check-out counter farthest from the entrance picking up several empty boxes and putting them on top of the check-out counter.

SM1: (Calling across the store to his cash department head.) Say, have you had coffee yet?
Cash department head: No, I haven't.
SM1: Well, when you get through having coffee, get these boxes out of here, O.K.?
Cash department head: Yeah, sure thing. (He left.)

SM1 and the researcher engaged in small talk for a while, during which time SM1's eyes roamed around the store. One of the things they lit on were several small price signs lying on top of some merchandise by the check-out counter. As a clerk came by he said:

SM1: Say, what are those signs for over there?

The man silently picked up the signs and left.

SM1: (speaking to another clerk) Here's a present for you (giving a few rags and an empty coke bottle to a grocery clerk who silently took them).
SM1: (calling over to his grocery manager) Would you send Joe over to help out the dairy man?

Grocery manager: Sure thing. I've got him on a job now and as soon as he's through I'll send him over, O.K.?

Again we see SM1 in a relaxed manner keeping his eyes on the entire store operation and giving straightforward directions as required. Notice that on minor housekeeping details he gives instructions directly to grocery clerks but in reassigning a grocery clerk he works through his grocery manager.

Relations with Merchandisers

On another visit SM1 was discussing his relationship with the produce merchandiser in response to a question of the researcher's.

SM1: I get along fine with the produce merchandiser for this store. We get along fine—always have. We get our information from headquarters on Tuesday or Wednesday about the special promotions we should have that week in both our perishable departments. Then the produce manager uses one of these diagrams to lay out his display for the week. Then he brings it to me and I look it over and usually make a few notes on it like, "Check Blank Markets for prices on corn," or something like that—there are certain items we have to be locally competitive on—and then we come to an agreement on the display. Usually Wednesday afternoon or Thursday the produce merchandiser will come in and check over our display to see how he likes it. Usually he doesn't change a thing. I get along very well with him, because I figure if you work with a fellow like that, he'll help out in a pinch—and he does, too. Sometimes, a couple of my fellows will be out sick and the produce manager will be behind the eightball and not set up for business and, without a word, the produce merchandiser will just take off his coat and go to work for an hour and straighten everything up for you. But if I didn't work with him, he'd have a perfect right to report something like that to headquarters. But he never does, and we get along just fine.

A few minutes after this conversation about the produce

merchandiser, he entered the store and, after greeting SM1, went into the back room where he found the produce manager. He asked to see the display plan for the week and, taking it with him, went out and looked over the setup for about five minutes. After he had finished this, he talked with SM1 and the produce manager for a few minutes about some personnel difficulties he was having in attempting to fill the opening week personnel for a new store, and then left.

As was pointed out in the preceding chapter, one of the new relationships that the reorganization called for was that of the merchandiser working with store personnel in a staff rather than a line capacity. Here we see SM1 talking about the way he works with his produce merchandiser and then we see that the actual behavior fits the description. SM1 sees the merchandiser as a welcome source of help—not as a threat to his authority in the store. The merchandiser also apparently feels satisfied with his staff relationship to the store personnel.

Comments on DM1—SM1 Relationship

To round out our picture of what was going on in the relationship between DM1 and SM1, we shall look at some of the comments these men made to the researcher on the topic.

DM1: SM1 runs a happy store, and for my money that's one of the most important things there is. He's not developing quite as fast as I'd like, but I certainly have all the confidence in the world in him and I'm sure he'll come along. You know, several of the district managers criticized me when I put him into that store because they felt that he wasn't quite aggressive enough, or "pushy" I guess would be the word for it. But in these smaller communities, I think that aggressiveness can be more of a drawback than anything else. He wears well with the trade and he wears well with his help. I think that's very important, particularly in this kind of community.

He knows how to assign work, too, and that's very important. He can give an order and it'll be followed up and it'll be done. I think he's going to be a real executive. He's not like some others who do a simply terrific job in running a store but do a lot of the work themselves.

One of the most interesting things to me that's happened in store 45 is what's happened to the people who work under SM1. I remember ten years ago I had a conversation with his grocery manager in which I told him outright I just didn't think he had the interest of the company at heart, even though he was doing an acceptable job. But, if you go in there today and talk to him, you won't find a more enthusiastic person; and everybody in the store is like that. Of course, we picked him for that job because we felt he had this ability, and most of the things I try and do in the store are to develop it further. But I'm really proud of him. I think he's got a real ability to organize people, and that's what we want in our store managers.

Notice in DM1's comments how he is judging SM1's performance by many of the same standards that top management desired to attain in these new store managers: skilled handling of personnel, development of subordinates, and customer relations.

At a later time SM1 commented on how he ran his store.

Researcher: One of the things we're interested in is when and under what circumstances do you transfer people from one department to another in the store?

SM1: (smiling) Well, I've got some opinions on that! That's one of those things that looks a heck of a lot better on paper than it really works out. But there are some times when we do do it in here. For example, if a fellow in one department is sick, we try to fill in if we can or, if there is a big rush up here at the front end and we need bundlers and checkers, we try and get them from the other departments. Or, once in a while, we'll give the produce manager a hand, particularly on a Friday morning if his load has come in all mixed up.

So those are the times when we do it, but as I said before it's one of those things that really looks a lot better on paper than it works out in practice. And another thing—I've been running a payroll of between 5.4% and 5.1% here for the last five months. Now every single one of my departments has been cut right straight down to the bone on payroll or I wouldn't be able to have a store average like that. So what does that mean? That means that if I find that I can really spare a man from one department to another one for longer than an hour or two then I really don't need him where he is and, of course, that never happens. I can't spare my men. The way our payroll is running, if I cut a man loose for more than an hour, that whole department is really shot.

On paper it says it is easy to do but.... (laughs softly) Of course you figure at one end you've got zero per cent and at the other end you've got 100%, and if you've gotten as far as 50% then you figure you're pretty well off. And in this store we are pretty close to 100%; we're pretty far along. For example, when you have a fellow like my meat manager saying to you, "Look, I'm short-handed. I'm going to have to put some more hands on, but I really think I can do it with only a part-time person and maybe you can use the other half of that week's salary to give them a hand over in the grocery department." Well, when you've got a meat manager that thinks like that you are really pretty far along. You are pretty close to that 100%.

Yes, I've really got a good deal here in this store, because I've got good boys, and we work together pretty well. Of course the meat manager has only been with us five years and that's a good thing. Before that he was with another chain and that's a hell of a lot easier for me than if I had one of those twenty-year men in here. When those twenty-year meat men find a grocery manager who they thought was their equal for the last twenty years all of a sudden coming over to them as a store manager, they're not too happy about it. They don't like the idea that an equal of theirs is now their boss.

And that reminds me of something else—about how you have to use discretion when you move into a store. You can't just be a boss because your boss says you're a boss. That's not the important thing. You've got to take four months or six months or maybe a year, and you've got to try and bring harmony into the store rather than just barge your way into everything in one month.

You have got to continually keep in mind how it is these fellows are going to feel when you tell them something. You can make them feel good about a bad decision or you can make them feel bad about a bad decision, but it's their feelings you've got to keep in mind and not just go trampling over them.

There's a lot of little things that go together that make a good store, and that's only one of them. It'll all work out. It's working out pretty well now. There's a lot of little things that have to go together. The district manager has to be on your side. He can't be doing things that will keep you from moving in as boss, but there's a lot more to it besides that. You've got to have good personalities in the store on a department head level and on the store manager level, and, if your district manager is going to criticize somebody, or pay somebody a compliment, he should have you along and maybe he could mention it was the store manager's idea. So if you get all these things working together, and they are really all just little things, you're going to have a good store.

SM1's comments again reflect his confidence in handling his job and clarify some of his methods. He expresses his awareness of the need to work on the building of good relationships with his key subordinates. He sees this as taking time, but he feels that he is making real progress. And while he gives credit for the help of his department heads and of his district manager, he still feels that this is something he is doing. In other words, he seems to feel independent—maintaining a sense of choice. He is clearly getting personal satisfaction from his work and feels he is developing himself and learning.

Summary

The picture given above of the DM1–SM1 relationship is remarkable for the exactness with which it follows top management's organizational plan for the desired store manager and district manager roles. By and large, the communication in this relationship is two way, the quality of understanding and problem solving seems good, and it is following the approved new channels. Here is a district manager who is seen working actively and effectively in getting the store manager to assume more initiative and sense of responsibility for his store. He is doing this so effectively that the store manager does not give him much credit for his own development. Here is a district manager who is helping the store manager establish his leadership in all parts of the store and a store manager who, over time, is succeeding in doing it. Even in the area of establishing a different relationship with the staff merchandiser, the limited evidence indicates that top management's plan has been translated pretty well into daily behavior. While we have not attempted to track down signs of change at the level of the clerks, we have seen evidence of change in the direction top management desired in the attitudes of the grocery manager and the meat manager.

The full significance of this picture will only be apparent as we move on to look at our next DM–SM pair.

CHAPTER V

A Changing Supervisory Pattern

IN THE SUMMER of 1955, SM2 was picked for promotion from his job as grocery manager to a position as store manager under the supervision of DM2. These two men were no strangers to each other or to the company. DM2 had supervised SM2's work for several years. SM2 had worked for the company for more than twenty years, and DM2 had been a district manager for more than twenty years. It is the work of these two men that we shall be observing in the next few pages.

BEHAVIOR PATTERN, DM2 AND SM2

Initial Indoctrination

Our first look at these men is in a meeting called to introduce SM2 as store manager to the personnel in his new store. The store operations manager and his assistant had arranged for the meeting and the assistant acted as chairman. Also present in addition to DM2 and SM2 were the meat and produce merchandisers who covered the store, and the heads of the store's four departments—the grocery, meat, produce, and cash departments. The meeting was held in the store office.

Assistant Store Operations Manager: I'd like to get this started and I'll keep this meeting as short as possible. I know you men all want to get back to your customers upstairs.

DM2: (interrupting) We'll give you fifteen minutes.

Assistant Store Operations Manager: I might even be able to make that. We are holding this meeting today to inform you all of something that, of course, you all know about. It is that

SM2 will be taking over in a few days as store manager here. We thought this would be a good time to review with all of you, and most of you know some of these things already, what we have in mind with this whole store manager program and how we think things could best work out here in the store. After I've talked to you a little bit about this, I'd like to have you raise any questions you might have about the whole matter. I know that with something new like this there's always a few problems that come up and have to be worked out, and I know that all of you people might well have some questions you'd like to raise that would help us see that things get clicking just right under this setup.

Now the whole idea of this store manager program is to bring into the store a person who will have complete responsibility for all aspects of the business. He'll be responsible for all departments and all phases of those departments and we'll have that responsibility right in one person. That's the chief advantage of this program. It's a program that stores in other parts of the country have gone to and it has proven to be a success. It has a number of advantages. It allows the whole store and all the store personnel to think of themselves more as working toward a common objective and working as a team. It gives us more chance to have interchangeability of people from one job to another in the store which gives people a chance to learn more than one job. It gives the individual a chance to move ahead and gives us more flexibility in running our stores efficiently. We want the store manager to be, in effect, what we call a resident supervisor. He will be like the district manager for this particular store and have over-all responsibility for getting things done and getting results.

This program has some real advantages from the standpoint of you department heads, too. It gives you somebody you can go to quite readily; somebody who will always be around and give you faster action in solving your problems and getting things done you need to do your job. It also gives you a chance to be a member of a very close management team right in the store. Working with one another as a team, you can get results for the store as a whole. We'll expect you to work as a team and you've got to try and work it out that way. Now SM2 is known to some extent by all of you. He's a fellow who has had about two weeks' experience in meat, one week in produce, and years and years of experience in the grocery business. I heard he isn't going to come into the different departments of the store and act as if he knows all the answers and can tell you just exactly how to run every part of your business. He isn't going to do that because he really doesn't know that much about it. He has been trained enough so that he can take a look into the different departments of the store pretty much as the customer would look at it and see some things that he would call to your attention that will need taking care of. I think he can be of help to you in that way, and, of course, he can help in a lot of other ways too.

Another thing I thought I would mention is just how we would expect the store manager and the merchandisers to work together. There has been a little confusion about this in a few places, and I thought it might be worth mentioning what we expect on this. We expect the merchandiser, when he first comes into the store, to check in with the store manager if he's at all available and tell him he's here. Probably the store manager will go right with him as he goes around and looks at the departments he is concerned with. Now he, of course, is going to have some ideas that he will pass on to the department heads, and we expect before the merchandiser checks out of the store he will go back to the store manager and tell him about the principal ideas he has passed on to the department heads. We expect this to work this way for a number of reasons. Primarily because it is awfully hard on the department heads, as we all know, to have somebody like the merchandiser come up to him and tell him to do something one way and about a half hour later have the store manager come up and tell him to do it some other way. We have to keep together on these things. Now there may occasionally be an incident where the idea of the merchandiser doesn't check with the idea of the store manager about how to do something. We don't think that will happen often but we have to be prepared for the times it will. When that happens those two men along with the department head ought to sit down and try to thrash out the differences and come to an agreement. If they find it impossible to do that after they have talked about it for awhile, then the final decision as to what will be done will have to be made by the district manager.

Another point I want to make clear is that the store manager is working exclusively for the district manager. He is the boss of the whole works, and that means that even a merchandising manager who might come down here in the store doesn't have any business telling people what to do. They can make suggestions and their suggestions are to be taken seriously, but the final authority on what's to be done in the store rests with the district manager.

Now I wonder if any of you have any questions you want to voice about these arrangements and how they work out.

The produce merchandiser asked about the policy for managers taking days off in a store manager store.

Assistant Store Operations Manager: Well, I don't think there are any rules on the thing and I'm not in a position to make any rules on it. I think that sort of thing has to be worked out on the spot. SM2 will have to go into it and I am sure he would want to get your ideas on it too before he set up the days off. And of course this will also have to be worked out to work into the plans of the district manager.

DM2: I'd like to say something in here at this point about this program, and I'm going to address this to the cash department head. This may sound like criticism but I don't mean it that way and I don't think anybody here will take it that way. You all know me well enough to know what I mean by this. Now I want to make it clear that SM2 has a responsibility to me for running this store right, and each one of you as department heads have a responsibility to SM2 to see that you are running your own department right. Now I want to make this perfectly clear (standing up) that I don't think you (cash department head) are always carrying out your responsibility on this kind of thing. For instance, if Mrs. DM2 walks up to check out her food, you are all bowing and scraping and doing everything you can to be pleasant and nice and helpful to her. Now that's all right, and you have a responsibility to the customer, but I am not sure you are thinking at that particular moment—is my chief responsibility to this customer or is it to see that the five or six other people that are working for me at the different cash registers are doing what they should be doing to give the customers the service we want to give them? But, if that other thing isn't being taken care of, that should take priority over your being nice to Mrs. DM2. That is your responsibility. Of course you have to worry about the customer, but you must primarily worry about whether your men are looking out for the customer or not. I think that is something you've got to learn to do.

Assistant Store Operations Manager: Yes, I think what DM2 is trying to say, or rather what he is saying, is that all of you have the job of supervising the work of others and you are primarily responsible to see that they are performing their duties. You can't do them all yourself. If you follow through on this, it will make your own job easier and the whole situation more pleasant for everybody. Now would any of the rest of you like to raise any questions or comments on this thing? How about you (looking at the meat manager)?

Meat manager: I am perfectly happy about this whole thing.

Produce manager: Yuh, it's O.K. with me.

Assistant Store Operations Manager: Well, if there isn't anything else then we can break up. I'd just like to congratulate you, SM2, and give you our best wishes and I know it's going to go well.

At this point all the department heads and the merchandisers shook SM2's hand, and told him they would enjoy working for him. They all then left the room.

DM2: I'd like to say just one other thing to you, SM2, and that is that I'd like to make a bet with you. If and when you can get the volume of this store up to $70,000 a week, I want to take you and your wife out to dinner and to the theater. I mean that and I really think you can do it. I think the day will even come when you'll get to 75.

SM2: Well, thanks a lot.

DM2: I think there's another thing for you to remember too,

and that is I think you have to have a relationship with your department heads in which they have a certain fearful respect for you. I don't mean fear in the bad sense at all. I mean they have to really have respect for the fact that you're boss, and that you're in charge and responsible for running things.

The Store Operations Manager added some comments on the need to improve the clerks' attitudes toward customers and the meeting then broke up.

This meeting was, of course, important primarily for its ceremonial value. Higher management was giving SM2 its official and public endorsement of him as store manager. The meeting also gave higher management a chance to restate the official way in which the new store manager was to work with store department heads, the district manager, and the merchandisers. Then, after a couple of perfunctory questions, DM2 chose to use this occasion to criticize the cash department head. This may have been wise or not, but in any event it was not working through the new store manager in dealing with department heads. After the department heads and merchandisers left the meeting, DM2 gave SM2 a personal challenge to improve the performance of the store and urged SM2 to establish his leadership in the store on the traditional basis of "fearful respect." It is interesting also to note that SM2 said virtually nothing during the meeting.

Routine Supervision, DM2—SM2

Our next look at the evolving relationship between DM2 and SM2 is four days later on the occasion of SM2's first full day in the store as the new store manager.

DM2: I'm very concerned about the store's condition. Things are fouled up here. We're having a lot of trouble getting the merchandise onto the shelves. The basement area that is used for grocery storage is poorly laid out.

A CHANGING SUPERVISORY PATTERN

Shortly thereafter DM2 and SM2 toured the basement area.

DM2: How can your men ever take a decent inventory down here, SM2? I've seen the same items stocked in several different places.
SM2: Well, they can't under those conditions. We've got a lot of work to do down here.
DM2: Just look at this stuff here. This olive oil. I've seen that in two other places on the floor.
SM2: Well, look at this over here. It's the same story over here. This is really fouled up.

The two men continued to exchange remarks of this kind as they walked around the basement noting different things that were in bad shape. They talked about all the extra groceries which had been dumped on them by the warehouse a few weeks earlier because of the shortage of storage space.

DM2: Boy, this place gives me an ulcer. You can see what it is doing to me. Just look at that conveyor there. That's a real Rube Goldberg. We've got to get that thing changed around too.
SM2: Well if you'll be patient with me, boss, on this thing, I'll get it squared away for you. I know I can get it done.
DM2: Well, I know you can too. It's just going to be hard for me to be patient. I'm so anxious to get it cleaned up. But I know you'll get it done if I give you the time, and I certainly know you need time to straighten this out. It won't be done overnight, so don't think I think it will. You know last week our problems were in the front end of this store and now they're down here. Last week we had a lot of trouble getting people through the check-out booths and I spent quite a bit of time working on that. Of course, that will still take some time, and you know I want to tell you that I don't blame that on the cash department head. We can't expect our people to do those things unless we train them to do them.
SM2: That's right. If the pupil hasn't learned; the teacher

hasn't taught. I don't blame him either. We're just going to have to keep working with him on this thing.

DM2: That's right and I think he will do it, too. It's going to take some time. Certainly the fellow is willing and hardworking. He did a good job for us on the drug counters and on the frozen foods, so we move him up to the front end and give him the keys to the car and tell him to drive it, and he hasn't even had a driving lesson. That's one thing we don't do a good job of in our company.

It will take some doing to straighten out this basement. you're going to have a big job down here to clean this place up.

SM2: Well, I'll certainly have to agree with you on that.

DM2: (to researcher) You know this fellow will do a good job out here. He's really going to get on top of the store and handle it right. I'm sure of that. My whole problem in working with him is one of trying to be patient and stay out of here enough to give him a chance. I've got to hold my tongue while he gets going. (DM2 then pretended to be stuttering to indicate how he was going to have to try to keep from saying things to SM2.)

Here we see DM2 reviewing with SM2 the problems he faces in the store. DM2 is keenly aware that he needs to change his usual way of dealing with these problems. He knows and acknowledges that he must discipline himself to stay out of the problems. He expresses his confidence in SM2, and he knows he should give SM2 a chance to handle his store problems and thereby establish his leadership in the store. However, before he left the store that day he was talking to SM2 as follows:

DM2: One thing I want you to do as soon as you can in this store is to clean up that back room there. I see so many carriages out there full of junk that I just can't take it any more. I really want you to clean it out. I don't want to see it that way the next time I come back in.

(SM2 nodded in agreement.)

A CHANGING SUPERVISORY PATTERN 105

And the other thing is that I think you ought to get right on to fixing up that delicatessen table. That thing isn't set up right yet and I want you to get on to it and square it away.
(SM2 again nodded in agreement.)

So we see that DM2 is giving SM2 detailed instructions on matters that bother him in spite of his sincere intentions of giving SM2 time to work out his problems in his own way.

After DM2 had left for the day the researcher asked SM2 for his views of his assignment.

Researcher: Since this is the first full day you have had as store manager, I am interested in the fact that you seem to know quite a bit about the people here, about the routines, and about what needs to be done.
SM2: Well that's true, but you know I've been in this business for twenty years. You learn a lot about running a store in that time.
Researcher: So you've already seen some things that you are going ahead and doing something about.
SM2: That's right. Already I've got a few things lined up—like a change in the time that we order and do our inventory work on our groceries. With my experience I know that it will work out better if we change it. I am also looking over the payroll to make sure we haven't got any padding there. You know I've had to annihilate help before and I'll have to do it again here, perhaps. I found quite a bit of extra labor over at my last store and that's one of the things we did over there to get that place cleared away.
Researcher: I noticed you were talking quite a bit about the basement. How long will it take you before you get that in the shape you want it in?
SM2: Well in six or eight weeks I think I'll have this store in pretty good shape. I think in that length of time I can do it. You know I've had to clean up other basements before.

SM2 expresses confidence that he knows what needs to be done to improve the store and confidence that he can do it.

There was no sign that he was getting this sense of self-confidence from the qualified confidence that his boss had just expressed. Rather his confidence seems to be stemming from his experience and his job knowledge.

Two months later DM2 was still unhappy about the appearance of SM2's store. The following episodes give a sample of the problems that concerned DM2 and the way he handled them with SM2 during a lengthy visit to the store in early December.

DM2: SM2, I think you are short-handed on your grocery help. I think you are planning too tight. You ought to get some people in here and get these shelves loaded up. I suggest you get some more help in here and see if you can't get this cleared away a little better. Now, how about this matter of getting delivery on certain short items.

SM2: Well, I've called in about it and they told me they're going to do it the day after tomorrow.

DM2: Do you believe them? I'm glad you do. I wish I could. I've had some pretty sad experiences with that group. They've never proved to me since they began that they're really a service group. (Pointing to drug counter.) Now this is the kind of thing I mean over there. Now take a look at that. I'll be truthful to you, it looks a little better to me today than it did on Saturday when I looked at it, but it still doesn't look right. Now you've got two girls working part-time on this.

SM2: One and a half.

DM2: Yah, one and a half. It seems to me with that kind of help you should be able to keep that drug counter looking better. Now take a look at this, you see the price tags are all in the wrong places, and the shelf looks pretty sloppy. I think you've just got to make it clear to these people what you expect to get from them by way of results and see that you get it. You may even have to put a little more help on this, but we should get this thing looking better than this.

* * * * *

DM2: Say, I see you don't have much of this specialty appetizer line left. What's happened to all that stuff you had up here?

SM2: Oh, it's sold I guess.

DM2: Yah, guess. What I want to know is whether it's sold or stolen.

* * * * *

DM2: Now, what I'd like to have you do on this side is to get all your things centralized in this one spot and then it will look a lot better. And take these cones up here. I think the biscuit people are fine people, but I don't think you ought to give them that much space. You see you've got six rows of this stuff up there and I don't believe you'd sell that much in well over a week.
SM2: But those are really three different items—you see, three different kinds of cones.
DM2: Oh, you're right. I didn't notice that. Excuse me.

* * * * *

DM2: Now take this stand over here. I think you're giving just too much space to the produce people in this area right here. You see you've got all those displays of nuts and dried stuff in there, and you're cutting out your candy counter here. I think you ought to be able to push those things out and consolidate them in there so that you've got the line drawn right down here between the candy department and the produce department. You know I'll tell you something about the produce man. If you give him an inch, he'll want a mile. You give them a little space and they always want more; they never will have enough. I don't think you're going to sell enough of this stuff to make it worth giving him that much space.
SM2: O.K.
DM2: And I'll tell you something else. You see these marshmallows here. I wouldn't blame you a bit if you gave those about three rows. You've only got those packed in one. And I'll tell you something else, you see these small packages of raisins. I wouldn't think you had bad judgment if you made a big mass display of those and brought in about 25 cases and stacked them up and really moved them. I think they'd sell. I wouldn't say you were wrong. You see it's just judgment, judgment, judgment on all these items! How does this make you feel?
SM2: Oh, good. Good and lousy.

* * * * *

DM2: Take a look at that shelving there. That looks hot, doesn't it?

SM2: But look, these guys are trying you know. They haven't had too much time and they are trying to get this thing cleared away.

DM2: I don't say they're not trying. I know they're trying. (Pointing to a stack of boxes that were in one corner of the back room.) You know that just shouldn't be there, don't you?

SM2: Well, it wasn't that way last Friday. It came in since then.

DM2: Well, I know that's true, but you know it just shouldn't be in there. I don't blame you for it either. There is a place for this stuff, you know, and you've got to train these people to put it in the right place, but I really don't blame you. But you know you can't do all these things yourself. You can't be everywheres, and you're not good to me dead you know. You shouldn't have to be limping around here and trying to straighten out that kind of thing. You know what's right and what ought to be done the same as I do. I don't have to tell you. Say (speaking to the man who was working in the back room), look at that junk set up by that public address system there. How does that get there anyway?

Back Room Man: Oh, I keep after it.

DM2: Look, if you have to, go around and start breaking people's arms if they don't understand these things.

* * * * *

DM2: (walking around in the basement) Take a look at this stuff around here. I don't know how it gets this way, but you know as well as I do that it shouldn't be this way. Look at those carriages. If we're going to have broken carriages down here, why can't we have them in one place so that every time we bring one down we can put it over in that place. Then we'll know where they are and eventually we'll get them fixed. Now look at this stuff—all this broken merchandise. You see that's all over the place. Why can't we have a place where we can keep it together, and when anybody has this kind of thing, they'll put it in there and there it'll be.

* * * * *

A CHANGING SUPERVISORY PATTERN   109

DM2: (in basement) Take a look at those panda bears there. What are they doing? They don't look like they're worth selling. (SM2 took them down and looked at them and they were pretty dirty.) Why don't you just throw those things out and get rid of them? You shouldn't have that junk in here.

Well, things really do look lousy down here. Everything is done wrong down here. There's no getting around it. Everything seems to be in the wrong place and it all looks bad. Now I know, and you know, that you were in pretty good shape in here three weeks ago. You're as bad now as when we first came out here. These two holidays came along and you ordered according to your best judgment and now we're back in this shape. One of the keys is, of course, to get our merchandise down to a decent level to see what we're doing and stop stumbling over things.

The pattern of supervision we see in these incidents looks much more like the traditional pattern than like the new organizational model. DM2 is finding many details that he thinks are wrong and that he expects SM2 to correct. He takes some of the edge off of his demands by acknowledging the difficulties SM2 is working under. He focuses his attention on the technical details of the job and does not talk about the organizational aspects. He gives instructions directly to grocery clerks and thereby violates the required channels. All his attention is also on the grocery end of the business with the exception of his reference to the space desires of the produce people—and then he identifies with the grocery point of view.

Three days later the researcher had a chance to ask SM2 if he was bothered by DM2's visit described above.

SM2: No, it didn't bother me because I knew what the reasons were for the trouble and I knew we were going to lick it in time. You see it looks a lot better now, and I think we'll keep making it look better. It was just the holiday business that threw us off.

DM2's criticisms did not seem to have much effect on

SM2 one way or the other. He was still confident that he could handle the problems of the store.

Relations with Merchandisers

The researcher had several opportunities to observe DM2 and SM2 working with the two merchandisers. The following three episodes are typical.

> DM2, SM2, the meat department manager, and the meat merchandiser sat down in the store office to go over some personnel matters. The merchandiser outlined a proposal of his for a series of related personnel transfers. At one point he turned to the researcher.

Merchandiser: I want to make one thing clear. You know meat merchandisers are not supposed to spend any of their time handling personnel problems. You understand that, don't you? But it just so happens that is what we spend most of our time doing.

> When the merchandiser finished going through the sequence of personnel shifts, DM2 simply said, "I'll buy." The merchandiser then turned to the meat department manager and asked him which of two men he would like to send out of his store to another one. There was a little exchange of opinions on this and the meat manager finally made his choice and the merchandiser agreed to it. SM2 asked a few questions during this conversation and indicated by his comments that he knew the people and knew what these moves were, but his opinions were not requested or offered and he did not participate in the final decisions.

* * * * *

> The produce merchandiser came up to DM2 and spent some time in proposing to him that he hire a full-time man to work nights in the produce department in SM2's store. DM2's reply was that he thought the night produce boss was weak and they might have to do something about that. The merchandiser kept saying that they needed more time to test the night boss and one way to get more support for

A CHANGING SUPERVISORY PATTERN

him was to give him a good night helper. DM2 never did respond to this suggestion. A little later the merchandiser made the same suggestion to SM2 while they were by themselves. SM2 immediately said, "If you think that will help, why don't you go right ahead and do it. I'm all for it."

DM2 in these instances is condoning the traditional pattern of having the merchandisers (ex-ADM's) take the initiative in lining up personnel shifts between the perishable departments in different stores. While this practice does not conform to the new organizational model, it is not too surprising since the merchandisers were in a position to be well informed on the talents of people and the needs for people. However, DM2 also passively watched SM2 being left out of the discussion when the merchandiser asked the meat department manager to make a choice.

In the second incident DM2, for unknown reasons, did not respond to the merchandiser's suggestion on a personnel change. The merchandiser then decided to raise the question with SM2 who, without hesitation, gave his approval and in this way asserted his leadership in the produce department. Again we see that DM2 is not doing much to build up SM2 and his position but SM2 is going ahead confidently on his own to establish his position.

Routine Supervision, SM2—Store Personnel

This same pattern was observable in the following typical incidents of SM2's dealings with his own department heads.

> The grocery manager came up and asked SM2 for permission to order a special item. When SM2 agreed, the grocery manager then picked up a catalogue in the office and started looking for the item. SM2 suggested that he might try the specialty catalogue. The grocery manager laughed with embarrassment and said, "That's a good idea. I guess you're useful for something around here."

* * * * *

The produce manager entered the office and said something to SM2 in a complaining tone about the amount of money they got out of a load of celery they had to sell at a reduced price. SM2 told him he was lucky to get anything out of it and then did quite a bit of kidding with the produce manager while the latter made a phone call. Finally the produce manager turned to SM2 and in quite a loud voice but in a kidding manner said, "Why don't you shut up so that I can finish making this phone call?" Everyone laughed at this, and SM2 continued to kid the produce manager until he left.

* * * * *

SM2 walked into the produce department and spent quite a bit of time observing the work. Then he went into the back room and asked the people back there if they knew where the produce manager was. They said he was out to coffee and SM2 complained because just a few minutes earlier he had bought him a cup of coffee. SM2 asked, "Do you think that's grounds for dismissal?" SM2 then went out to the produce floor and looked at the way the manager had arranged the specials for the week, checked them against his merchandising plan, and pointed out that he had already discussed with the produce manager earlier in the week the way he would handle the specials. He said he was just checking to see if it was all done.

* * * * *

SM2 walked into the meat back room, and spent quite a bit of time kidding the meat wrappers and cutters as they stopped for a coffee break. The manager was not present. SM2 then walked out to the front end of the meat department and spoke to the meat manager about the specials for the week. He informed the meat manager that they were not going to run a newspaper ad on lamb legs but rather just on roasts. They discussed his displays.

As SM2 walked away, he explained to the researcher that since he had been in this store he made it a habit to check the code date on all the meat items, and the meat manager had adopted the practice of sending a man around the last

A CHANGING SUPERVISORY PATTERN 113

thing each day before the store closed and getting all the over-age items out of the counter, so that SM2 would not find any the next morning.

SM2: That's exactly what I wanted him to do. Now, of course, I can't find any over-aged items in his counters and that's what I want.

* * * * *

SM2 explained the layout he had planned for rearranging the basement storage area. The researcher asked what he was doing to get this conversion made.

SM2: I've spoken to DM2 about it and he's working on it. I also had an opportunity to speak to the store operations manager about it once when he was in the store. Then last night I discussed it with the head of our construction department and he seemed to think it was a good idea. I urged him to try and get it done next month when his setup crews would not have to be working on new stores.

* * * * *

SM2 explained to a store manager in training how he got results in his produce department.

SM2: I've got the produce manager competing against his own number two man to see who can get the most stuff in the display case the first thing in the morning. What I did was ask them to start at different ends of the counter every morning and work toward the middle. In that way I get them racing to see who will get to the middle first and finish up before the other one gets there. At first I asked them if they could get it finished by 10:30 and they came back and told me that they had made it. Then I worked them up finally until 10 o'clock, and now they're getting it done at least by 9:45 every morning. I sort of give them a challenge and the rest takes care of itself. They really get a big kick out of getting it done faster than I thought they could.

In these incidents we see SM2 assuming a leadership role in all departments of the store. He seems to combine a relaxed and kidding manner with a straightforward review with the department head of what he wants done. He does not hesitate to bring pressure not only on his own boss but also on higher officials to get the things he needs to run his store. In all of his behavior he expresses confidence in his own ability to run his store.

Summary

As might be expected, SM2 was rated by DM2 and others as an excellent store manager. One of the merchandisers commented that SM2 had shown an unusual interest in learning about the produce department and, as a result, really understood its problems and was able to make wise decisions in that area.

As with our last pair of supervisors, DM1 and SM1, the DM2 and SM2 combination appears to be getting the results in the store that meet the requirements of the organizational model. In contrast to DM1, however, it is a real question whether DM2 is helping or hurting these results. SM2 is meeting his new role requirements even though DM2 does not provide much help to him in establishing his leadership. We see that DM2 has a tendency to by-pass SM2 in dealings with the merchandisers and department heads. DM2 on occasion forgets his own good intentions by giving detailed and rather obvious instructions. He does, however, express confidence in SM2 and give SM2 the feeling that his boss understands the problems he is up against. From this look at DM2, it appears that he is not yet meeting his new role requirements even though he expresses some understanding of the new model and some interest in following it.

Our final pair will give us even a different picture.

CHAPTER VI

An Unchanged Supervisory Pattern

OUR FINAL district manager–store manager pair were also long-service employees of Food World. DM3 had held a number of supervisory positions in the company and was one of the most senior district managers. SM3 was being promoted to his new job from a smaller store where he had been grocery manager for many years and where DM3 had been his immediate supervisor for a number of months. Store 40 that SM3 was to manage was a new store. After SM3 had finished his six-week store manager training program, he had spent two weeks in the new store before it was open to the public. Our first glimpse of DM3 and SM3 working together comes on the opening day of the store and begins to build up a picture of the pattern of their relationship.

BEHAVIOR PATTERN, DM3 AND SM3

Initial Indoctrination

Before 9:00 o'clock of opening day, many of the top executives of the chain were in the store. Things seemed to be well organized and the store was ready to open.

Shortly after the crowd surged through the open doors, DM3 came over to SM3: "You better keep an eye on these grocery carriages; we are almost out. Try and get them out of the cashiers' tables and set up here by the front door as soon as you can."

SM3 nodded and from then until noon he remained at this task almost continuously.

Around 11:00 o'clock the opening surge fell off somewhat, and SM3 went out to the back room for a cup of coffee where he met DM3.

SM3: Say, DM3, we have some awfully slow cashiers out there.
DM3: I don't think so. You have four experienced people out there, don't you?
SM3: Yes.
DM3: Well, that's about as good as you can expect on an opening day with four good people in there.
SM3: Well, yes, that's right.

During the opening day rush these were the only two interactions that were observed between DM3 and SM3. They illustrate the kind of relationship that further observations revealed as a consistent pattern. Notice that DM3's first contact with SM3 on opening day was to give him an instruction, a simple and straightforward order to look after the grocery carriages. SM3 complied without comment and stayed with the job for the rest of the morning. At the time SM3 received the instruction he, obviously, was doing something else. He did not raise any question with DM3 about the relative importance of the two jobs. He did not question whether it might not be better to assign another man to the carriage job. He simply, without a word, did what he was told and this was clearly what DM3 expected him to do. And, in spite of all the other assignments he might have shifted to, he stayed with this job throughout the hectic morning.

In the second interaction we see SM3 taking the initiative in raising with DM3 his doubts about the cashiers. DM3 replies, in effect, that SM3 does not need to worry. He did not explore the question or ask if SM3 had any constructive suggestions. In both of these interactions DM3 makes the decision that closes the conversation.

Routine Supervision, DM3—SM3

Our next look at DM3 and SM3 is the occasion of one of DM3's routine supervisory visits to the store some weeks later. It gives us a chance to see more of the pattern of their relationship.

AN UNCHANGED SUPERVISORY PATTERN

DM3 entered the store and, after telling SM3 in some detail just what was expected of him at a women's club meeting at which SM3 was to represent the store, he asked SM3 to follow him upstairs to the lunch room.

DM3 spread out a list he had prepared in which he had located, in other stores, a number of different types of promotion dishes SM3 needed to meet certain of his customers' needs. He requested SM3 to produce his inventory of the dishes he had on hand and, when it became apparent that SM3 did not have one, DM3 sat down with SM3 and the two of them took inventory. DM3 directed this process and gave SM3 detailed instructions such as, "Just put down the letter 'P' there for that on your list. Don't bother to write out 'pink.' It takes too long. Just use the letter 'P.'"

After about an hour, SM3 left the room for a minute and DM3 explained to the researcher that SM3 was all mixed up on these dishes and that while he hated to spend the time to go over them and straighten them out, it was clear SM3 wasn't handling them correctly. He also expressed irritation about SM3's confusion about the luncheon meeting.

After SM3 came back, DM3 asked him about his list of slow-moving items. SM3 said he didn't know about that and would go and get it. Again he left the room.

DM3: (to researcher) That's the sort of thing that he should have the answer to. In most stores this conversation would only take two or three minutes but now he's got to go out and look it up. That's one way you can get a fast notion of whether or not the store manager is on top of things. This fellow doesn't seem to be in touch with what's really going on in his own store. I really shouldn't be getting into so many details of this kind, but in this instance it seems I just have to straighten things out.

SM3 returned and the two men discussed several items DM3 had on his list, returning again to the luncheon.

SM3: Should I tell the meat man about it?
DM3: I don't see why.

SM3: Well, I was just thinking he might not be dressed for this kind of a luncheon. He might just come in a sport jacket or something, and be embarrassed by the way he was dressed.
DM3: I think you've got a point there. I'll try to speak to him about it ahead of time.
SM3: Do you think we ought to bring the grocery manager?
DM3: Well, I think that's something we can decide; what do you want to do?
SM3: It just occurred to me that it might make a difference to the store operations manager whether we did or not.
DM3: Look, you don't need to worry about what he thinks. What I mean is I am sure he will go along with anything we agree on.

DM3 told SM3 to get some dishes out of the lunchroom, and, when SM3 carried them out and set them in the hall, DM3 then told him to take them down to the office.

SM3: Well, the trouble is the office is too full to put them in.
DM3: What have you got down there?
SM3: Some cases of tape.
DM3: Well, that shouldn't be in there. The thing for you to do is to move that tape out of there and then you can put these dishes down there.
SM3: O.K.
DM3: SM3, what I'd suggest for you to do is to get yourself a notebook just like this one I carry to keep these notes in that I'm telling you—to write down now. Then you'll have them in one place and be able to keep track of them. It's sort of a little date book. Well, that's all I've got. Any questions?

SM3 had none, and left, after which DM3 turned to the researcher.

DM3: You can see I had to get into a lot of details today. That isn't right and I wouldn't do that regularly but this man we've got here is pretty weak and you've got to get into these things with him. I hope in time he'll be able to do these things for himself.

AN UNCHANGED SUPERVISORY PATTERN

In this series of interactions we see more confirmation of the type of relationship that began to show up on the opening day. DM3 is giving detailed instructions which SM3 is trying hard to comply with. DM3 is somewhat unhappy about getting into such detail, but, as he sees SM3's troubles in keeping up with all his expectations (inventory lists, slow-moving items, etc.), he feels compelled to go into more details. When SM3 raises a question about the luncheon arrangements, DM3 checks his tendency to reject it and inquires for the reason. It seemed like a good point to DM3 so he accepts it, but decides to speak to the meat man himself instead of letting SM3 do it. So we see there is some upward communication in this incident but not much. In all the exchanges DM3 does most of the talking. A few more typical interactions will round out this picture of the relationship.

DM3 and SM3 were walking together across the grocery sales floor.

DM3: SM3, I'd like your opinion on something. You see this display over here where you're planning to put up your copperware. I was thinking that you've got your island a little off balance here. You see you've got a high pile and then four over there that are lower. I was wondering what it would look like if we put this high display right in the middle so it's sort of balanced out to give the proper effect here across the front.

SM3 nodded his head in agreement.

DM3: I'm not suggesting you change it now because you've got the thing set up. I don't like to push our people too much on this because then they start telling me they're going to run into too much payroll. But it's the sort of thing I think you might keep in mind when you lay out these things again.
SM3: Well I can get that changed in just a few minutes. It won't take more than about five minutes.
DM3: Now don't go ahead on that now. You've got it set up this way and I'd just as soon leave it.
SM3: No, I'll go ahead. It won't take more than a few minutes.

SM3 walked off and got a clerk and the two of them started moving baskets to change the displays around.

Here we see SM3 taking something that DM3 is ostensibly offering as a helpful suggestion, and treating it as an order for immediate compliance. There was no expression of SM3's opinion on the matter or his reasons for setting up the display as he had. DM3's suggestions had become SM3's commands.

During another supervisory talk between the two, DM3 asked SM3 to call in his grocery department head. When he arrived, DM3 spent quite a while going over a number of detailed items directly with him. At this point DM3 explained to the grocery manager why he was giving him instructions directly.

DM3: In the first place I'd like to get you in on this in order to keep you informed on what I'm instructing SM3 to do. It gives you a little more background as to what's going on and it's training you for taking over that kind of an assignment some day. The second thing is that getting you in like this saves SM3 the trouble of coming down and telling you what I want done. It will save time.

This explanation tells us a good deal about DM3's conception of the store manager's functions. He seems to see him as simply relaying DM3's instructions to the men in the store and sometimes he can be saved the trouble of doing this.

During a break in a discussion with DM3, SM3 commented privately to the researcher,

SM3: Notes, notes, I'm getting so many notes around here from everyone telling me what to do I'm not sure what I'm going to do with all of them.

* * * *

AN UNCHANGED SUPERVISORY PATTERN

SM3: (to the researcher) You know this was supposed to have been my afternoon off but I can see that is out of the question.

At no time did SM3 tell DM3 that he was scheduled to take the afternoon off.

* * * * *

On another occasion a meat specialist from the company headquarters called to the attention of DM3 and SM3 certain behavior he had seen in the store's meat department that did not conform to standard procedure. DM3 and the specialist discussed this for some time while SM3 remained silent. DM3 closed the conversation by saying that he would call the problem to the attention of the meat merchandiser who called on the store. Later SM3 gave the researcher a quite different explanation of the nonstandard behavior but he had said nothing about it in front of DM3.

The pattern of this relationship is now abundantly clear. DM3 is treating SM3 as a person who is to carry out his detailed instructions or relay them without change to his subordinates in the store. SM3 is desperately trying to comply with these instructions. He is offering but few suggestions to DM3 and is often not explaining to DM3 his view of a problem situation (as in the meat incident). DM3 is following the traditional pattern also by continuing to deal directly with SM3's subordinates on several occasions and by looking to the merchandisers to correct problem situations in the store's perishable department.

Routine Supervision, SM3 and Store Personnel

Now we can turn to how SM3 was handling himself with his subordinates in the store. The following five incidents have been selected as fairly typical of SM3's interactions with his store people.

SM3 was observing the bulletin board in the produce back room.

SM3: (to the produce manager) Oh, jeez, that's not the way to do those cards. We've got to make them last a long time. (He was referring to the personnel cards on which the hours for each employee are recorded. The produce manager had used one card to record a single week.) You should do it the way it is on the sample card that I gave you. We have to use them for several weeks.

Produce manager: O.K.

SM3: (walks away and comments to the researcher) Look at these cards. I showed him how to do this when I gave him the first cards and look what I get back. Well, I'll draw lines on these for six weeks so they can't possibly go wrong during that period. But you bet your life that after these six weeks are up they'll be doing it in the same messed up way and I'll have to show them all over again.

* * * * *

Meat manager: (to SM3 as he walked by) Say, SM3, I'm going to need some kind of space to move all these hams. Is that a good spot? (Pointing to a rear grocery island.)

SM3: Well, I thought I'd give you this spot. It's a pretty good place where all the customers can see it. (Walking up toward the front end of a short table and pointing to the grocery island which faced the produce department.)

Meat manager: Well, that's a pretty good spot. I just wanted some place to move those hams in case we get a lot of them in because they seem to go pretty well this time of year.

SM3: Yes, I think this is a good spot and we'll be able to dummy up the display and make it look pretty good.

* * * * *

SM3: (to researcher) Take a look at these cans. They look pretty good, don't they? Well, last night I was standing over here (he indicated a spot about 15 feet away from the display), and I just kept looking at two of the fellows who were putting up this display. They were jawing with each other and putting them up upside down (he demonstrates), sideways, the labels facing all different ways, and that kind of stuff. Then I waited until they put up the whole display and then I walked up to

AN UNCHANGED SUPERVISORY PATTERN   123

them and said, "O.K., fellows, now go get a couple of carriages." They didn't know what I wanted but they went and got them. When they came back, I said to them, "Now you boys are supposed to be smart high school boys. There may be some excuse for you putting up a display like this with the cans facing every which way. I don't know. Maybe you haven't had enough training or something. But it seems to me that you just don't need any training to know the right way to do a job from the wrong way to do it. I can't understand it because you fellows are supposed to be smart. Now you take every single one of those cans down and put them up right." I guess they felt kind of stupid. But they really learned how to put up cans. You know, sometimes you just can't figure out how these kids can be so dumb. They just don't use their heads.

* * * *

SM3: (to grocery manager who had just entered SM3's office) Here's the payroll for grocery last week—6.8%. (This figure was quite high by chain standards.)
Grocery manager: Well, ain't that romantic.
SM3: Yeah, it's romantic all right.
Grocery manager: Well, they've got worse. (He went over and picked up some signs and left.)

* * * *

SM3: (to researcher) DM3 wants me to hold these meetings with my department heads every day because he's a great guy on meetings. But it's hard. There's all kinds of things going on in the store, and, if a fellow is trying to get up his corn or put his meat up on the counter, they start bitching if you take five or ten minutes away from them every morning. Five or ten minutes doesn't mean much to me one way or the other, but I think the fellows really resent it. Everybody seems to do these things differently.

In these incidents we see SM3 trying to carry out with his subordinates the instructions he has been given. But we also see him being quite uneasy in his relationship with his men. He gets annoyed and frustrated when they don't fill out the cards or stack cans the right way. He corrects them but he expects that they will continue to do things the wrong way. His grocery manager is flip when SM3 is serious in talking about the payroll figures. And finally SM3 feels squeezed between DM3's direction that he hold daily store meetings and the resistance of his men to these meetings. He is clearly having some trouble establishing his leadership in the store. The comment that the meat and produce managers both made to the researcher about SM3 was, "Oh, he's all right. He just leaves us alone and we run our own departments."

Relations with Merchandisers

This lack of much respect for SM3 and his position in the store was apparent also on the part of the merchandisers who called on the store. The following conversation indicates this.

Merchandiser: (speaking to SM3 and looking at the cash department head who was standing some distance away) Say, is he sick?

SM3: No. Why?

Merchandiser: Well, I left him there by that register on opening day, and he is still there. He'll get to weigh 300 pounds if he stays in one spot like that. Do they have one of these guys in store 45?

SM3: Sure they do.

Merchandiser: You're damn right they do. And he handles the drug counter and the candy table and a lot of the other stuff.

SM3: Well, this fellow will do that too.

Merchandiser: Yeah, when?

Comments on DM3—SM3 Relationship

To wind up our picture we shall quote DM3 and SM3 as they spoke individually to the researcher about their relationship to each other.

DM3: The thing I'm most interested in looking for in picking a store manager is aggressiveness. I think that's a quality that's most important. I know everybody wouldn't agree with me on that. There are some store managers in other territories that are doing an excellent job but they wouldn't appeal to me very much because they're not aggressive enough. I like to have a man who can stand up to criticism. I like to have them argue back if necessary. I like to have them willing to take risks and gamble on their own decisions. I'm having some trouble finding people like that in my territory. Most of them don't seem to be very aggressive.

Yes, I have something to say about selecting the store managers in my territory. I picked SM3, for instance. I've known him for years. My chief problem with SM3 is that he isn't very aggressive. I would say his chief fault is he's too anxious to please me. I am surprised sometimes at his questions. He asks me questions that he ought to be answering for himself. I've got to get him to assume more initiative and to be more aggressive. I think he'll make out all right but you never know. He may never acquire the necessary aggressiveness to do that job. I've been trying to think of some way I can get him to assume more initiative. I'm thinking of telling him that he's got to find his own answers to some of the questions he is asking me to handle for him.

* * * * *

SM3: You know, DM3 seemed pretty happy about our recent store figures. Of course we've got to do some more work on this payroll—we can't stay up above 6% forever. We've got to bring that down, but I feel pretty good about it because I think that we've really got a chance to make some money in this store if our volume only goes up. As long as that volume goes up, the payroll will come down, and we'll really be making the money.

I really like it here in a big store a heck of a lot better than I ever liked it in a small store. Of course there's a few more details that you have to keep on top of, and there's a heck of a lot to learn. You take a fellow like me and put him in a store like this, why even in five years he won't know everything there is to know about it. Every time DM3 comes in here he gives me a list much too long for me to do everything on it, or even know how to do everything on it. It'll just take time, that's all. . . .

You know DM3 really goes by the book on those things and does things the way the company wants. He really sticks by the book and that's the way it should be because, of course, if you go by the book, you're going to keep out of trouble. Now I know there's a lot of district managers who wink at unauthorized practices because they realize that, if a fellow has got a few cases of junk merchandise that he wants to move, island wings and carriage displays are usually a good way to do it. I know that my grocery manager has got a hell of a lot of stuff down there in the back room that he'd like to clean out but, gee, if I ever let him start putting up carriages of merchandise around the store, he'd have those carriages all over the place. You know they don't stay in one place either. You put a carriage down there by that drug table that has a few items on it, and you come back in a half an hour and some damned little kid has pushed it way over there to the coke machine. And you just can't have stuff like that.

Of course, it's the same sort of thing in any job, you have to figure out what kind of a fellow your boss is and play the game his way. You figure out how your boss wants it done, and that's how you do it. That keeps you out of trouble. I've got about three cases of Japanese tuna fish that I'd love to push down there by the drug table in a carriage because I bet you by tonight I'd have all that stuff gone. They're always after us to move that kind of merchandise, but if DM3 or any of the headquarters people came in here and saw a carriage of tuna sitting there, well, it just wouldn't be by the book, and it would be all wrong, and I'd be wrong, so I just don't do it.

Summary

The pattern we see in the observations of DM3 and SM3 at work is quite consistent. Their habitual relationship is one of DM3's telling in considerable detail what he wants and SM3's agreeing verbally but having no sense of choice in the matter. DM3 is making the decisions, not only on matters like display arrangements, but also on details such as what is to be stored in the office. There is very little flow of suggestions or voluntary "bad news" going up the line from SM3 to DM3. SM3 is trying to conform to DM3's instructions principally from a fear of DM3's displeasure and criticism. He is not being treated by his superior with the respect that was planned as a positive incentive to help induce the desired behavior. Witness DM3's tendency to ignore and by-pass SM3 and the way this treatment is also present in the tone of the merchandiser's comment to SM3 about his cash department head, a man for whom the merchandiser had no official responsibility.

Finally, we can see that almost all of DM3's conscious attention in these episodes is on the technical details, the handling of inventories, display technique, control procedures, etc. We do not see him raising for explicit attention questions relating to the changes in the required roles or other aspects of the organizational system.

The over-all picture of this relationship at this time is that it is virtually a stereotype of the traditional pattern described in Chapter II. DM3's influence at this time is to hold it to this pattern, and our observations give no sense of movement toward a new pattern even though DM3 was being asked by his superior to use his new store managers in a different manner and make the necessary changes in his own supervisory behavior.

As we would expect, given this supervisory pattern between the two, SM3 comes to the conclusion that his job is rigidly to "follow the book" of DM3's instructions. His efforts to do this, however, are not satisfying DM3, who sees SM3 as lacking in "aggressiveness." This appraisal of SM3 is probably accurate in the sense that most observers would judge SM3 to be less aggressive than the other store managers, SM1 and SM2. However, DM3 is apparently not aware that his own behavior is at least to some degree a contributory factor to SM3's failure to take more initiative. And to round out the picture, we see that SM3 is having some trouble in finding a basis to establish his leadership as a communication center for his subordinates in the store. Again at this level the daily behavior is not coinciding with the new organizational model.

Conclusion

We have now seen three patterns of supervisory behavior by reviewing and analyzing selected episodes of the behavior of three pairs of individuals working with each other. This review has given us three rather clear patterns of response to the initial formal efforts of top management to move the behavior of its management people from the traditional pattern to the new model. In our first pair we saw that their behavior coincided to a remarkable degree with the new required roles. In our second pair we saw DM2 making a conscious attempt to change but often reverting to the traditional pattern, while SM2 was moving rapidly toward achieving the new role for store managers. We were in doubt as to whether SM2's behavior was because of, or in spite of, DM2's behavior. In our third pair DM3 was holding to the traditional pattern and SM3 was not making any discernible progress toward the new model. Management's initial efforts to introduce organizational change were not resulting in a uniform response. To the contrary, our clinical look at the behavior patterns of three district managers has uncovered some remarkable differences in behavior.

In our next chapter we shall be going further into the analysis of the differences in the behavior of these three district managers with their store managers. We need to answer more questions. Are the differences we see in these episodes reliable? Can we check these differences by quantifying the supervisory interaction patterns of these three men? Will this help to illuminate the nature of the differences?

In all of this, we have been treating the variable of the district manager's behavior as the focal point of our analysis.

This is not, let us be reminded, because these individuals can be expected to have any less trouble than others learning to modify their customary behavior but because they are playing such a strategically important part in changing the entire organizational pattern.

CHAPTER VII

Interaction Patterns — Three District Managers

THE PRINCIPAL organizational changes that the top management group wished to make were in the overt behavior between superiors and subordinates at certain key spots in the organization. To succeed in effecting these changes, they had to get the members of their supervisory forces to actually change their interaction patterns—their customary conversational practices with their subordinates. Top management could not be content with gaining a mere intellectual understanding of what they wanted, nor would it be enough to secure merely verbal agreement with their plans. And, since all the district managers spent most of their time talking to subordinates in the stores, the important question was not who the district managers talked to, but rather how they talked to their subordinates. The on-the-job, moment-to-moment, verbal behavior of people had to change or the new organizational model would not become a reality. Because this overt behavior was the true test of the success of the change, it also had to be the researcher's way of measuring the change. This fact ruled out the use of many research methods for checking the degree to which the change was actually implemented. It ruled out the use of questionnaires or various pencil and paper tests. It forced the researcher to search for ways to observe and record the overt interactions of the key individuals in the change.

In the last three chapters we have presented one way of reporting research on the behavior of people in an organization, the reporting of a sample of episodes of their behavior. This method has the advantage of helping us get a "feel" for these people and of seeing some of the dynamics of their behavior. However, this method used by itself leaves us with some doubts and shortcomings. Was the sample biased? Can we be sure that a change has occurred between one point of time and another? To overcome these doubts and problems, the researcher decided to supplement his direct recording of behavior episodes with a way of quantifying the overt interaction pattern between a superior and a subordinate. This chapter will briefly describe this research method and then give the results of using it with our three key district managers.

The Research Method

On a somewhat trial-and-error basis and by borrowing ideas from Bales' interaction analysis methods,[1] the researcher evolved a research method that was simple enough to be practical in making direct on-the-job observations and that provided a quantified measure of the interaction pattern between a superior and a subordinate. In practice the method worked as follows. The researcher entered a store with the supervising district manager. Every time the district manager and the store manager engaged in conversation with each other, the researcher noted: who talked; the length of each separate speech; the category of speech involved (that is, was it (1) asking a question, (2) supplying information, (3) giving an opinion, or (4) giving directions or suggestions); the type of topic involved; and finally who initiated new topics. The topic classifications that were used were, (1) discussion of people, (2) merchandise, (3) record systems, (4) physical plant, and (5) small talk. A more detailed description of this observational method, and its implicit assumptions, is given in the Appendix.

These observational categories follow closely the descrip-

[1] See Robert Bales, *Interaction Process Analysis* (Cambridge, Addison-Wesley Publishing Co., 1950).

tion in Chapter III of the required changes in the interaction aspects of the new supervisory role. It follows, then, that if we can get reliable quantitative data on these items, we can measure the degree to which the behavior of our three district managers is meeting the new role requirements for interactions. The data will also serve as a check on the validity of the descriptive analysis of the district managers' behavior presented in the preceding three chapters.

The interaction patterns of our three key district managers were systematically observed over a period of five months in the summer and fall of 1955. This was roughly the same time period in which the episodes occurred that are reported in the three preceding chapters. At this time each of these men was supervising the work of several newly appointed store managers. The theory behind the store manager program had been fully explained to them. They had had enough exposure to the new arrangements so that the first novelty of the system had worn off. All the formal steps to implement the program had been made, but it was still a very new thing. Our data should give us a measure, then, of the degree to which the behavior of our three district managers coincides with the new model at an early date, but after all the formal and direct organizational steps had been taken to implement the new system.

The researcher was anxious to get a representative sample of the interactions of each key district manager so that the resulting data would reflect accurately the supervisory characteristics of the district manager and not other extraneous factors. To do this, the district managers were observed working with several different store managers to minimize the effect of the personality of a particular store manager on the interaction pattern. The district managers were also observed calling on stores on different days of the week, and for considerable amounts of time. This was done to minimize the possibility of seeing a district manager handling only a few types of problems in a store. Because

EXHIBIT 6

Prevailing Conditions During Observation of DM Interaction Patterns

District Manager	Total Interaction Time Observed	Time Early in Week	Time Late in Week	No. of Separate Comments Recorded	No. of SMs Involved	No. of Separate Store Visits
DM1	227 min.	157 min.	70 min.	1,115	3	9
DM2	277 min.	134 min.	143 min.	1,173	3	5
DM3	466 min.	293 min.	173 min.	2,092	3	4

of the need to suit the job convenience of the district managers, it was not possible to get a perfect distribution of observing time in all these factors, but, as is indicated by Exhibit 6, interactions were observed under a variety of circumstances to reduce the possibility that the differences between the three men could be ascribed to factors other than the habitual interaction pattern of the men themselves.

RESULTS

The systematic observation of the interaction patterns of the three district managers turned up some striking differences between them. The most important differences are indicated by Exhibit 7. This exhibit presents a profile of each district manager's interaction pattern with three of his subordinate store managers (on the right-hand page) and each district manager's average profile (on the left-hand page). The exhibit shows the percentage of total talking time that was used by each party to the conversation and the category of speech used. There are three observations that can be made from these data that are of special importance.

First, the total talking time used by each district manager relative to his subordinates indicates the degree of dominance of the district managers in these conversations. The relatively balanced talking time between DM1 and his

EXHIBIT 7

Percentage of DM and SM Talking Time by Categories

	Average with 3 SMs DM1 / SMs	Average with 3 SMs DM2 / SMs	Average with 3 SMs DM3 / SMs
Questions	13% 9 / 4	16% 14 / 2	11% 9 / 2
Information 30%	17 / 23	15 / 13	43% 26 / 17
Opinions	27% 17 / 10	37% 28 / 9	16% 12 / 4
Directions or Suggestions 20%	15 / 5	19% 16 / 3	30% 28 / 2
Totals	58% / 42%	73% / 27%	75% / 25%

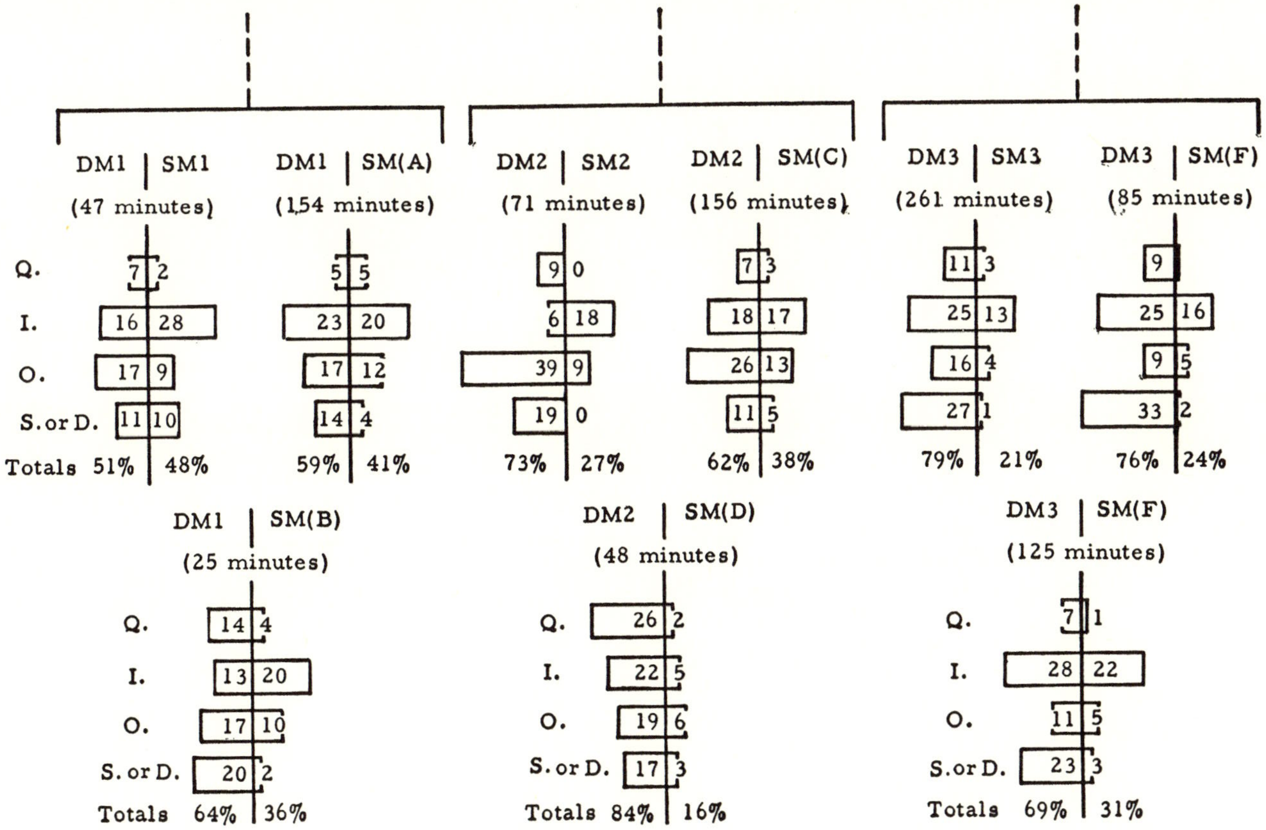
DM1 | SM1
(47 minutes)
DM1 | SM(A)
(1,54 minutes)
DM2 | SM2
(71 minutes)
DM2 | SM(C)
(156 minutes)
DM3 | SM3
(261 minutes)
DM3 | SM(F)
(85 minutes)
Q. 7 2 5 5 9 0 7 3 11 3 9
I. 16 28 23 20 6 18 18 17 25 13 25 16
O. 17 9 17 12 39 9 26 13 16 4 9 5
S. or D. 11 10 14 4 19 0 11 5 27 1 33 2
Totals 51% 48% 59% 41% 73% 27% 62% 38% 79% 21% 76% 24%
DM1 | SM(B)
(25 minutes)
Q. 14 4
I. 13 20
O. 17 10
S. or D. 20 2
Totals 64% 36%
DM2 | SM(D)
(48 minutes)
Q. 26 2
I. 22 5
O. 19 6
S. or D. 17 3
Totals 84% 16%
DM3 | SM(F)
(125 minutes)
Q. 7 1
I. 28 22
O. 11 5
S. or D. 23 3
Totals 69% 31%

store managers indicates that DM1's behavior most nearly coincides with the model requirement of two-way communication in this relationship. The figures indicate that DM3 deviates the most from the new organizational model. For DM3 the words going down the line are three times as much as those coming up the line.

Secondly, the breakdown of talking time into categories of speech gives us another check on the degree of balance in each district manager's interaction pattern. The breakdown indicates that DM1's interaction behavior was not only balanced over-all, but also relatively well balanced within each category of speech. This is especially evident in comparing DM1's record with the others in the categories of *questions, opinions,* and *suggestions or directions*. DM3's behavior is again the furthest from coinciding with the organizational model, going to an extreme of imbalance in the *suggestions or directions* category. For DM3 giving suggestions or directions was distinctly a one-way street.

Thirdly, the exhibit indicates the relative amount of time spent in each category of speech. This indicates the type of conversation that predominated in these exchanges and provides some clues to the problem-solving values of the conversations. When DM1 was talking with his store managers, most of the time was spent in exchanging *information,* with *opinions, suggestions or directions,* and *questions* following down in that sequence. This is the same sequence of time distribution followed by his average store manager and, in fact, by the averages of the store managers working for DM2 and DM3. This suggests that this particular sequence of time distribution among categories reflects a useful problem-solving type of discussion. This hypothesis, of course, could only be established by much more research.[2] This sequence contrasts with DM2's which is very heavy on *opinions* and of DM3's which is heaviest on *suggestions or directions*. In

[2] The research studies of Robert Bales on problem-solving patterns in discussion groups tend to support this hypothesis.

summary, Exhibit 7 indicates that DM1's interaction pattern most nearly coincides with the organizational requirement of a two-way, problem-solving interaction pattern in this critical relationship. DM3's behavior coincides the least with this model.

Exhibit 8 presents the breakdown of the amount of DM-SM talking time that was devoted to the major topical headings. Again some clear differences emerge between the three district managers. These figures indicate the principal topical orientation that each district manager brought to his work. DM1 clearly put his emphasis on the handling and development of people. DM2 puts his chief stress on handling the merchandise, while DM3 was heavily oriented toward the record systems with a secondary emphasis on merchandise. All three gave about the same amount of time to the topic of the physical plant of the store. In the small talk category it is interesting how little time DM3 spent on this in relation to the other two men—DM3 stuck consistently to business in his conversations with subordinates.

EXHIBIT 8

Percentage of DM and SM Talking Time by Topics

Topic	DM1	DM2	DM3
People	48%	17%	11%
Merchandise	16%	41%	32%
Record Systems	22%	25%	47%
Physical Plant	7%	11%	10%
Small Talk	7%	6%	.5%

It is not too easy to say which topical pattern most nearly coincides with the new organizational requirements since the model itself is hard to define in terms of topics. However, the emphasis of DM2 and DM3 on merchandise and record systems indicates their concern with the activities that had traditionally been the focus of management attention. While it is not quite so clear, DM1's emphasis on the topic of people would seem to indicate that he was giving conscious and explicit attention to discussing the interaction patterns (delegation, coaching, coordination procedures) and sentiments (morale, discipline, feelings about promotions, demotions, and transfers), all of which more directly involve the people in the business. In this sense DM1 seems to be most nearly following top management's model for changing organizational behavior.

Exhibit 9 shows the ratio between the number of new conversational topics initiated by the district managers and

EXHIBIT 9

Percentage of New Topics Initiated by
DMs and SMs

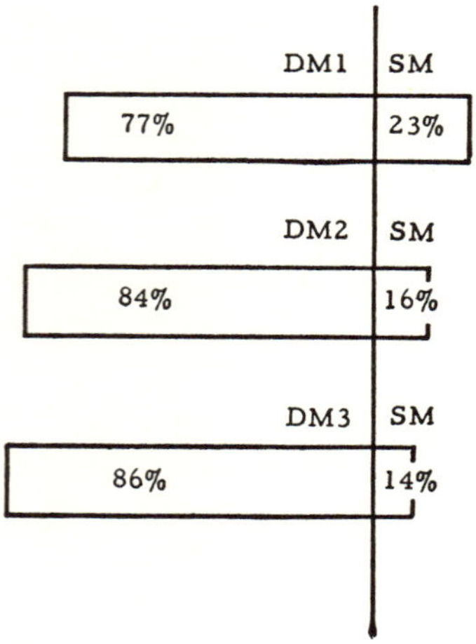

	DM1	SM
	77%	23%
	DM2	SM
	84%	16%
	DM3	SM
	86%	14%

those initiated by their subordinate store managers. While each of the district managers initiated many more topics than their subordinates, DM1 was slightly more balanced on this score than his two colleagues. This provides another test for two-way communication.

Exhibit 10 gives the average length in minutes of a single speech (or comment) by the district managers and their store managers. The exhibit indicates what the earlier data would lead us to expect, namely that DM1 again shows the best balance in the average length of his single speech in relation to his subordinates and DM3 shows the least balance. DM1 gave the shortest single speeches of the three men and his subordinates gave the longest speeches. This would seem to indicate a relative lack of a sense of restraint on the part of DM1's subordinates in conversation with him and again indicates two-way communication.

EXHIBIT 10

Average Duration of a Single Comment in Minutes

DM1	SM
.20	.17

DM2	SM
.28	.16

DM3	SM
.26	.13

Summary

The quantitative data given above consistently confirm the tentative conclusions we reached in Chapters IV, V, and VI. Without exception, every measure of the interaction pattern of all three district managers shows that DM1's behavior was most nearly coinciding with the desired model while DM3's was furthest from the new model.

The data in this chapter allow us to make some additional observations about the nature of the organizational behavior changes that were being attempted at Food World. First of all, the data help clarify an essential characteristic of the change that needs emphasis. The interaction pattern of our three district managers has been quantified by observing them making hundreds of discreet acts of speech at a rate of several per minute. It was this overt behavior pattern that top management wanted them to change. Changing this pattern is a far cry from the more customary changes, such as introducing new forms or work procedures, changing the allocation of job time, transferring to a new district, and so on. Such changes, by comparison, would be easy to effect. The desired changes involve a man's intuitive, instantaneous responses to the entire range of supervisory issues. They involve some of a man's most intimate and persistent assumptions about himself and others. Of course, top management did not define in such concrete operational terms the changes they desired but, nevertheless, this is what their expectations meant in terms of actual behavior. The point is that the desired changes constituted severe demands on the key individuals involved.

One of the district managers used an analogy to explain to the researcher how difficult it was to make this transition.

> This organizational switch-over that we are going through now is really tough. I can only make a rather earthy kind of comparison to give you an idea of how difficult it is. I think it is about like a woman who has lived with one man for

thirty years suddenly becoming a widow and marrying a second husband. I think her adjustment in trying to live with that second husband and the difficulties that it must put her through is comparable to what we are going through.

The quotation above suggests our final observation. The figures in this chapter reflect the external manifestations of behavior—those which can be seen by a third party watching a conversation. We must remember that behind these external manifestations are the thoughts, beliefs, feelings—the personalities, if you will—of the men doing the talking. And these interaction patterns are so much the natural expression of this inner man that they will not significantly change unless many of the man's basic beliefs about himself also change. This statement is not proved—it is a hypothesis. But we shall begin to see evidence in support of this hypothesis in the next chapter as we take a look at the personality systems of our three district managers. We shall be seeking some further understanding of the distinct differences in response that have showed up in the past four chapters.

CHAPTER VIII

Self-Concepts — Three District Managers

WE HAVE BEEN looking at the contrasting ways that our three district managers were working with their new store managers in the initial stages of the planned reorganization. We saw some remarkable differences both in the descriptive and in the quantitative look at these men at work. These differences in overt behavior are all the more striking when we remember that all three of these district managers had for many years been working in the same organization, for the same bosses, with similar job responsibility, and with similar and, in many cases, the same subordinates.

These differences were crucial to the company's reorganization plan. While the top executives could not wisely expect complete uniformity in their district managers nor complete and perfect adoption of their new model for organizational behavior, they could not ignore the degree of difference represented by DM3's behavior and still mean what they said about the future of the business hinging on adopting their new organizational model. We saw that they had worked out their plans carefully. They made careful explanations of the new procedures and gave the reasons. They had every reason to think that the plans were understood and accepted by the key people—the district managers. And yet we see extreme variation in performance in the actual daily work routines of the three district managers. Of course, our experience tells us that changes of the kind that are involved in this instance will take considerable time to implement if they are ever to succeed. But why is this true? If the changes are logical and sensible from an organizational standpoint, what makes them hard to implement? What is the stubborn stuff they are bumping into? And why do we see such contrasting responses, ranging from almost complete adoption to almost complete nonadoption? If we can provide additional understanding of the differences, we may cast new light on what makes such a reorganization so difficult to translate into daily behavior.

It will not be easy, however, to account completely for the differences in behavior between the three district managers. There are, in theory, several possible ways of doing it. We could try to explain it by a historical analysis of the personal backgrounds of each of these individuals. We could try to explain it by analyzing the effects of the historical pressures and influences that have been working on these men over the years as members of a management group in this particular organization. We could do it by means of various psychological tests by which we would strive to categorize these men by psychological types and characteristics. All these methods could be valuable to us, and later on we shall refer back to them, but we have chosen to start seeking for the meaning of these differences by another method.

The approach we shall take to arrive at an understanding of the three district managers draws on the theory and research of an increasingly accepted school of thought about individual behavior. This school of thought is called "self" theory or "phenomenal field" theory. Many psychologists have contributed to its development but one of the best and most complete statements of it is by Snygg and Combs.[1] In essence this school of thought holds that we can best understand the behavior of individuals by looking at the meanings they assign to themselves and the world around them. These meanings, taken together, form a pattern that is internally consistent at any point of time and constitutes "reality" for the individual. The individual's overt behavior is an outward expression of this pattern of meanings

[1] Donald Snygg and Arthur Combs, *Individual Behavior* (New York, Harper & Brothers, 1949).

and is consistent with it so that his behavior always "makes sense" to him. While the pattern of meanings, the phenomenal field, of an individual tends to persist over time, it has been built up by the internalization of the meanings of past experience and will change over time in an orderly way as the individual has new experiences. The central part of any individual's set of private meanings is the picture he has of himself, his self-concept. The theory holds that, in everything the individual does, he is striving to maintain and enhance his self-concept.

In this chapter we shall be applying this theory of individual behavior to our three district managers to supplement our other methods of understanding and describing their behavior. The theory's chief advantage to us in this situation is that it will provide a kind of understanding of our three district managers that will be relevant to taking action in living and working with them. We shall proceed by looking at how these men perceived themselves as district managers, and how they perceived their relations to others in the organization. We shall look at these perceptions in the terms the men themselves use. We shall try to enter into their own personal frame of reference for seeing and evaluating their world of work. The data we shall be using in making this analysis will be quotations from the men themselves as they talked to the researcher on many different occasions. Out of all such available comments we have selected those that seem to reflect best the persistent meanings or attitudes these men brought to their work. We shall be examining these data to find a pattern that links the parts and makes a self-consistent framework that, in total, constitutes the self-concept that these men brought to every job situation they faced. This method of analysis will not tell us how these self attitudes came to be—simply what they are in the here and now. We shall start by looking at DM1.

Self-Concept, DM1

As a District Manager

We shall start our look at DM1 by setting forth in our own words four statements that the researcher believes best capture DM1's view of himself as a district manager. Or to express it differently, it seems to the researcher that DM1 acted and talked as if he held these four statements about himself to be true.

1. I am a competent, hard-working district manager but I can make mistakes and I always have more to learn.
2. I am a person who says what I think to anyone, even if it is unpopular, but I am willing to accept good ideas from any source.
3. I face up to unpleasant realities, even about myself.
4. I am something of a nonconformist.

These statements were derived by the researcher from many comments made by DM1 of which the following are typical and particularly revealing:

> One thing I've done lately is stop worrying about being fired. It happened mostly last summer when I was sick. I had a lot of time to think. I decided that it wasn't worthwhile worrying about things like that and that I might as well go ahead and do what I was going to do and stop worrying about it. I also decided I was going to speak up more when I disagreed about something. So I go ahead and say what I want to say and I'm perfectly willing to take what follows. I don't think I'm going to get fired because actually I think I'm doing a pretty good job as a district manager.

* * * * *

> I'm the sort of person who's pretty critical of himself and so when I think I'm doing reasonably well, that must mean that my bosses think I'm doing pretty well.

* * * * *

I don't think any of us should be too proud to use the good ideas that somebody else has.

* * * * *

The important thing is to teach yourself the new tricks first and then you might have a chance to teach someone else.

* * * * *

I've always been known as a maverick in this organization.

As a Superior

DM1's concept of himself is reflected in the prevailing point of view he took toward his organizational subordinates. The researcher has summarized DM1's view of himself as a superior as follows:

1. I do not want to dominate the thinking of my subordinates.
2. I want to push responsibility on them as fast as I can and get them to answer their own problems.
3. I operate by giving them my advice and suggestions and taking a keen interest in their problems and suggestions.
4. I treat different employees differently and do not expect perfection.
5. I look for administrative ability as the primary requirement for my subordinate supervisors.
6. I candidly tell my subordinates where they stand with me.

These statements of DM1's thinking about himself as a superior were derived by the researcher from many comments, some samples of which are given below.

> My notion of a good supervisor is one who doesn't talk any more than his subordinates do. Of course, you've got to do some of the talking to explain to him the kinds of things he ought to know about what the company wants him to do, but you've also got to give him plenty of chance to talk

about his problems and the things he has on his mind or you're not going to get very far.

* * * * *

I'm interested in my store managers' opinions and, of course, I want them to know what mine are.

* * * * *

I don't do the same thing every time I go into a store. If I did, I would blow my brains out after awhile because this job would be so dull. Of course, I don't do things the way I used to a few years ago either. Even in the stores without store managers I've been letting the department managers handle more matters, like working out displays, than I used to or than I imagine some of the other district managers do. Besides, how the hell am I going to develop my men if I don't let them do things like that?

* * * * *

I believe that if a store manager can come up with his own answer to a problem, it is going to be the best answer in almost every case. I may not agree exactly with the way he would do it, but, unless he's really wrong, you ought to go ahead and let him do it his own way and he'll be better off. That's the only way you teach them to take the initiative on these matters.

* * * * *

I believe in giving my men suggestions instead of giving them hell.

* * * * *

He is a very good meat manager, but you have to be kind of careful how you talk to him because he's apt to take criticism in a rather childish way. He's apt to get defensive and feel hurt if you criticize the way he runs his meat counter. That's why I stepped to one side to speak to him about his hamburg. I've learned to handle him all right and he does a very good job.

* * * * *

You know you can't expect perfection out of people and different people work differently. They can't all be as fast as some.

* * * * *

As far as I'm concerned, the number one part of a store manager's job is that he's got to have administrative ability. He's got to get people to do the job—that's the best definition of administration I know of.

* * * * *

I let the store manager know where he stands. At set times I sit down with the fellow and we work out a written report evaluating and approving his performance for the period. It is done with the man right there because it isn't going to do him any good if we just file a report in the head office. Sometimes these sessions are pretty frank and a little tough on the fellow, but as far as I'm concerned he has to know his shortcomings and straighten them out.

As a Subordinate

DM1's concept of himself is again reflected in the pervasive attitudes he took toward his relations with his organizational superiors.

1. My superiors are approachable, hard working, decent, and competent, but not always right.
2. I am not afraid of being fired and I say what I think to my superiors.
3. No organization is perfect.
4. I expect, as a district manager, to be consulted by my superiors on all issues affecting the stores.

This summarization by the researcher of DM1's orientation toward his superiors is drawn from many comments of which the following are typical.

The V.P. of Sales is a great guy to work for, a fine boss. The people who run this business make some mistakes but they are really decent people. I don't hesitate to disagree with him on something or other and you can really discuss things with him. He's hard-working too. Of course, after we discuss things he has to decide what he is going to do, and, if he says we're going to do something, I'll do the best I can to make it work.

* * * * *

A couple of things came up recently that I think the district managers should have been consulted on by top management. On one item I was so upset I got hold of the store operations manager on the spot. It was a matter that affected the people in our stores, and the district managers should have been consulted before the decision was made. We are closer to the situation and I think, actually, most of the top men would be glad to get our opinions. They just didn't bother to ask us.

* * * * *

This is a very friendly company and I don't know any one in the company who is afraid to speak up to anybody else. It's always been like that since I can remember and I think it stems largely from the top.

* * * * *

It's like in any organization you get into, there's always a certain amount of politics in it and you have to expect that.

Summary of DM1

We could at this stage try to characterize the personal attributes of DM1 that are implicit in this material. We could say that he is self-confident but not self-centered, etc. But the selected material seems to speak for itself and the reader can, if he chooses, apply his own labels to the resulting picture. The more important fact to note, however, is the internal consistency of this set of perceptions and sentiments. Without being able to "prove" it, the data do give a picture of the man that has a unity to it. This is not a random collection of attitudes. DM1's self-concept as a district manager is linked to his orientation toward his superiors and his subordinates. For example, he does not feel submissive to his boss nor does he desire to dominate his subordinates. Instead he sees himself making an adaptive response to the demands of his superiors and he expects, in fact insists, that his subordinates be on this give-and-take basis with him. He accepts his own fallibility and, in turn, that of others while still maintaining high performance standards for himself and others. He knows he has things to learn and welcomes sound ideas from others. Many other such interconnections could be traced. The point is that this set of perceptions is a unified consistent system. This means that one aspect of it cannot be changed without forcing some realignment of all other aspects. It provides a consistent self-concept by which DM1 guided his behavior.

Attitude Toward Reorganization

Given the above picture of DM1's way of looking at himself as a district manager and the world around him, we could quite easily predict his response to top management's reorganization plans if we knew nothing else about him. But let us look at some of his initial reactions to the plans and see how they fall in place with what we know about the man.

> I know most all of the district managers will tell you they are sorry the assistant district manager system is gone. They miss not having those men as their assistants. Well, I think it was a good system but I think our present system can be better when we get it working right. I think the store manager system is working out fine because I think of the store managers as my assistants and I can do a better job with them than I ever could with the assistant district managers.

* * * * *

SELF-CONCEPTS—THREE DISTRICT MANAGERS 151

The store manager is my representative in the store.

* * * * *

This store manager program is still pretty new . . . but I think it is already showing it is paying for itself. We can add the store manager's salary to our store payroll and still have a better over-all performance in that store. He can give us a lot of valuable supervision in there.

* * * * *

I have to keep watching myself on working consistently through the store manager. Every once in awhile I slip back into the habit of speaking to whoever happens to be handy when I see something I don't like, but you really lose the effectiveness of what you're trying to do if you do that. Sometimes I have to remind other people too that come into the store to deal with the store manager.

* * * * *

You know the store manager was upset with what I found in his perishable departments and he should be. It takes a lot of time to supervise and keep track of the perishable departments. I think we used to get a little better coverage in our stores when we had the assistant district managers in there looking over these perishable departments. Now those things must be carefully watched by the store manager. I consider it his responsibility to keep on top of these things and make sure they don't happen. I think this incident will make the store manager a little more alert on these things.

In the preceding chapter we looked at DM1's interaction pattern in supervising his store managers and we saw that his behavior most nearly coincided with top management's new required role for district managers. We can now understand much better why this was true. The set of sentiments required by the new role was virtually identical with DM1's existing self-concept. The two were a natural fit. For DM1, getting his behavior and thinking to coincide with the new required role was no problem. It required no reorganization of DM1's self-concept. True, he had to remind himself to work directly with the store manager, but this was a minor problem. On the potentially more difficult question of his interaction pattern, DM1 simply had to do what made sense to the inner man anyway. Management simply had to announce its plans to DM1 and make the formal changes, and he was immediately in line. To state this observation in general terms, *when a desired change in an organizationally required role complements the existing self-concept of the individual, the formal aspects of the change are sufficient to effect the necessary coincidence in behavior.*

The observation that DM1 found himself in harmony with the reorganizational changes leaves a question of how DM1 had handed his relationships under the traditional organizational setup with which his self-concept must have been in conflict. Three comments of DM1 throw light on this question.

> I worked for Mr. X for many years, and I never did agree with his ideas about how to run things. I always did things somewhat differently than he would have. We grew to respect each other in spite of that.
>
> * * * * *
>
> I have always been something of a maverick in this organization.
>
> * * * * *
>
> I go ahead and say what I want to say and I'm perfectly willing to take what follows.

These comments are most significant. They tell us that DM1 had been something of a deviant as regards the organizational pattern, that he was fully aware of his deviance, and, furthermore, that he had learned to live with the feelings of insecurity that go hand-in-glove with deviant behavior. In effect, when in the past DM1 had been asked to conform to the traditional pattern, he had *chosen* to be different. He was aware of major portions of his self-concept; he was aware of most of the organizational (external culture) demands on him; he was aware of the difference or conflict relationship between the two; and he was aware of the feelings of discomfort the conflict generated. This over-view of these elements or "awareness of self–environment" made it possible for him to see the opportunity for exercising a *personal choice*. The choice might have been to get in line with the organizational demands, be deviant, or leave the organization. The making of any of these choices would have been an adaptive response to the conflict rather than a rote, conforming response. DM1 chose to maintain his somewhat deviant position and "take what follows"—the frequent discomfort that goes with being a deviant. We can diagram DM1's perceptual field (everything within the heavy line) at the time as follows:

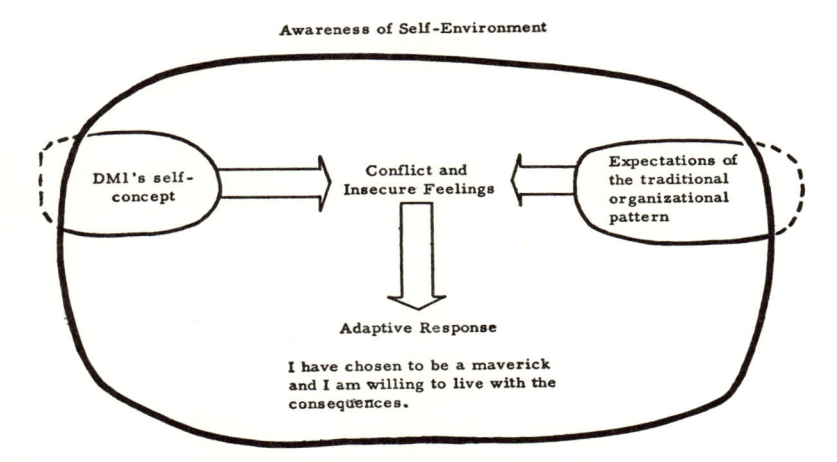

Awareness of Self-Environment

DM1's self-concept → Conflict and Insecure Feelings ← Expectations of the traditional organizational pattern

↓

Adaptive Response

I have chosen to be a maverick and I am willing to live with the consequences.

This analysis of DM1's adaptive response to his past conflict with organizational demands is based on hindsight of earlier events. We shall see a current example of the same process as we go on to look at the self-concept of DM2 and his response to conflict.

Self-Concept, DM2

As a District Manager

DM2's concept of himself as a district manager is, in many ways, the most difficult of the three to describe. It contains more apparent inconsistencies, and our job is to find the underlying consistency of it. We shall start with the researcher's summarized statements of DM2's self-concept.

1. I am a reasonable, hard-working man trying to handle the many conflicting pressures on me.
2. I can see and feel both sides of most any problem.
3. I have to be an s.o.b. at times with my subordinates but I still take care of them.
4. I can see the funny side of things.
5. I don't have all the answers, but I am good at handling people and at getting merchandise sold.
6. The most important thing to work for is the satisfaction of doing a good job.

The direct quotations below are some of those from which the summary statements of self-concept are derived.

> You'll notice this store looks clean. Because it looks clean, do you know what I'll do as a dirty s.o.b.—excuse me, I mean district manager—I'm going to look at the cash register to see if we are doing any business. That's the way we are, you know. If it looks good at one end, we ask questions about the other end.

* * * *

> Mind you, I think we do need to have a strict rule on [meat] prices. If we didn't, we'd have the thing going all haywire and it would be all over the place. So I think it's right at both ends. You've got to have strict rules and you also have to understand occasionally why [the people in the store] have to make exceptions. And the district manager is in the middle. We have to learn to talk both ways.

* * * *

The store does need to have us act as a cop. You may not like that word, but I think that's what we've got to do. You still need a guy to come in and be the s.o.b. The headquarters man can come in here and be a goodwill ambassador and I tell the store operations manager that's what he ought to do when he travels with me. But I'm the guy that's got to tell them they've got to obey the rules and regulations of the company. I'm the one that's got to tell them to clean up the floor and make sure they do it. Somebody's got to be that s.o.b.

* * * * *

This is just my opinion, but I've always thought that my great strength as a district manager is in my handling of people. I've always prided myself in districts I've had before in knowing every individual in my stores. I can't claim that now because there are too many stores working such long hours, but I do try to get to know them.

* * * * *

One of my strengths in this business is rotating merchandise between stores to get everything cleared up and sold.

* * * * *

It seems to me that the district manager's number one job is handling people and that's what he has to spend most of his time on. Our number two job is worrying about getting our merchandise displayed and sold.

* * * * *

I've been in this business an awfully long time but I don't consider myself a meat expert.

* * * * *

You know I would go nuts if it wasn't for my wise-cracking. In this kind of a business and the kind of pressures you're under, if you can't see the funny side of things, you'd really blow your top and I really mean that, too.

* * * * *

The important thing to work for is to do something you can really be proud of.

* * * *

One thing you can say about this company—you'll never find anybody goofing off. That is something the company can be proud of and it's true all the way up and down the line.

* * * *

The old-timers in this organization are doing what they have been trained to do for the past thirty years and they are doing it well. It's hard for them to try something else.

As a Superior

Some of DM2's concept of himself in relation to his subordinates are indicated by his comments stated above. Other aspects of it are summarized by the researcher below:

1. You have to listen to and appreciate their problems and still tell them what they have to try and do.
2. If a subordinate has a healthy fear of the boss, it helps in handling him, but you can put too much pressure on subordinates and get poor results.
3. We owe something to the loyal old-timers.
4. You have to check up on people to get results but you can't expect perfection.

Most of the statements above are presented in a two-sided, ambivalent fashion. They reflect DM2's view of himself as a person who can see and feel two sides of a problem and as being in the middle of conflicting pressures. The more extensive quotations quoted below show this pattern of understanding and identification alternating with pressure and distrust.

I have to take time to listen to the way these fellows [store managers and grocery managers] feel about their problems. The way he feels is very important, but I also have to point out to him eventually that he still has to make the effort to do these things the way we want him to.

* * * * *

Everybody is touchy in this business. When people's talents are in demand, they get pretty touchy; otherwise they do what they're told. It's pretty hard to run a business when people are in demand this way. You can't get any leverage on them.

* * * * *

We've got to think of a better place to put the time clocks in this store. We've got them in the basement where nobody can police them. In other stores we have them where people can keep an eye on them but here nobody knows what is going on.

* * * * *

One thing I've learned is that you're never going to find perfection in this business so you might as well never expect it.

* * * * *

Did you hear that question? The store manager wants to know if he should take down his required displays and put up the sale displays. What should I tell him? He's instructed to put up both and he doesn't have enough room. Somebody from the office could come in and ask where his displays are and have a perfect right to ask that question. That's the kind of thing you're always up against in this business.

* * * * *

In this business we are always getting our lines crossed. There are an awful lot of people who can come into this store and tell people how to do things. Take the produce department. The produce manager feels subservient to the merchandiser and the produce sales manager. Now I don't blame him for feeling that way. He's got to survive. Those people tell him to set up his displays one way and I come along and others do and tell him something else. They get driven crazy by that sort of thing. But we are always crossing up our lines that way.

* * * * *

I think there's too much pressure on that guy, and in that frame of mind he's not doing the best job he can do on the bread and butter business of running a good store.

* * * * *

One thing you have to learn about this business is that you can't program everything. You get your plans set and then something happens—any one of a dozen things can throw you off.

As a Subordinate

DM2's orientation toward his superiors can be characterized as:

1. The top management people are no fools, but they don't always appreciate what we are up against in the stores. They sometimes give conflicting directions.
2. You can afford to resist a top management proposal only so much, regardless of what you think of it.
3. My bosses are very decent and are interested in doing a good job.

Here again DM2 is seeing both sides of the matter. He sees his bosses' point of view but he still feels somewhat misunderstood and some restraint in saying what he thinks in this relationship. He feels a loyalty to top management but still resents the conflicting pressures he sees being put on him. A sample of direct quotations gives a little more of the feel of this mixture.

People at headquarters often don't appreciate how much planning is going on in the stores. It's there, even if it isn't on paper.

* * * * *

The store operations manager knows what the problems

are pretty well. He's no dummy. A man here asked me for a raise and I didn't see how I could make a final decision on the matter until I went higher up, so I spoke to the store operations manager about it and he told me what he thought I ought to do. I said, "Well, should we clear it on up then?" He said, "Well, you asked me for an answer and I've given it to you and that's your clearance." I was glad he said that to me. He was telling me that he had certain responsibilities and he is willing to assume his responsibilities and give me an answer, and that it did not need to go any further. Well I'm glad to know that, that's the way you get oriented. I'm perfectly willing to get my answers from him, but I had to make sure he is willing to assume responsibility for that.

* * * * *

There is some pressure in this organization to say "yes" when your boss asks you how you like a new program. When I report problems, they think I am resisting just because I don't like change. So I can say it just so often, and then I have to stop because I'm beginning to get a bad reputation for bucking everything.

* * * * *

My boss is not working so hard because he's hungry. He's not hungry, but he keeps trying to do things better all the time. It's his interest in the achievement. He wants to do something he can be really proud of.

Summary of DM2

DM2 sees himself continually as the man in the middle. He feels caught in the middle between conflicting instructions from different superiors; in the middle between the pressures from above and the daily problems of his subordinates. He is good at understanding both sides of these issues but does not often feel confident he can resolve the conflicts. He sees himself giving his conscious attention to the problems of people but mostly to the problems of loyalty, discipline, and morale. He is good at building the loyalty of his subordinates to himself and the company on a personal basis that is consistent with the traditional organizational practices. And yet he is also expressing an interest in changing toward the new organizational model. He is again in the middle as regards the new model and the old practices. This is consistent with his overt behavior that we saw in Chapters V and VII. It shows up even more in his comments about the reorganizational plans.

Attitude Toward Reorganization

The following comments reflect some of DM2's early responses to the company's plans for change.

> The big problem of the whole [store manager program] is the problem of teaching old dogs new tricks. It's a tough one. You can't overrate it. It's not the fault of the old-timers either.

* * * * *

> This decentralization thing is really a good idea and so is the store manager plan.

* * * * *

> Sometimes we don't have the people we should have to move into these new assignments as store managers. Some of them don't seem to have what it takes.

* * * * *

> The most important thing for a store manager to be able to do is handle people, and I think it's terribly important that he be a good man with customers. After that he best pay attention to merchandising problems and be a good merchandiser.

* * * * *

> If the store manager plan was working right, they would be carrying the ball in almost all of these problems and we'd just go in and give them a little steering and criticism on

SELF-CONCEPTS—THREE DISTRICT MANAGERS 161

things we noticed and help them on problems they couldn't swing for themselves. That's the way it ought to work but we haven't gotten there yet.

* * * * *

A lot of people in the stores still like to see me about whether they are going to get a raise. I suppose this is to be expected. I always try and get the store manager in on these conversations even though I still have to handle these things. I just can't cut them all off over night.

* * * * *

All these changes they are putting in are probably good things but there are just too many of them coming too fast, I think.

These comments reflect DM2's ambivalent reactions to the new model. He is for it but he is also against it. He sees values in both the new and the old. He is experimenting with changing his customary way of thinking and behavior while he is still retaining many of his habitual attitudes and practices. He is similar to DM1, however, in certain aspects of his reactions. He is consciously aware of certain aspects of his self-concept (I have to be a cop, etc.). He is aware of a good part of the new organizational demands (new tricks for old dogs). And he finally is aware that this puts him in conflict and creates for him feelings of insecurity and uncertainty (it's a tough problem). In other words, his perceptual field at this time includes the same elements that we saw in DM1's. He can see what is happening. This gives him a sense of choice about his own behavior. He apparently is choosing to try out, cautiously and tentatively to be sure, thinking and acting in line with the new role requirements. He is a man in the process of painfully redefining the basic elements of his own self-concept. As the reader might suspect, he is the district manager that was quoted at the end of Chapter VII comparing his own personal adjustments to those of a second marriage. Because he can see and admit the differences between his own self-concept (the traditional one for district managers), the new demands, and the resulting painful conflicts, he has achieved a degree of awareness of self-environment. He is capable of making an adaptive learning response to the new demands. His adaptive response could have been to leave the organization, to maintain a deviant position, or to try changing his self-concept. He has tentatively chosen the latter course. We need to emphasize that this is not an easy road for him to follow and he will be sustained in taking this road by an appreciation on the part of others in the organization of its difficulty. We can diagram his phenomenal field at this time as follows:

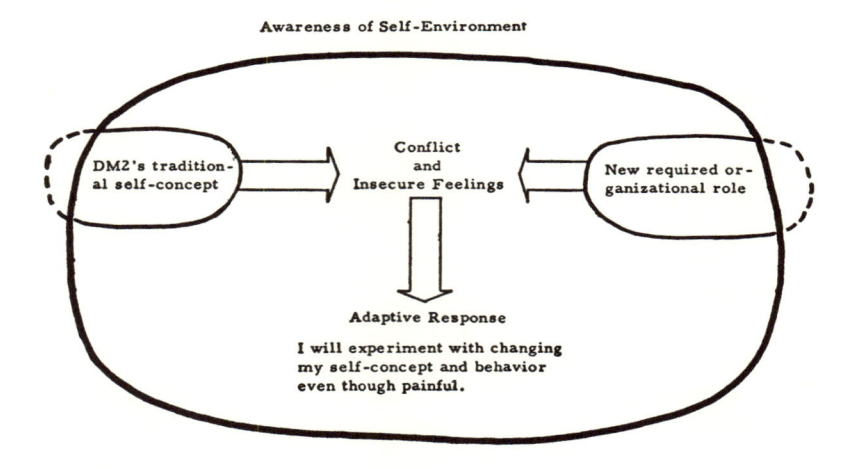

Awareness of Self-Environment

DM2's traditional self-concept → Conflict and Insecure Feelings ← New required organizational role

↓

Adaptive Response
I will experiment with changing my self-concept and behavior even though painful.

SELF-CONCEPT, DM3

As a District Manager

One of the significant characteristics of DM3 was that he was not very much aware of or explicit about his self-concept. We have seen that DM1 and DM2 could be quite specific in their statements of the way they saw themselves as district managers. This was not so true of DM3, which means that we shall have to do more interpretation of his comments to discover the nature of his self-concept. DM3's view of himself as a district manager is summarized by the researcher in the following three statements.

1. I am a systematic and tough supervisor who gets things done.
2. I am an all-around expert on running supermarkets.
3. I am too honest and forthright for my own good.

These statements of DM3's self-concept are, of course, simplifications of a very complex matter. They do provide a starting place for understanding DM3's persistent orientation on the job. The direct quotes of DM3 given below are the sort of data these statements were derived from.

> That man is the best store manager in the whole chain. I never saw a guy who was so much like me in the way he acts in a store. He sometimes is tough on the people but he really gets the work out and gets things done. For my money he is the best.
>
> * * * * *
>
> I was the one who started the first self-service store in the chain. In that store we tried out a great many of the ideas that have since come into common use in the company.
>
> * * * * *
>
> I think the first thing you're in here for is to make some money for the company. In order to do that, you've got to go out and get a volume of business. You've got to be selling things and selling them in a way that doesn't run your costs up too much. To do that you've got to keep your shelves filled up with good merchandise properly presented. These are the fundamentals. If you are doing those things right, it will show up in the figures.
>
> * * * * *
>
> I'm getting paid to have good merchandising ideas.
>
> * * * * *

Anybody who is a district manager has got to be interested in merchandise and selling merchandise.

* * * * *

When I've got something on my mind, I want to get it done today and not put it off. I suppose I carry that to such an extent that it is a fault of mine.

* * * * *

We've got too much heart in this company. We're just not businesslike.

* * * * *

I never give the store one figure on projections and the office another. The reason is that I simply can't lie. That's my biggest weakness. I'm not a diplomat. If I've got something on my mind, I just spill it. I can't hide it.

If we do a modest amount of interpreting, these views of DM3 about himself and his role as a district manager are fairly clear and we shall not stop to analyze them until we see how these views fit in with his concept of himself as a subordinate and as a superior.

As a Superior

DM3's view of how his relations with his subordinates ought to work was quite clear cut.

1. I tell my subordinates what to do, answer their questions, and follow up to see that things get done.
2. I expect my subordinates to listen to my instructions and then do them without a lot of argument.
3. I expect subordinates to be aggressive in getting things done with their own subordinates.

This summary is drawn from comments of DM3 such as the following:

You really have to train store managers to look after these details, and I have to follow up to make sure it is done.

SELF-CONCEPTS—THREE DISTRICT MANAGERS

You see, I have written out complete notes on everything I talked to [this store manager] about today so there's no excuse for his not doing something about them. Then I'll check these notes with him when I come back.

* * * * *

You have to spend a lot of time with some of these fellows explaining things to them.

* * * * *

I find in my own experience that I can work much better with the people under me who have learned to accept my criticisms and welcome them instead of those who seem to be fighting them.

* * * * *

(To store department heads.) I want each of you fellows to know that the store manager is constantly getting demands from above on how to do things. When he comes to you with something it's not just personal, he's getting orders from the district people to do things, and he has to follow through on them.

* * * * *

I like a supervisor who is really the boss, really running things, a take-charge guy.

Most of DM3's statements about his subordinates concerned what he expected of them. He did much less talking about his own behavior toward them. In essence he expected his subordinates to follow his instructions and treat him as an expert on store management.

As a Subordinate

DM3's persistent view of himself in relation to his organizational superiors is summarized by the researcher as follows:

1. I am fully willing and able to do what I am told to do by my bosses.

2. Superiors should give me clear-cut policies and instructions to follow.
3. I tell my bosses exactly what I think (but not so much lately because it has gotten me into trouble).

These statements are drawn from the following kinds of comments by DM3:

> I may argue about something ahead of time, but once a decision is made, right or wrong, I will carry it out.

* * * * *

> This is the first time I've found out what this new system is all about. Can you imagine that! They ought to tell us about these things if people are going to come in and put them into our stores.

* * * * *

> I used to be pretty outspoken and that was part of the thing that got me in trouble. I was known as the great dissenter but I've stopped all of that now.

* * * * *

> In this business you can't do anything right. It gets you one way or the other.

* * * * *

> No one in the front office is much interested in my opinions.

The dominant belief of DM3 as a subordinate was that he expected to conform to instructions. He saw himself as arguing ahead of time but then following orders. Notice his use of the "right or wrong" phrase—a conflict of views tended to be a black or white matter for him rather than a difference of opinion. He preferred specific instructions from his superiors to general ones and often asked for clear-cut orders even in circumstances when he knew in advance he would not agree with what was coming. Implicit in his perceptions of a lack of higher management interest in his views is the attitude that his views, as an expert, should be respected and recognized.

Summary of DM3

DM3 has a set of beliefs about himself as a district manager from which his expectations about others flow in a completely consistent manner. He sees himself as a hard-headed, systematic expert on store management. He expects to be treated by others as such. He wants clear orders from above with which he will comply, right or wrong, and he expects his subordinates to treat his orders in the same way. This set of beliefs and expectations constituted a self-concept that is both internally consistent and self-re-enforcing. It is a self-concept that put DM3 in harmony with the traditional organizational pattern of the company. It makes the overt behavior of DM3 that we saw in Chapters VI and VII much more understandable. Seeing himself as an expert on the substantive problems of the business, what could be more natural than that he would spend so much time giving his subordinates instructions. Seeing himself as conforming to his boss's orders, what could be more expected than that SM3 would say that DM3 expected him to "go by the book."

One aspect of DM3's phenomenal field needs special emphasis. In spite of the fact that DM3 frequently did not agree with higher management's decisions on particular issues, he never saw himself, as a person, in conflict with the organization, as a system. He admitted no such conflict or uncertainty. He conceived of himself as perfectly willing and able to do what he was told without inner conflict, and he expected others to do likewise. His was a conforming response to orders. This was DM3's reality. He saw no other way of conceiving of his job and relationship to the organization. Any latent feelings of conflict must have been denied conscious attention.

This picture of DM3, it must be noted, is not a picture of the whole man. It would more accurately be called the social man. We have not looked at DM3's capacity to solve the technical problems of the company. There was considerable evidence that DM3 deserved the label of an expert on supermarket problems. He had outstanding skills in the presentation of merchandise. He was highly interested and skilled in working out special promotions in his stores. He was a keen analyst of record-keeping procedures and work methods. DM3's capacities in these areas were not only witnessed by the researcher; they were also testified to by his colleagues in the company. Needless to say, these capacities were very important to the company even though the reorganizational plans called for an emphasis on organization change rather than technical improvements. This fact, that we are looking at our district managers from a limited standpoint, needs to be kept in mind as we proceed to look at DM3's initial response to the reorganization plans.

Attitude Toward Reorganization

The available evidence indicates that DM3's overt response to the new plans was that he was perfectly willing to comply and confident of his ability to comply. At least this was the response he gave to his superiors in meetings on the subject that the researcher attended. DM3 did not express enthusiasm for the change but neither did he express doubts about its wisdom or his ability to execute it, and others did express such doubts. Instead, it was the observation of his peers that he seemed to be "quieting down" and, in effect, withdrawing somewhat from the open discussion of these changes. This behavior fits with his concept of himself as fully willing and able to comply with orders.

In private to the researcher, however, DM3 did express antagonisms toward the change in the following kinds of statements.

> I'm one of the few guys in the business who thinks this whole inventory control theory simply won't work.

* * * * *

The old assistant district managers are having some trouble in changing over to the new merchandiser setup. They're a little puzzled and when they come to me and ask what they should do I tell them to go ahead and use their own judgment in situations.

* * * * *

I'm one of the few people that doesn't like this new setup with merchandisers and store managers. I thought the old way was much better. I had a team operating in my territory that you just couldn't beat. But I'm not arguing with them. I'm doing what I'm told these days.

These statements carry a certain tone that was characteristic of DM3's initial reaction to the changes. He seems to see the changes in an impersonal way, and he considers them to be a mistake in business judgment. Significantly, he does not say that they upset him, threaten him, or in any way disturb his capacity to comply with what is wanted. Even in his private comments of antagonism DM3 is still maintaining his self-concept as a fully competent and obedient district manager who is meeting the company's new role requirements.

This initial response of DM3 to the reorganization is inconsistent with his overt behavior that was presented in Chapters VI and VII. It will be recalled that he was the district manager most out of line with the desired behavior. Yet we know that he saw himself as a person who complied with higher management expectations, and he gave no open resistance to the reorganization. In effect, management had asked him to meet the new role requirements, to be more adaptive in his response to orders, and to teach his subordinates to do likewise. His response was, in effect,—"Yes, sir, anything you say." And by giving this response he proved to his superiors that he was still out of line, still giving a conformist response. This lack of an explicit awareness of his own self-concept and its conflict with the new demands did not even permit him to see that any alternative response existed. He had not achieved an awareness of self–environment, and without it he could not see the possibilities of *personal choice*. So by definition he could not make an adaptive response. We see the paradox of a man trapped into a deviant position by his own desire to conform—and committed to denying that he is deviant. It is also clearly evident, if there was ever any doubt, that *ordering a conformist to be adaptive is not sufficient to induce the change*. DM3's perceptual field (again the area within the heavy line) and the other components of his situation are diagrammed below:

Awareness of Self-Environment

DM3's traditional self-concept → Conflict and Insecure Feelings ← New organizational role requirements

↓

Conformist Response

I am willing and able to comply with the new demands.

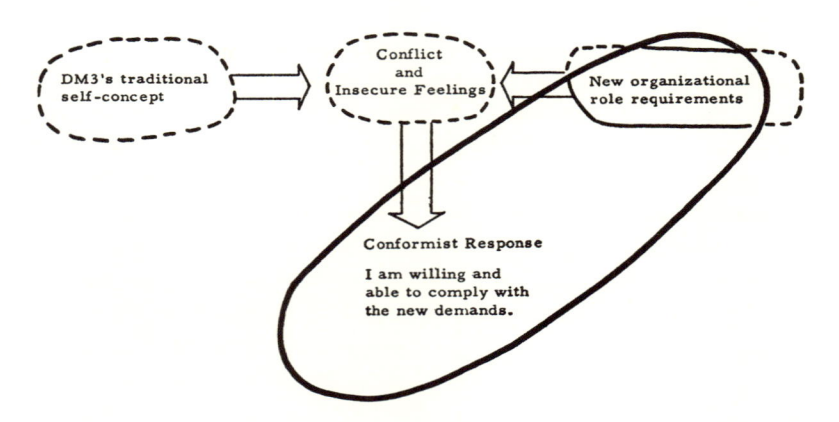

This response of DM3 is only his initial response to the changes. Over the months that followed the formal announcement of the plan, DM3, along with the other district managers, was subject to a variety of influences which higher management hoped would foster the execution of their plans. In the next chapter we shall look at the evidence of the results achieved after two years of operation under the new plans, and at the various organizational influences that contributed to these results. We shall focus primarily on DM3, since all our evidence indicates that he would have the greatest difficulty in meeting the new expectations. Thus our questions will be: Is it possible for an organization, given time, to make significant changes in the behavior patterns of people? What practical day-to-day influences affect the final results? What is involved in helping an individual with a conformist response, such as DM3, develop a more adaptive type of behavior? Before addressing these questions, certain conclusions can be drawn from the evidence in this chapter.

Conclusions

This chapter was designed to help us account for the differences in the overt behavior of our three district managers. Have we accomplished this objective? What do we now know about these men?

We have been looking at the self-concepts of the three district managers, comparing them to one another, and relating them to their overt behavior in response to the organizational pressure to change. This line of analysis has *not* told us where the differences among the men came from. It would, however, be very easy, since we have been focusing so long on these particular individuals, to jump to the conclusion that the differences are caused by inherent personality differences from some vague and distant origins. Such a conclusion would be most unwarranted. We need to remind ourselves at this point that such pure psychological determinism ignores the fact that all three of these district managers have for years been working in an organization where the assumptions of DM2 and DM3 about themselves as district managers were customary. It would not be at all unlikely or unnatural for two of our three district managers to have, over time, internalized these organizational codes into essential aspects of their self-concepts. Or it could be argued that earlier social conditioning could have brought our DM2 and DM3 to the organization with these assumptions about themselves already formed. Additional study of these past social influences could help us further in accounting for these individual differences. But, lest we swing to the other pole of sociological determinism, we should remember that one of our district managers apparently existed in the same organizational environment without internalizing its traditional codes. Neither a purely psychological approach nor a sociological approach seems to account adequately for the origins of the differences. Let us now face the conclusion that *we do not have and cannot secure a final answer to our query about the origins of the differences among our district managers.* However, we need not worry about this conclusion if we look at what we have learned by the approach we have taken to the differences among the three men. The analysis we have made does provide us with some useful leads to action.

We have seen that these self-concepts were not random collections of attitudes but integrated self-consistent ways of perceiving and dealing with the outside world. This consistency is what is often referred to as the basic integrity of the individual. All our district managers had this personality integrity and deserve our respect for it. The other side of the coin is that these self-concepts do not change quickly or easily in response to the needs of the organizational system for change. Regardless of the urgency for change from an organizational standpoint, the individual must maintain the consistency of his concept of himself. One of our district managers was lucky in that his prior self-concept so neatly complemented the new role requirements and he was not put into conflict (even though it was not by luck that he had developed his awareness of self–environment). DM2's self-concept was in conflict with the new model, but his way of thinking about himself and the organization (awareness of self–environment) allowed him to choose to start down the painful path of rethinking his self-concept and experiment with new behavior patterns. We saw that he was in the middle of the changing process. DM3 was also put into conflict by the changes, but his lack of an explicit awareness of self-environment would not initially allow him to see this conflict. This put DM3 in the most difficult dilemma of all to resolve. Regardless of the outcome, however, we now know what the "sensible" organizational plans of top management were bumping into that made their execution so difficult. They had come into conflict with the individual interaction patterns that were persistently sustained by the self-concepts of our key individuals. Because of the very nature of this conflict, *the desired changes were not going to be executed successfully until what made "sense" in the realm of organizational welfare was reconciled with what made "sense" in terms of the self-concepts of the strategic individuals.* The evidence indicates that there was no easy short cut for effecting this reconciliation. This stubborn fact must be faced up to by administrators who would introduce significant changes.

By putting together the self-concepts of these men, we have also seen how the outward behavior of each man makes "sense" to him as an expression of his inner assumptions. Once we identified these self-concepts, we could predict with some certainty what the response of each man would be to the organizational changes. This has the obvious value of providing clues to the source, kind, and degree of resistance to the desired change that should be anticipated.

Finally, spelling out these self-concepts has allowed us to know these men in a more intimate "internal" way. We now have some depth of understanding of what their differences in behavior *meant* to the men involved. This kind of "internal" picture gives us a chance to acquire an empathic understanding that would provide a better basis for building a learning relationship with these men than many other forms of understanding them. In the next chapter we shall get a glimpse of the value of such a relationship.

CHAPTER IX

Two Years Later — Results and Interpretation

NEARLY TWO years after the data reported in the previous chapters were secured, the researcher renewed his intensive study of the company to see what, if any, evidence existed of a change in behavior patterns within the organization. In essence, the evidence two years later indicated that a significant change had occurred in the way the organization operated. The researcher picked up signs of this change as he talked to people from the level of top management down to the level of store manager. The change struck the researcher as being no dramatic miracle but a clearly discernible movement in the direction of top management's desired model. District managers and store managers were behaving more in line with their new required roles. This impression of change, of course, could be deceptive so the researcher sought to check his observations by again focusing on the behavior of the three strategic district managers and their immediate subordinates. Had their interaction patterns changed? Did their self-concepts and related assumptions seem to be different?

EVIDENCE OF CHANGED BEHAVIOR

District Managers — Changes in Behavior

In the early summer of 1957 the researcher again observed the interaction patterns of DM2 and DM3. It was not possible to get new data on DM1 since in the interim he had been temporarily assigned to an important new position at the central office. In collecting the new interaction data on DM2 and DM3, the researcher used precautions to get comparable and typical data.[1] Exhibit 11 summarizes the principal results of these observations and compares them with the earlier observations.

Exhibit 11 indicates that both DM2 and DM3 made some important changes in their customary interaction patterns with store managers. These changes are in a direction that brings these men closer to congruence with the desired organizational model. DM2 has moved very close to achieving a 50–50 balance in total talking time with his subordinates while DM3 has moved 13 percentage points closer to such an over-all balance. This better balance is also seen in the breakdown by categories of speech. These two patterns still show some of their earlier characteristics (DM2's for giving many *opinions* and especially DM3's for giving many *directions*) but these tendencies have been reduced and a better balance has been achieved. As to the relative amount of time spent in each category of speech, both men have shifted to spending most of the total talking time in the *information* category with *opinions* second. This sequence of time allocation now coincides with the sequence that DM1 demonstrated earlier and fits our desired model for a more problem-solving type of interaction.

Exhibit 12 presents the comparison between 1955 and 1957 in the average duration of a single comment. These data again indicate a movement toward the desired model of a balanced interaction pattern.

The changes in interaction behavior demonstrated by Exhibits 11 and 12 were corroborated by the observations of people in the company who worked closely with DM2 and DM3. The vice president of sales commented that in his opinion DM3 had made a remarkable change in his supervisory practices that brought him more in line with what the

[1] DM2 was observed for 219 minutes with 1,116 separate comments recorded in interactions with 6 different store managers. DM3 was observed for 233 minutes with 1,160 separate comments recorded in interactions with 4 different store managers.

EXHIBIT 11

Comparison of DM—SM Talking Time
in 1955 and 1957

1955
Average with 3 SMs

	DM2	SMs
Q.	14	2
I.	16	13
O.	26	10
S.or D.	16	3
Totals	72%	28%

1957
Average with 4 SMs

	DM2	SMs	
	12%	9 3	Ques.
	55%	25 30	Info.
	23%	14 9	Opin.
	10%	7 3	Dir. or Sug.
Totals	55%	45%	

1955
Average with 3 SMs

	DM3	SMs
Q.	9	2
I.	26	17
O.	13	4
S.or D.	27	.2
Totals	75%	25%

1957
Average with 4 SMs

	DM3	SMs	
	11	3 14%	Ques.
	27 26 53%		Info.
	12	7 19%	Opin.
	12	2 14%	Sug. or Dir.
Totals	62%	38%	

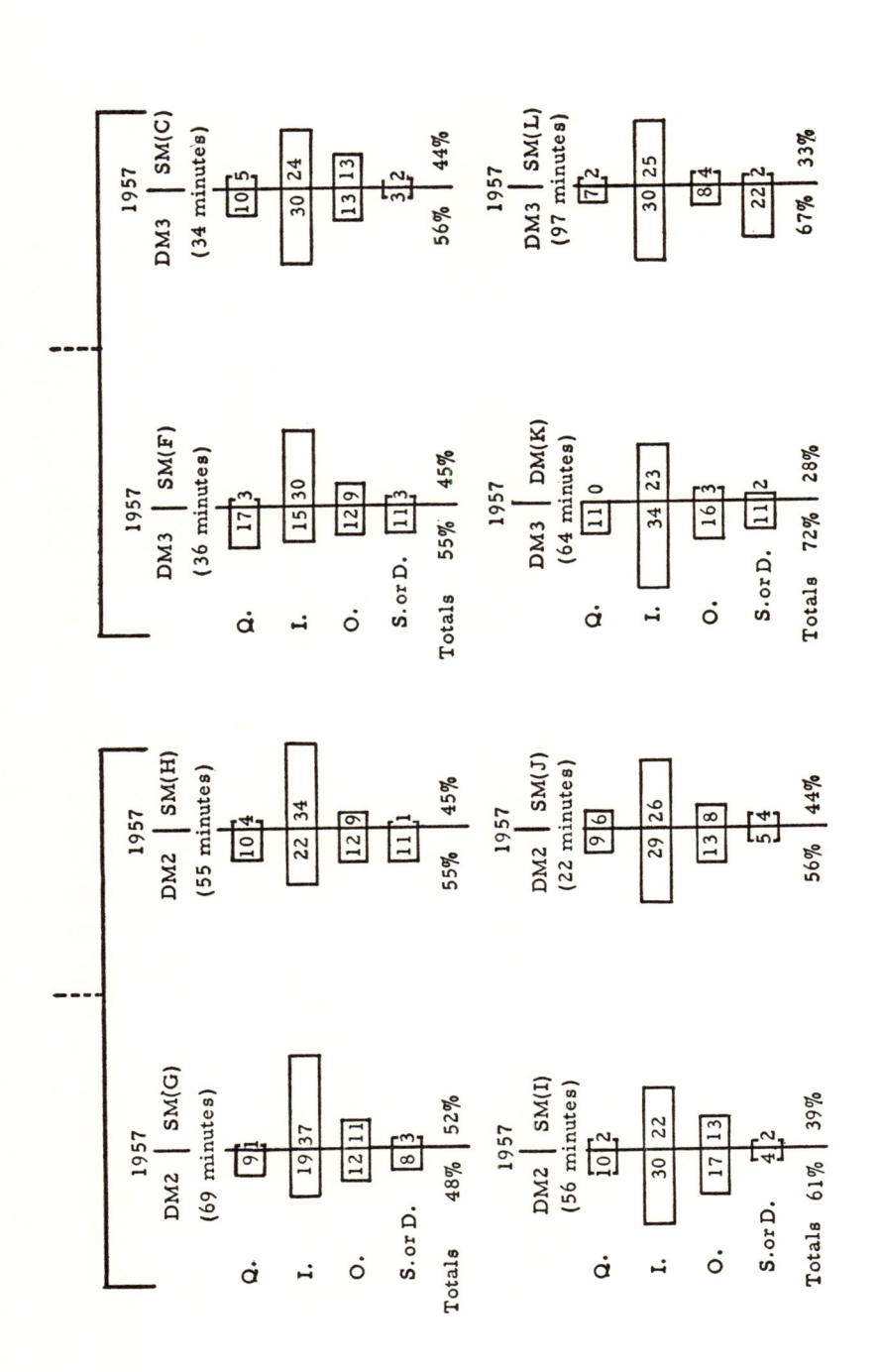

	1957 DM2 | SM(G) (69 minutes)	1957 DM2 | SM(H) (55 minutes)	1957 DM3 | SM(F) (36 minutes)	1957 DM3 | SM(C) (34 minutes)
Q.	9 | 1	10 | 4	17 | 3	10 | 5
I.	19 | 37	22 | 34	15 | 30	30 | 24
O.	12 | 11	12 | 9	12 | 9	13 | 13
S. or D.	8 | 3	11 | 1	11 | 3	3 | 2
Totals	48% 52%	55% 45%	55% 45%	56% 44%

	1957 DM2 | SM(I) (56 minutes)	1957 DM2 | SM(J) (22 minutes)	1957 DM3 | DM(K) (64 minutes)	1957 DM3 | SM(L) (97 minutes)
Q.	10 | 2	9 | 6	11 | 0	7 | 2
I.	30 | 22	29 | 26	34 | 23	30 | 25
O.	17 | 13	13 | 8	16 | 3	8 | 4
S. or D.	4 | 2	5 | 4	11 | 2	22 | 2
Totals	61% 39%	56% 44%	72% 28%	67% 33%

EXHIBIT 12

Comparison of Average Duration of a Single Comment in Minutes, 1955 and 1957

1955		1957	
SM1	SM		
.20	.17		
DM2	SM	DM2	SM
.28	.16	.19	.21
DM3	SM	DM3	SM
.26	.13	.22	.18

company desired. The store operations manager made the observation that, while he thought people did not change certain basic characteristics, these two district managers were making real progress in meeting the new organizational requirements. One of DM3's immediate subordinates testified that the changes in his boss during the time period were most dramatic. The researcher heard no comments from any source that contradicted this evidence.

It was more difficult to capture the extent and nature of the corresponding changes these two men had made in their self-concepts as district managers. DM2 told the researcher that he felt more "on top of his job" and attributed this partly to an improvement in his health. He spoke with pride of the way his store managers had developed in their capacity to run their stores and indicated an increased confidence in what he could accomplish by working through them. He no longer talked of himself as being in conflict as we saw him do in Chapter VIII. He now seemed comfortable in conceiving himself as a man who could help some competent store managers develop their capacities and solve their problems.

In turn DM3 made several statements to the researcher that indicated a shift in his concept of himself as a district manager. Some of these statements follow.

> My job of adjusting to my new job setup [2] is like the problems of a grocery manager becoming a store manager. You have the same old problems to deal with, but you have to learn to handle them differently. I have to be very conscious of how I get things done. I'm trying to delegate more details.
>
> * * * * *
>
> This job isn't too easy. I can use all the help I can get on it.
>
> * * * * *
>
> I am trying to learn as I go along.

These comments by DM3 were mixed in with others that were more like the way he was talking two years earlier. But the fact that he could make any statements of this kind is most significant. Here he has expressed awareness of his own supervisory behavior pattern and its difference from what management desired. He expressed his feelings of uneasiness and discomfort at this conflict and his interest in modifying his customary behavior pattern. In other words, a diagram of his phenomenal field at this point would look more like DM2's in Chapter VIII—a picture of a man in change, a picture of a man who was developing an awareness of self–environment. Both DM2 and DM3 had come a considerable

[2] The specific "new setup" referred to by DM3 was a move in 1957 that enlarged DM3's district and gave him two staff assistants. This change was a further step in top management's over-all plans for reorganization.

way in two years toward meeting the new role requirements. They were working out of a conformist response to organizational pressure toward a more adaptive, choosing response.

Store Managers—Changes in Behavior

As an additional way to determine the extent to which the company's reorganizational effort actually changed behavior, the researcher observed the work habits of store managers at two different times. For this purpose the new store managers, SM1, SM2, and SM3, whose behavior was described in Chapters IV, V, and VI, were selected for study. Some six months after these three men had been appointed store managers their work was systematically observed. This provided a picture of their early response to their new job and the kind of supervision they were receiving from DM1, DM2, and DM3. They were again observed two years after they had become store managers. The results of these observations are presented in Exhibits 13 and 14.

Exhibit 13 shows the amount of time each store manager spent in two basic functions, interactions (talking to people) and activities (working without talking). These times are again broken down into time spent interacting with (1) department heads, (2) clerks, and (3) all others including customers, salesmen, nonstore employees of all kinds, maintenance men, delivery men, etc. The activity time is broken down into time spent (1) observing store operations, (2) doing paper work, (3) working directly with the merchandise or on the upkeep of the store's physical facilities, and (4) helping customers.

It will be recalled that our firsthand observations of SM1, SM2, and SM3 in earlier chapters indicated that SM1 was meeting the new role requirements for the behavior of a store manager. SM2 seemed to be fairly close to the requirements also, while SM3 was not meeting the requirements in several ways. Exhibit 13 presents in quantitative terms certain indications of these differences. Of particular signifi-

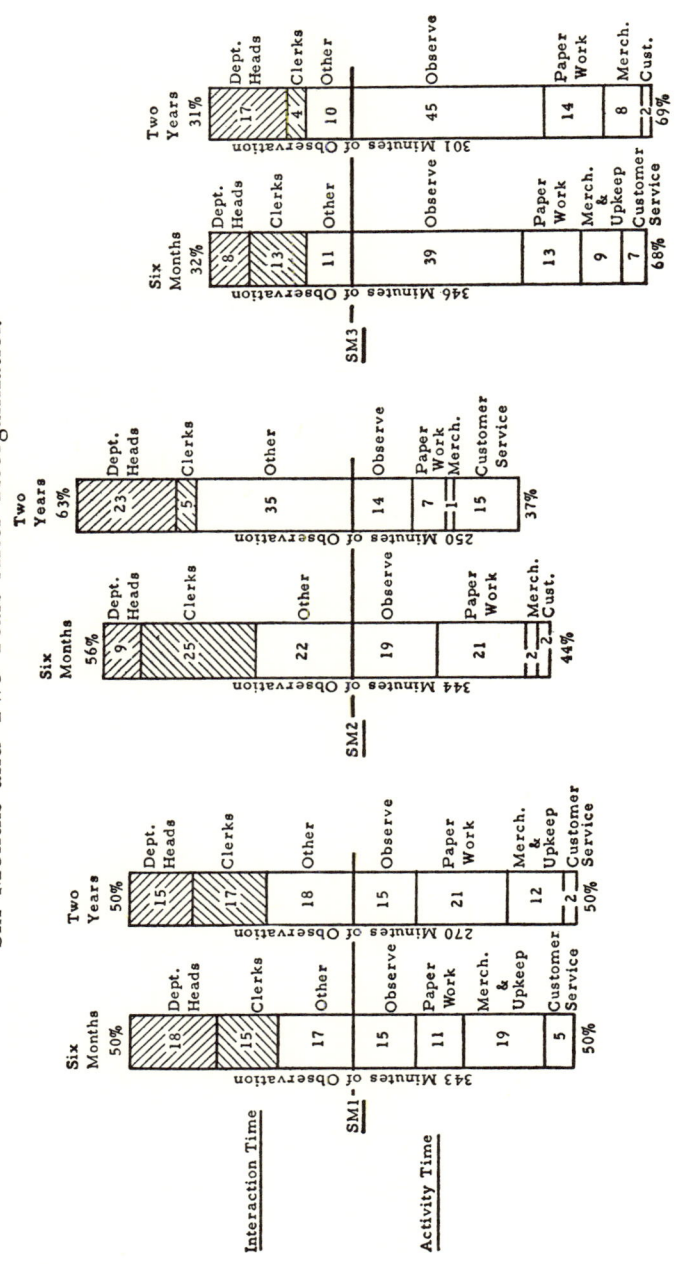

EXHIBIT 13
Interactions and Activities of Store Managers Six Months and Two Years After Reorganization

EXHIBIT 14
Initiation of Interactions by Store Managers Six Months and Two Years After Reorganization

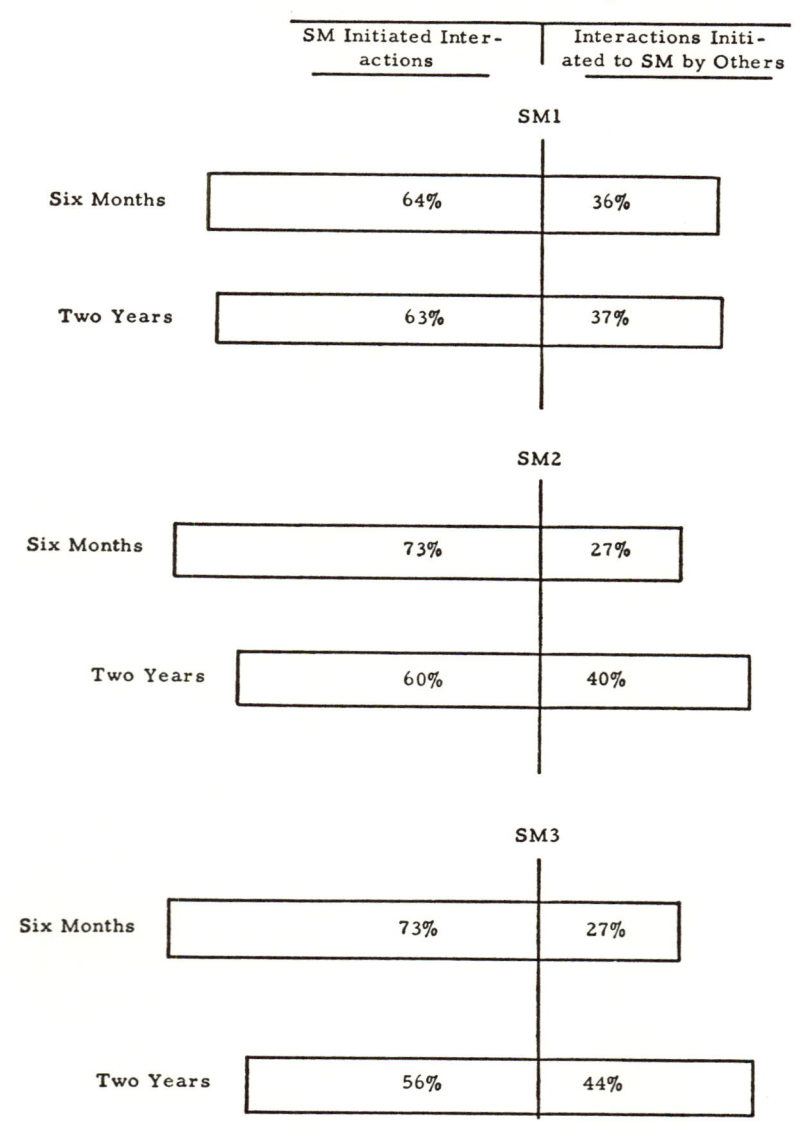

	SM Initiated Interactions	Interactions Initiated to SM by Others

SM1

	SM Initiated	Initiated by Others
Six Months	64%	36%
Two Years	63%	37%

SM2

	SM Initiated	Initiated by Others
Six Months	73%	27%
Two Years	60%	40%

SM3

	SM Initiated	Initiated by Others
Six Months	73%	27%
Two Years	56%	44%

cance are the figures on the time spent interacting with department heads and clerks. We note that at the first point of observation SM1 was spending 33% of his time talking to department heads and clerks and that the time was about evenly split between the two groups. This contrasts sharply with SM3 who was spending but 21% of his time in this manner and mostly with the clerks. SM2 was between the two with a high of 34% of his time spent in these interactions but mostly with clerks.

A year and one half later the figures indicate that certain aspects of behavior changed while others did not. The behavior of SM1 remained virtually unchanged except for minor shifts in his allocation of activity time. For SM2 and SM3 the most significant shifts were in the distribution of their interaction time between department heads and clerks. Both of these men virtually reversed the proportion of time they spent with department heads and clerks while maintaining roughly the same amount of total time so spent. This shift would bring these two men more into congruence with the required role for store managers since it would indicate that they were working more through the expected organizational channels or, in other words, acting less like grocery managers and more like store managers.

Exhibit 13 also indicates certain behavior characteristics of these three men that did not change over this time period. Their allocation of time between interactions of all kinds and activities of all kinds was remarkably consistent. SM1 was consistently balanced in this regard. SM2 consistently had a high amount of interaction time, while SM3 consistently had a low amount of interaction time. Management did not set up anything like a role requirement for this behavior characteristic, and wisely so. There is no reason to think that a "successful" performance cannot be turned in by managers that vary a great deal in this characteristic even though we would predict that an extreme of imbalance in either direction would be undesirable. Perhaps SM3 is approaching such an extreme of a low amount of interaction time. In any event, the evidence at hand indicates that this characteristic is less subject to rapid change than the allocation of time within these two broad elements of behavior.

Exhibit 14 presents some additional data on the behavior of SM1, SM2, and SM3 at the same two time periods. It indicates the proportions of interactions that were initiated by the store manager as against those initiated toward him by others. SM1 again shows a consistency between the two time periods while SM2 and SM3 show a similar shift in behavior. Of course, top management was not specific about its role requirement for this characteristic, but it did desire to see more of a two-way, give and take between store managers and their subordinates. This requirement would translate into desiring a balance in the initiation of interactions. By this criterion SM1 was initially meeting the role requirement better than the other two men (as our earlier observations also indicated). A year and a half later, SM2 and SM3 had significantly shifted their behavior in the direction of closer congruence to the required role. Thus, Exhibit 14 tends to confirm the evidence in Exhibit 13 that the three store managers, taken together, had shifted their overt behavior during the two-year period to meet more nearly the new role requirements for store managers.

Summary

All this evidence adds up to the conclusion that the behavior of people in the strategic spots in the organization was actually changing. The reorganizational plans were being converted from the realm of ideas into daily routine behavior. A small group of management men were on the road to changing, as planned, some of the most persistent behavior patterns of people in an organization. This is a highly significant finding. In Chapter I we referred to man's belief in the importance of organizations as change agents. The findings of this one study support this belief. Even in as short a time as two years, some basic behavior patterns were changed to a limited but measurable degree. The behavior by no means changed easily or readily but it did change. As soon as this statement is made, it pushes us on to the next question. Can more light be shed on how this was done? What were the influences that brought about these changes? Before we tackle this question, we need to take a quick look at the ground we have been over.

In Chapters II and III we looked at some of the traditional behavior patterns of the organization and at management's plans for changing these patterns. Management proceeded to make some specific formal moves to institute the changes, and in Chapters IV, V, and VI we had a description of three district managers' response to these initial changes as they broke in three new store managers. We saw the characteristic supervisory behavior of these men and the basic stubborn nature of it. The initial formal moves were sufficient to bring the behavior of DM1 and SM1 into congruence with the required roles and to start DM2 and SM2 making the required changes. The behavior of DM3 and SM3 was considerably out of line with the new requirements.

Our description of the behavior of these key individuals still left some things to be desired. We needed a more systematic way of analyzing and measuring their behavior patterns. For this purpose we conceived of their behavior in three basic elements: interactions, activities, and sentiments. The new role requirements for district managers called for virtually no change in their customary activities of calling on stores, but they did call for a considerable change in their interaction patterns and their underlying sentiments. We devised a way of measuring quantitatively the interaction pattern of these men, and those results were presented in Chapter VII. The variable of sentiments, or more precisely, in this instance, the self-concepts of the key individuals, was presented in Chapter VIII. The analysis of these two variables gave us a more precise picture of what had to change to

186 THE CHANGING OF ORGANIZATIONAL BEHAVIOR PATTERNS

reach management's objective and some of the problems of effecting the change. In this chapter we have seen already that two years later the evidence indicates that a significant change did take place in these two variables.

To account for these changes we need to face up to a problem concerning the nature of the relationship between our variables. Did the change in sentiments, in the inner self-concept, *cause* the change in the overt interaction behavior? Our common-sense answer would probably be yes. But such a causal relationship cannot be proven. It seems safer to assume that our two variables are interdependent, that each can be influenced by the environment directly, and that a change in either variable must create a change in the other. Thus for this study we shall conceive of the chain of influence as follows:

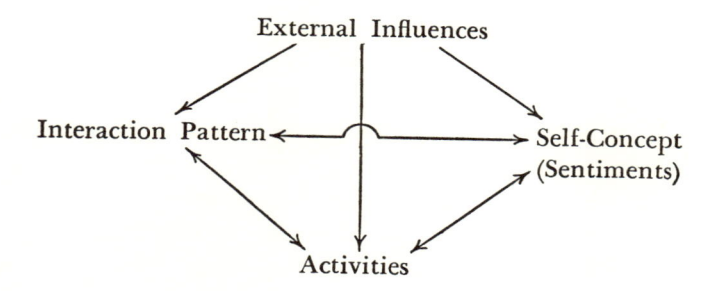

```
              External Influences
             ↙        ↓        ↘
Interaction Pattern ⇄     ⇄ Self-Concept
             ↖        ↓       ↗ (Sentiments)
                   Activities
```

rather than:

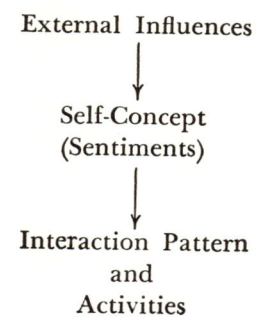

```
External Influences
        ↓
   Self-Concept
   (Sentiments)
        ↓
Interaction Pattern
        and
     Activities
```

We shall start our examination of the influences on behavior by looking at the direct organizational influences on the interaction patterns of our key individuals. The reader needs to be cautioned as we proceed that the questions we seek to answer are very difficult to answer in a definite way. It would have been ideal from a research design standpoint to run a series of controlled experiments that could have checked the effectiveness of each of several different ways of influencing behavior. This was not a feasible methodology to use in this study. Instead the researcher had to accept the reality that a number of influences were working on the situation at the same time and also accept the limitations of his own eyes and ears in observing these many influences and their consequences in the behavior of our three district managers. These limitations mean that our evidence will be rather thin in spots. It means that we cannot state our findings as firm conclusions but rather as insights and hypotheses that can be leads to further research. In spite of these limitations, the questions are so important that they seem well worth addressing.

Influencing Behavior Patterns

Direct Influence on Interactions

By quite a variety of means higher management had a direct influence on the interaction patterns of key subordinates like district managers. Two important examples were the budgeting procedures and the employee rating procedures. These two procedures were ostensibly set up to improve sales forecasting and expense planning, and to improve employee development and selection. The particular means used for accomplishing these objectives had an influence on the district managers' interaction patterns. These procedures required the district manager to ask (not tell) his store managers what their sales and expense forecasts were, and what their opinions of employees were. For several of the district managers, requiring them to solicit their subordinates' opinion was requiring a rather novel kind of interaction for them. The fact that they had to secure their subordinates' opinions to fill out the forms did not necessarily keep them from dominating those opinions or perhaps disrespecting them. But the requirement of asking for opinions time and again could well have pushed the district manager's sentiments toward more respect for, and confidence in, the store manager's opinions and likewise altered the store manager's concept of his own function. The budget and employee rating procedures are examples of major continuing influences on interaction patterns, but nonrecurring incidents of lesser importance were having similar effects.

The following incident illustrates the way that top management took advantage of ordinary events to foster a different kind of interaction pattern.

> In early 1955, the vice president of sales was discussing with some of his top people the dissemination of current information about union contract negotiations. This information had been customarily handled as confidential to higher management. The vice president of sales proposed that the information be passed on to the newly appointed store managers.

V.P. Sales: I personally think it is a good idea to inform them. I think we'll reach an agreement with the union soon to take them out of the union. I think including them would sort of build up evidence that we really do want to treat them like management by giving them management's side of the negotiations. We may be taking some risks but I don't see what they are. How do you people feel about it?
Produce Merchandiser: I think it is a bad idea. If just one of those men started talking to a union representative, we'd be in hot water.
V.P. Sales: Well, I should think we'd be able to trust those men. Do you think that is a safe assumption?
Store Operations Manager: Well, I think it is.

Advertising Manager: I think so, too. After all, we're just going to give them the facts of the situation. We're not taking much of a risk.

V.P. Sales: I think we're going to go ahead on that unless I hear from some of you in the next few days with some good reason why we shouldn't.

Of course, the sequel to this conversation was that the district managers were asked to pass on this information to store managers. In other words, they were required to interact by conveying information that was customarily held in higher management. Again the district managers' interaction pattern had been directly influenced and probably their sentiments indirectly influenced.

The examples given above could be multiplied because the top management people involved were constantly seeking for opportunities to influence directly the interaction pattern between district managers and store managers. They were trying to handle the ordinary affairs of the business in a manner that required the use of the interaction pattern that they desired. The researcher cannot provide a measure of the magnitude of this kind of influence, but he personally was impressed with its importance. We shall now proceed to examine a variety of different influences on the relevant sentiments, the self-concepts, and the related assumptions of the key individuals.

Influence by Prior Consultation

It has become well established in management beliefs that prior consultation with the people concerned will facilitate the introduction of changes. This belief has been tested and validated, however, around the introduction of technological changes and not changes in fundamental supervisory behavior patterns of an organization. This study has not provided a rigorous test of the validity of this belief for the type of change under consideration, but we can reach a few tentative conclusions.

The researcher began his active field work about the time that the organizational changes were announced and, hence, did not personally observe the prior consultations. By secondhand evidence we can, however, reconstruct some of this picture. We know that several top management people conducted their own research into the workings of their organizational system in order to diagnose its troubles. As they observed their middle and lower supervisory people going about their work, they discovered that these men were eager to discuss on an informal basis their views of the strengths and weaknesses of the existing organization. While these conversations were not about specific proposals for organizational change, they did constitute an effort by consultation to come to a common diagnosis of the strengths and weaknesses of the organization. They also tended to alert people down the line to the likelihood of some organizational changes. There is evidence that the formal announcement of the changes did not surprise many people even though some of the specifics of the plans were news. There is no evidence that these consultations had actually changed the customary behavior of people, but they did create in many people a state of readiness for change. If the change had not come, there would have been a letdown. To this extent the prior consultations were useful.

All the evidence indicates that top management did not conduct prior consultations with the district managers as a group on the specific details of their plans in advance. DM1 discussed the plans on a confidential basis with some of the top people. He passed on some of this information to the district manager group and suggested that they, as a group, ask for an advance exchange of views on the plans with top management. The rest of the group decided not to make this move and thereby indicated they were still following the traditional pattern. On the basis of hindsight, we can say that top management would have been well advised to have taken the initiative in soliciting the views of the district manager group in advance of the change. In view of the deep-seated nature of the behavior patterns that were required to change, however, there is no reason to believe that this step would have done much more than improve the readiness for change and serve as the first example of the newly desired relationship between district managers and higher management. It certainly would not have been a cure-all.

Influence by Changes in Personnel and Structure

The management of any organization that wishes to make a major change in its organizational behavior probably considers the possibility of facilitating that change by discharging certain individuals and hiring new ones. Some might argue quite simply that, if you want a different kind of organization, you have to get different kinds of people. The top management of Food World briefly considered this possibility when it introduced these changes. In Chapter II we reported one conversation on this topic. The reader will recall that a member of top management was questioning the capacity of some key people to adapt to the required changes. The vice president of sales asked his colleague if he was prepared to fire these people. When the answer was "No," the comment came back, "Then we have no choice but to tackle the job of training them." Another executive stated, "When we initiated this change we committed ourselves to the difficult job of working it out with our present personnel." Management consistently followed this policy of firing no one and of working out the change with the existing personnel.

The top management did, however, make some important changes both in the formal structure and in personnel assignments that constituted strong influences on sentiments. Chapter III described these formal changes. These changes brought promotions to a number of men but they also brought demotion to three incumbent district managers.

Thus, top management, by rewarding certain people and punishing others, was trying to influence behavior directly. We have already seen some of the consequences of this form of influence, but we now can explore other consequences and the possible alternatives.

During the early transition period there were three district managers who were demoted, two to jobs as store managers of big stores, and one to the job of product merchandiser. These three men were of the "old school" in that they were judged by management and the researcher (on admittedly little evidence) to have a view of themselves and the organization that fitted the traditional pattern. Management judged that the transition to the new pattern would be most difficult for them. The evidence is insufficient on these men to say if they had an awareness of self–environment that facilitated the adaptive response to change pressure that we saw in DM_1 and later in DM_2 and DM_3. This criterion apparently did not enter into top management's thinking.

The principal facts that swayed management to demote these men while keeping others with a similar pattern (DM_2 and DM_3) were the record of profitable results of these men and their general reputation. In other words, these three men were considered marginal district managers under the old system in contrast to DM_2 and DM_3 who had excellent reputations under the old system. This means that top management made its choices of district managers for the new system more on the basis of past performances than on the basis of anticipated difficulty in fitting in with the new required roles. This basis for judgment might be criticized but there were some good reasons for it. It would have been a gross violation of the sense of equity of many people in the organization if the district managers who were generally thought of as most successful were demoted to introduce the new program. This would have put a most severe strain on the loyalty sentiments of the organization.

Furthermore, the very past success of these district managers testified to their having considerable talents regardless of their kind of interaction pattern or sentiments. In addition, the top management people making the selection decisions were quite naturally and appropriately involved in the prevailing sentiments of the company, and it would have hurt their own sense of justice to demote "successful" district managers. In this instance their own sense of justice in making these personnel moves was probably a sound guide to the reaction that others in the organization would have felt. This sense of fairness influenced top management also in arranging the demotion of the three district managers in such a way that none of them were cut in salary. The reasons for the demotions were explained to the men involved, and by all reports these men found it possible to accept their transfers gracefully and were doing good work in their new assignments.

While management was demoting these three men they were also promoting many more to be store managers as well as district managers. In selecting people for promotion, management was weighing the capacity of people to meet the new role requirements against the obligations and loyalties built up by past relationships. As with the district manager selections, they compromised between these criteria. Thus they hoped to move toward the new organizational model without doing too great a violence to the existing sentiments. They hoped to signal the organization that they were not completely repudiating the obligations of the past but that they did mean business about making the necessary changes. Almost everyone seemed to understand this signal, but the trouble was that it was not too clear what management specifically meant business about. We have already seen the differences in the reactions of DM1, DM2, and DM3 to these formal changes in structure and personnel and their reactions pretty well mirror the diverse reactions of others.

In summary, for DM1 these formal moves were sufficient

to secure in him the type of behavior that was expected. The formal change in management's expectations had the effect on DM1 of removing him from conflict. Our review of his self-concept in the preceding chapter showed why this was true.

The formal moves were sufficient to put DM2 into a position of internal conflict between his desire to meet management's new expectations and his traditional self-concept. We saw that DM2 recognized this conflict, wanted to reconcile his self-concept with the new role requirements, but often was at a loss as to how to do it. The formal change had therefore set up in DM2 a willingness to change, but he was dependent on other influences to find the specific ways in which he could effect this change.

The reaction of DM3 to these new formal expectations is of special concern to us if we are to throw light on the changes that occurred over two years in his behavior. DM3 had a view of himself and his place in the organization that was in close congruence with the traditional organizational pattern. From an external point of view the formal changes put DM3 into a conflict position. We have seen, however, that his initial reaction was to give no overt sign of conflict. Instead his initial reaction can best be characterized as withdrawal. This initial withdrawal of DM3 is very understandable. He had felt somewhat sidetracked in the organization when he was given his current district manager assignment some time earlier. The new organizational changes were another indication that he was out of line with management's expectations. And yet his self-concept was that he was an expert who also kept in line with management's expectations. The new changes were so challenging to this self-concept that he could not overtly acknowledge the conflict. To pull back and withdraw seemed to be the only possible response to him at this time.

The reaction of our three district managers to the formal changes in the organization gives us some fairly clear leads on how such changes can influence the behavior of people and the limits of this type of influence. Changed organizational expectations, as signaled by changes in structure and personnel, will, by definition, put many people in the organization into a conflict position as regards their established self-concepts. There is no way of escaping this conflict. It seems, in fact, to be a necessary prelude to effecting any real change in behavior. The evidence of this study indicates that making the conflict clear cut is a necessary step for resolving the conflict. By making their new expectations clearcut, management can highlight this personal conflict. This step can be difficult because some tend to deny the existence of the conflict. The evidence also indicates, however, that clarifying the new expectations and the conflict is not by itself sufficient to induce the desired change in behavior. It certainly was not sufficient with DM2 and even less so with DM3. The making of the formal changes seems therefore to be a necessary but not sufficient (in all instances) influence to effect the desired changes in actual behavior.

Influence by the Behavior Patterns of Superiors

The store operations manager (SOM), as the immediate superior of the district managers, exerted an important influence on them by the example of his own personal behavior. In order to get a picture of his customary supervisory practices, the researcher recorded his interaction pattern in separate conversations with three district managers. The resulting figures (Exhibit 15) can be compared with those secured in the DM–SM relationships presented in Chapter VII and Exhibit 11. The figures summarize a total conversation time of only 149 minutes so that the resulting data are not so reliable as those for the district managers.

The interaction pattern of SOM that shows up in Exhibit 13 meets the new organizational model and then some. It is the first pattern in which the superior talked less than the subordinates. The amount of time spent in different speech

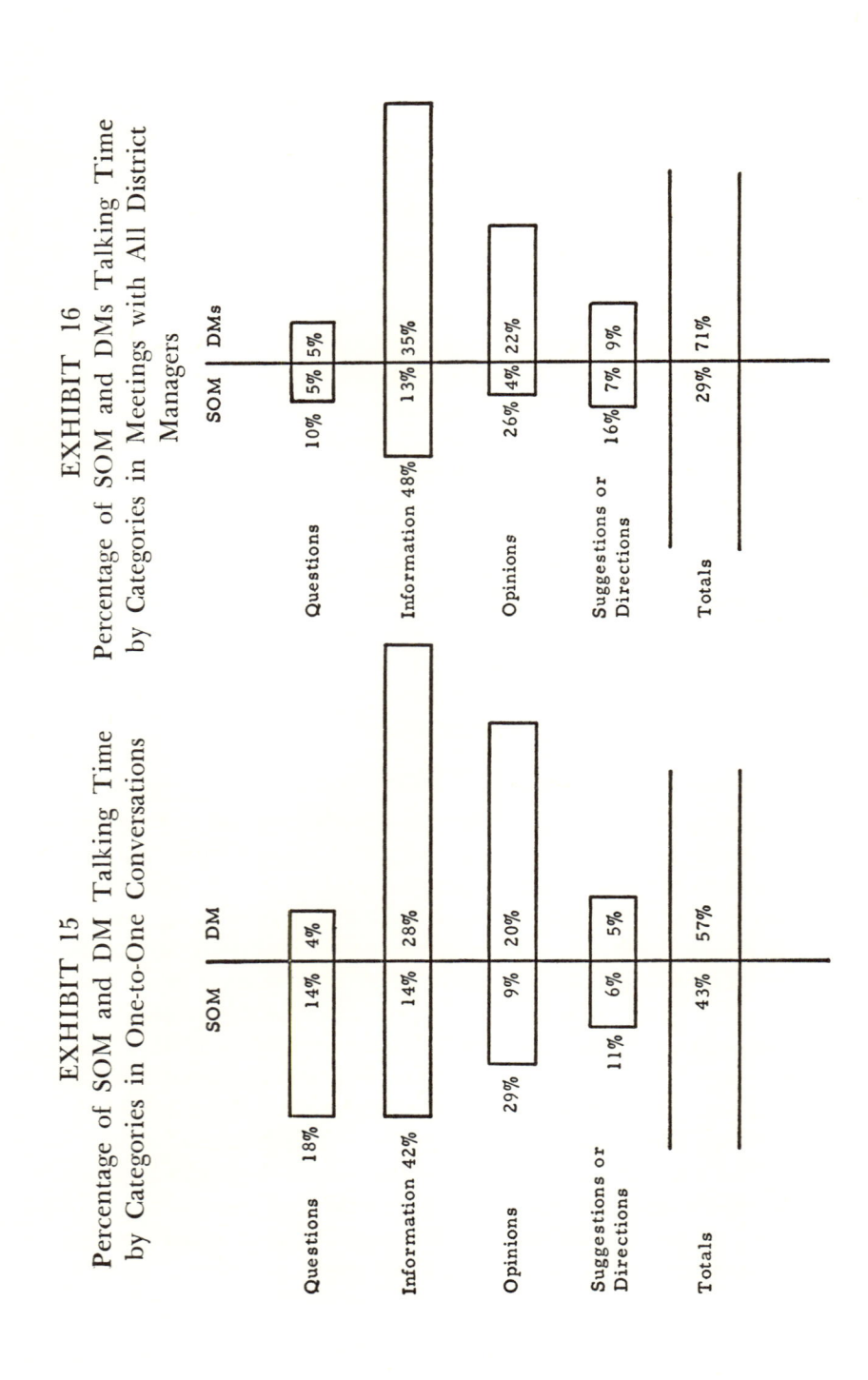

EXHIBIT 15
Percentage of SOM and DM Talking Time by Categories in One-to-One Conversations

	SOM	DM
Questions 18%	14%	4%
Information 42%	14%	28%
Opinions 29%	9%	20%
Suggestions or Directions 11%	6%	5%
Totals	43%	57%

EXHIBIT 16
Percentage of SOM and DMs Talking Time by Categories in Meetings with All District Managers

	SOM	DMs
Questions 10%	5%	5%
Information 48%	13%	35%
Opinions 26%	4%	22%
Suggestions or Directions 16%	7%	9%
Totals	29%	71%

categories follows the "problem-solving" sequence of information, opinions, questions, and suggestions or directions. However, there is an interesting lack of balance in the categories with SOM asking most of the questions while the district managers give most of the opinions and information. SOM seems to be using these conversations to inform himself as well as for mutual problem solving. The time spent in the suggestions or directions category is more nearly balanced than in any of the interaction patterns we have seen. It is clear that, if the different district managers were using their superior's behavior as a model to follow, their own behavior would move toward meeting the new role requirements.

In addition to his contacts with district managers on a one-to-one basis, SOM chaired biweekly meetings with all the district managers. SOM seemed to the researcher to be running these meetings in a fairly permissive manner. Certainly there was two-way communication. On the basis of systematically recording two meetings for 188 minutes it was found that SOM talked only 29% of the time. Further details on the interaction pattern in these meetings is given in Exhibit 16. He usually reached decisions by stating the concensus of the group discussion, and occasionally by explicitly overruling the concensus.

The influence that SOM's behavior had on the district managers is difficult to trace. Most of them respected SOM and probably tried to use his supervisory behavior as a model for their own. Others did not have such a high regard for his methods and to these his behavior did not provide an example to follow. DM3 was one of these. He was at least initially inclined to see SOM's supervisory behavior as evidence of vacillation and weakness. He responded by pressing SOM for detailed operating rules in areas where SOM did not feel detailed rules were wise. DM3 did not initially feel understood by SOM nor did he feel that SOM was militant enough in fighting the district managers' battles at headquarters.

One kind of contact between SOM and DM3 was of special importance. This was the annual session when SOM gave DM3 his evaluation of DM3's job performance. SOM reported that in one of his early reviews, he told DM3 that he was making progress in his handling of his subordinates but that he was still badly upsetting some of his people by his manner of criticism. SOM reported that, as he expected, DM3 became defensive and denied the validity of the comment. DM3 apparently got the impression that SOM wanted him to be more easy going with his people.

This evidence does not provide a very positive impression of SOM's influence with district managers like DM3. And yet, over-all, the researcher concluded that the influence was distinctly positive even with the district managers who were least inclined to model their behavior after SOM. In his reviews SOM was at least shattering DM3's idea that he was meeting the new role requirements. DM3 also found, over time, that SOM listened to his ideas with respect and acted on them when they were useful. SOM demonstrated his capacity to understand DM3 in the "internal" manner we discussed in Chapter VIII. As time went on and this relationship strengthened, DM3 found that SOM was less of a threat to him and did get results on the things DM3 asked for help on. In this environment it appeared to the researcher that DM3 found it possible to be less insistent on his expertise and more willing to look at and question his own behavior. In this manner SOM was providing the conditions that allowed men like DM3 to begin making some choices about their own behavior, even though these men may not have been inclined to try and copy SOM's behavior. And certainly it is very doubtful that, if SOM's own day-to-day behavior had not so well met the new role requirements, the kind of changes we have witnessed would have occurred.

Influence by the Peer Group

This entire study may have created the impression that all the influences toward change were coming from top management down the line. This was not true. Of course, the change we are studying happened to be initiated by top management so that most of the influences were stemming from that source. But both the district manager group as a peer group, and the store managers as a subordinate group were also influencing the sentiments of men like DM2 and DM3. The influence of the peer group contacts was most frequently observed in the district manager meetings. Two examples will be given of this influence.

At one of the early meetings after the reorganization was started, SOM asked the group how the new arrangements with the merchandisers were working out. He went around the table asking each district manager to comment on his experience. DM3 complained that he was getting slower action on the problems he expected the merchandisers to handle. DM1 commented that he had had misgivings initially but that he now thought the system was working fine. DM2 gave a qualified endorsement of the new system. The next five district managers said the system was working well with one very minor difficulty. Some of these comments may have been inspired by a fear of being critical. But regardless of their origin, they put DM3 in a minority position as the only one reporting any serious trouble.

Shortly after this event DM3 told the researcher that he now thought the merchandiser part of the reorganization was working fine for him. He then proceeded to describe how he had made the merchandisers in his district responsible for payroll and profits as well as technical assistance. In effect he was using them in a line capacity as he had done with his assistant district managers in the past. And the merchandisers seemed to welcome the treatment. In this way DM3 could report success with the new system and feel that he was conforming to management's desires.

The second incident is similar but it involves the store managers rather than the merchandisers. The district managers at their meeting were discussing their progress in getting store managers to perform as desired. Some of the district managers spoke in glowing terms and with obvious sincerity of how much more effectively and easily they could supervise stores by working through the store managers. DM3 had no comment to make on the subject at the meeting. Later he renewed his complaint to the researcher that so few men in his district had the aggressive characteristics it took to make a good store manager.

We cannot know the exact influence of the peer group on other district managers, but the repetition of episodes such as these must have left its mark. Even when it only pushed them into rationalizing about their own performance, it still made them uneasy enough to be somewhat more aware of their own behavior pattern and its divergence from the new role requirements.

Influence by Subordinates

The first few store managers formed a rather tightly knit group during their first few months in their new positions. As a group they felt a distinct excitement about the opportunities and challenges of their new positions. After a year many of these men felt somewhat disillusioned. They found that they were not exactly independent businessmen but still part of a large organization. Their initial exaggerated sense of freedom was replaced by frustration. After two years most of these reactions of the group had run their course. Most of the group now felt that they had made real progress toward establishing themselves and achieving the company's objectives, but they were no longer living in a world of illusion. This cycle of feeling is, of course, very understandable and probably could have been predicted. This cycle also had its effect on the behavior of the district managers. The initial exaggerated enthusiasm was met with apprehension, and some steps were taken to curb it. For a while it looked as though the net effect of the subordinates on their district managers was to foster behavior that was designed to stifle independence and initiative down the line.

However, the researcher did see a number of instances of store managers directly influencing the thinking and behavior of their immediate supervisors in the direction of the required roles.

In an earlier chapter we saw an example of this when SM1 reminded DM1 that he was pre-empting SM1's duties by directly answering a question from the meat manager. DM1 stated that he welcomed such reminders to avoid lapsing into old habits.

We saw in Chapter V the self confidence SM2 felt in moving into his new job as a store manager. Having a store manager like SM2 must have helped DM2 ease out of his needs to "be in control" and adopt a more problem-solving, two-way relationship with his subordinates.

On one occasion DM2 was approached by one of his store managers with the complaint that the head meat buyer was conducting a chain-wide contest with prizes going to several winning store meat managers and their respective merchandisers. The store manager complained that leaving the store managers out of the contest implied they were not responsible for the results of their own meat departments. DM2 agreed with the complaint and brought it up the line where it forced a re-examination of the assumptions behind the contest.

DM3 entered one of his stores on a warm summer day and immediately noticed that the air conditioning system was not keeping the temperature down. He immediately commented on this to the store manager and the following conversation took place:

SM: I know, it has been broken for a couple of hours.
DM3: It's really getting hot. We've got to do something about this.
SM: I've called the office and they're sending out a maintenance man.
DM3: Would you like to have me call again?
SM: I don't think that is necessary.

DM3: Have you looked over the equipment?
SM: Yes and there's nothing that can be done until the man gets here.

This ended the conversation and DM3 seemed to be left feeling a little uncomfortable. Clearly his store manager felt competent to handle this problem without DM3's help.

These episodes are simply examples of the many ways some of the more able store managers were acting to influence the behavior of their bosses toward the desired organizational roles. It will be recalled that in Chapter II we saw signs of restlessness with the job constraints at the levels of store department managers. This feeling provided a readiness for change among the managers and a willingness to "stick out their necks" to a modest degree. On the other side of the coin, of course, were many acts of store managers that signaled to the district managers that they still expected to be treated in the traditional fashion. This holdover behavior was to be expected and, by contrast, the acts of store managers that fitted the new model were unique enough to draw the conscious attention of the district managers and to make them more aware of their own behavior. For their part, higher management tried to encourage store managers to "speak up" to their superiors, and to protect them from any adverse consequences of doing so.

Influence by Organized Training Programs

During the two-year period after the reorganization was started, the company conducted several formal training programs that were designed to help implement the desired changes in behavior. The first of these programs was conducted for district managers, and subsequent ones were run for groups of store managers and merchandisers combined. Half of the time in these sessions was devoted to discussing case descriptions of problems other business organizations had had in introducing organizational changes. These discussions were intended to give the groups some perspective on such problems and some experience in thinking about them explicitly and systematically. The other half of the time was devoted to discussions of different aspects of Food World's own organizational changes. Such topics were discussed as the new relations between district managers and store managers in terms both of what was expected by management and of what was actually happening. Often actual company problem situations were described to give the discussions a specific focus.

Again it was hard to assess the influence of these meetings on actual behavior patterns. The meetings were another means by which the new required roles could be explicitly analyzed and compared with the individual's concept of himself and his job as this gradually emerged. For many in these groups the discussion provided their first opportunity for concentrated attention on these issues.

Some of the reactions of the district managers with whom we are familiar will help us assess the influence of these meetings. At one of the last meetings with the district managers, DM2 gave a moving and highly personal account of his own difficulties in learning to live with the new role requirements. When he finished, DM3 blurted out, "Speak for yourself." And yet at the end of the program DM3 commented to the instructor, "Don't be discouraged about me. I've got some things to learn and I'm learning some of them."

Summary

At the first of this chapter we presented the available evidence on the behavior (interaction patterns and self-concepts) of our key individuals some two years after the reorganization was started. The evidence indicated that these individuals, both district managers and store managers, had to some degree brought their behavior more into congruence with the required roles. The evidence of this change

204   THE CHANGING OF ORGANIZATIONAL BEHAVIOR PATTERNS

is not conclusive but it is substantial. The researcher can testify that for the key people involved the making of these changes had not been easy. He witnessed their conscientious efforts to rethink their daily practices and change long-standing habit patterns. They deserve great credit for the results achieved. The top management people would probably view the two years' results as good but not nearly enough. But when one looks at the built-in, self-reinforcing persistence of the historical behavior patterns, it is remarkable that *any* discernible changes had occurred.

In the latter part of this chapter we have been reviewing the different influences on behavior during the two-year period that could help account for the observed change. It is clear that we cannot assign any precise cause and effect relationship between specific influences and changed behavior. Instead the impressive fact that emerges from this review is the multiplicity of ways in which behavior was influenced. To use a favorite phrase of the store operations manager, they had "more than one string in the bow." It was the combination of influences that deserves credit for the change. The top management people had supplemented their initial formal organizational moves by an array of continuing influences—by their own personal behavior pattern, by designing the required interactions into routine procedures, by performance reviews, by meetings, and by formal educational programs. They were assisted in this by the influences that came from peers and subordinates. The resulting changes in behavior patterns had been achieved by the initial formal changes together with this combination of persistent and consistent daily influences.

This assortment of influences used in the Food World situation provides us with a kind of cookbook approach to changing organizational behavior. A pinch of this, a jigger of that, stir well, and behavior has changed. Such a look at organizational influences on behavior can be useful to other administrators. Certainly any administrator, undertaking to effect *similar changes,* would be wise to check the suitability of each of these kinds of influence for his own organizational situation. We probably need to be reminded of the importance of the phrase, similar changes. The top management of Food World wanted its supervisory hierarchy to move from a conformist response to organizational pressure to an adaptive response. If an administrator wants to move an organization in the opposite direction, he has quite a different problem on his hands. And in any situation a literal, unthinking application of the Food World recipe would, of course, be foolish.

Our cookbook approach to understanding behavior changes is useful but not enough. In our final chapter we shall attempt to look at the whole question of behavior changes in organizations from a more general perspective—the perspective of the chemist rather than the cook.

CHAPTER X

Conclusions

THIS CHAPTER will mark a sharp departure from the previous ones. We will be going beyond what is clearly demonstrable from the research data and will be extrapolating from those data to address the general problem of changing organizational behavior. At least one conclusion that has emerged from our study so far is that changing the basic behavior patterns of people in an organization is a very difficult and complex matter. Now that we have seen many complex aspects of the problem, can we find a more unified, consistent, and useful way of conceiving of the entire matter of changing behavior patterns in an organization? Can we take an over-all look at the problem that will provide a general framework of thought for the administrator who must all too frequently be concerned with the details of the process of change? This review will draw together ideas that are scattered throughout our study and restate them in a summary that runs all the risks of simplification for the advantage of perspective.

Throughout this study we have used the term, organizational behavior. The literature of the behavioral sciences is also full of terms like group behavior, cultural behavior, and individual behavior. When we see all these labels in one place we are reminded that the actual, concrete, observable behavior of a person comes unlabeled. It is behavior period. Any label we attach to it is done to highlight certain aspects of behavior that can be understood better by tying them to sets of abstract ideas we shall call dimensions. For our present summarizing purpose we shall look at behavior and the changing of it in terms of three dimensions: (1) the achievement of organizational purpose, (2) the achievement of self-maintenance and growth, and (3) the achievement of social satisfactions.[1] These dimensions are sets of ideas that act as goals for men and thereby act as powerful basic influences on concrete, human behavior. The relevance of these three dimensions to our problem of change will emerge as we proceed, but first let us explore the nature of our first dimension, the achievement of organizational purpose.

ACHIEVEMENT OF ORGANIZATIONAL PURPOSE

There exists a wealth of terms and concepts that man has invented to talk in abstract terms about organizational systems. The Food World people used a currently popular term, decentralization. Other familiar terms are: delegation, assignment of authority and responsibility, chain of command, division of labor, span of control, coordination, line and staff organization, and so on. Let us be presumptive enough to push these concepts to one side for a moment and to make a somewhat fresh start at constructing our own conceptual model for talking about organizations.

Certainly any organization to achieve its purpose must have a set of activities designed to perform its purpose—it must have a production system. The exact nature of these required activities can be logically deduced from its purpose. In a business organization, they will normally include both the activities required to produce the desired goods or services (ideally using the best available technological knowledge on both methods and division of labor), and also a set of distribution activities (ideally using the best available knowledge for determining the precise needs of the external market and the least costly means of filling these needs at the proper time and place). But our ideal organization could not function on this alone.

[1] For the underlying ideas in this approach the researcher is heavily indebted to F. J. Roethlisberger, et al, *Training for Human Relations: An Interim Report* (Boston, Harvard Business School, Division of Research, 1954). See especially Chapter VIII.

Our organization must also have a set of interactions that serves to bind the required activities together—it must have a communication-decision system. Such a system would ideally function to provide each person in the organization with all the available information that could help him perform his assigned activities. It would also function so that the necessary choices or decisions between alternative actions would be made for the organization by the individual who was most expert on the issue involved, regardless of his title or position. By the very nature of their required activities, the people in higher management would presumably be experts on different things from those performing other activities, such as operating machines. But whatever his position, this appropriate decision-maker would also have provided to him all the available creative ideas and suggestions that bore on the issue. This model of a communication-decision system could not properly be labeled either a centralized or decentralized system but simply a functional system. If an organization was getting almost all its decisions made by top management, it probably would be more functional for it to move toward decentralization of decisions, but in another case a move toward centralization could be more functional. The required interactions (our communication-decision system) would then serve to bind the required activities into a purposive whole and to make the necessary adjustments to external changes in technology, the market, or the economics of the field. Still our model is not finished.

We need a set of sentiments that would function to insure the full contribution of those working in the organization. Ideally we would want one sentiment to be dominant in all employees from top to bottom, namely, a complete loyalty to the organizational purpose. This would be the most functional sentiment system conceivable and would serve to bind the contributors into the organizational system.

Finally, we would need a set of organizational codes and

a set of rewards and punishments to enforce the codes. It is not enough that certain activities and interactions be performed and backed up by loyal sentiments. These required activities, interactions, and sentiments need to be explicitly codified and understood by all the employees with an arrangement for rewarding (financially and otherwise) and punishing people for compliance or deviation from these codes. Such a sanction system would ideally use the best available knowledge from the behavioral sciences to design incentives that would both induce and pressure individuals into meeting the requirements for maximizing organizational purpose. This sanction system would be the final functional element that would assure the continued maintenance over time of the required activities, interactions, and sentiments.

This, then, is our model for an organization that is designed to be ideally functional along one dimension, the achievement of organizational purpose. Drawing up such models have been the primary concern of a school of thought known generally as "scientific management" and to some extent by economists. Obviously, many of the ideas expressed above have been drawn from the literature of these fields. By now the reader may be a little horrified (and I personally hope he is) by our model of an ideally functional organization. He may have visions of "1984" [2] or of the epitome of "Organizational Man." [3] We may be assured that there never has been an organization that met this ideal nor do we have any reason to think there ever will be. Nevertheless, while we recoil from the extremes of the model, let us remind ourselves that the purpose it is designated to reach has in it important and essential human values. If our business organizations did not do a reasonable job of achieving their purpose, we would simply not have the material means

[2] George Orwell, *1984* (New York, Harcourt, Brace & Company, 1949).
[3] William H. Whyte, Jr., *The Organization Man* (New York, Simon and Schuster, 1956).

of sustaining our complex civilization. This is so obvious that we sometimes forget it. Man needs goods and services, and it is the purpose of our business organizations to produce and distribute them.

So a model of this kind can be very useful if we remember that it represents a set of ideas working along but one dimension, not a picture of the more complex and messy realities of everyday life. Such a model can serve as a guide to the long-range planning and broad-brush thinking of management in assessing the strengths and weaknesses of their own organization and establishing some goals to strive for to make their organization more functional in achieving its purpose. The planning efforts of the management of Food World can serve as an example of the utility of such a model.

We saw in Chapter III the statements of the Food World management on the objectives of their reorganization. They, of course, wanted to make their organization more functional but their thinking about what they wanted was not so clear cut as it could have been. And clarity of thought in stating objectives is a tremendous aid in meeting objectives. They were not satisfied with the term "decentralization" as a label for their objectives but they could not come up with a better substitute. Using the terms of our model, the top management of Food World would have said instead:

> In the past decade Food World and its industry has concentrated on making our production system more functional in tune with a rapidly changing market and technology. The rate of change in technology and market is slowing down and the organization is reasonably functional in the area. We are also reasonably functional in the area of sentiment; our people by and large feel a strong loyalty to us. Perhaps the only weakness there is that it is directed to the president as a person more than to the organization as such. We hope to change that.
>
> The area in which we are least functional is in our communication-decision system. The most expert people are not

making the decisions in all cases. The flow of necessary information, ideas, and suggestions is not adequate. This results in our production activities not being adequately related to one another or in allowing us to meet quickly rapid changes in our external market. It also is tending to weaken the necessary loyalty sentiments of our middle management people.

This requires us to concentrate on the reorganization of our communication-decision system and of the codes (and rewards and punishments) that tend to perpetuate our present communication-decision system. This then is our over-all plan based on assessing our strengths and weaknesses in each area seen in the light of our changing environment.

Our next step is to translate these over-all plans into operational terms—just what kind of an interaction pattern do we expect of our key supervisors and do we also expect changes in their activities and sentiments? How will we codify these new requirements? What specific steps could be taken now and in the future to try and implement these objectives?

The planning soliloquy above cannot by any means be the whole story of the reorganizational planning as we shall see below, but it does at least provide a way of clarifying what is required to make the organization more functional in achieving its purpose. The limits on the utility of such a model are set by the fact that it is one-dimensional in a world that is multidimensional. The goal of achieving organizational purpose is only one of several major influences on the behavior of people in organizations. The next dimension we shall consider, the achievement of self maintenance and growth, was of great importance in the Food World situation.

Achievement of Self Maintenance and Growth

Our culture places a very high value on the development of the individual personality. The emphasis our society places on this may wax and wane with the times, but to some degree we hold to a belief in giving everyone a chance to fulfill his capacity as a person or, at least, maintain his personal integrity. And, of course, it is a personal value of the highest order to each of us to try and maintain our self respect and realize our own potential. This objective of self maintenance and growth is such an important influence on concrete human behavior that it is certain to become involved in any attempt to change behavior in an organization. What do we know about this dimension that will throw light on organizational change?

In Chapter VIII we presented certain aspects of the "self" theory for understanding individual behavior. In summary, this theory holds that every individual has a self-concept that he strives to maintain and enhance in all of his behavior. This self-concept is a set of ideas, beliefs, and attitudes about self that the individual attempts to keep internally consistent. This theory has facilitated the study of individual development and certain major findings have emerged. The self-concept *tends* to change over time along certain trend lines; from the simple, dependent, and immature; by a process of learning, complication, and growth; toward a condition that has not been very clearly defined but has been variously labeled self-actualization,[4] maturity, fully-functioning,[5] or self-determination.[6] These tendencies are never completely fulfilled in any individual. However, if these growth tendencies are sufficiently blocked, an individual will develop psychoneurotic symptoms. While these tendencies for growth seem to exist in all people, the findings indicate another conclusion that also is of the utmost importance to

[4] A. H. Maslow, *Motivation and Personality* (New York, Harper and Brothers, 1954).
[5] Carl R. Rogers, "Toward a Theory of Creativity," ETC., Vol. XI (1954), II–III.
[6] Urie Bronfenbrenner, "Toward an Integrated Theory of Personality," in Robert R. Blake and Glenn V. Ramsey, "Perception," New York, 1951, pp. 206–257.

us, namely, that the self-concept changes very slowly and can most stubbornly resist outside efforts to change it that are perceived as nothing but threats to the self. Both of these findings (the tendencies for growth and the stubborn resistance to change) tend to be confirmed in this study by our observations of the district managers.

The psychologists have also studied and defined the conditions that seem to facilitate the growth tendencies of the individual.[7] When a person feels accepted for what he is, he can develop increased conscious awareness of his own self–environment relationship. As a person becomes more aware of his behavior, inconsistencies can be recognized (sometimes by an outsider's help) between what a person believes he is (self-concept) and what he does. When inconsistencies are perceived, the person will seek some way to become consistent, generally by choosing to alter his self organization along the growth lines described above. The limited findings of this study in this area again check with these conclusions. DM3 showed no signs of change as long as he remained unable to acknowledge consciously that the reorganization had created an inconsistency between his view of himself as the expert on all store problems and his view of himself as complying with management's directions. As he began to recognize this inconsistency, he chose to begin making some changes.

All these findings indicate that, if an organization wanted to become ideally functional along this one dimension of achieving self maintenance and growth, it would be useful (1) to adopt the way of thinking about individual growth described above, (2) to try and work with, rather than against, the built-in growth tendencies of people, and (3) to try and create the conditions in the organization in which self growth is fostered. These conditions provide a model for an organizational setting that would be ideally functional

[7] See especially Carl R. Rogers, *Client-Centered Therapy* (Boston, Houghton Mifflin Company, 1951).

along this one dimension. Again we must recognize, however, that an exclusive concentration on achieving self growth in an organization would also become a perversion. The seeking of nothing but the optimum development of all the "selves" in an organization would not only ignore the need to relate to others and do a job, but it would probably also demonstrate that we cannot even develop ourselves apart from an involvement in organizational purpose and a small group.

Achievement of Social Satisfactions

This study has had very little to say about the relationship between changing behavior patterns in an organization and the nature of small work groups. There exists, however, a rapidly growing body of literature that addresses this issue. This study did not center on this issue because it was designed to study attempts to change behavior at the middle management level where the intensive study of key people as individuals rather than groups was more rewarding. Nevertheless, any effort to change behavior in an organization must take account of the influence small groups have on behavior.

Small groups offer their members the satisfactions of sociability, spontaneity, and a sense of belonging. There is considerable research evidence that, to attain these everyday human satisfactions, people who are in contact with one another in larger organizations tend to form small informal groups.[8] These groups spontaneously build up routines of interactions and activities to achieve the satisfactions of membership. These behavior routines are developed into

---

[8] See especially:
George C. Homans, *The Human Group* (New York, Harcourt, Brace and Company, 1950).
George F. F. Lombard, *Behavior in a Selling Group* (Boston, Harvard Business School, Division of Research, 1955).
A. Zaleznik, *Worker Satisfaction and Development* (Boston, Harvard Business School, Division of Research, 1956).

group norms that are strong influences on the behavior of every group member. We saw a quick picture of such a group in Food World in our description of the grocery clerks in Chapter II.

These small groups can become very stubborn resistors to change, particularly changes solely designed to improve the achievement of organizational purpose. Several studies have documented this process; the group resists externally initiated change that the members perceive as threatening the routines that give them social satisfactions. These are known as frozen groups, and while they may be securing a fair amount of social satisfactions for their members, they are blocking complications along other dimensions.

If an organization desired to be ideally functional along this dimension, it would give people the widest latitude in choosing the form of their routine interactions and activities so that socially satisfying routines could emerge along with informal group leadership. Once these routines had emerged they would be left strictly alone. Once again, as soon as we state this ideally functional model, its potential for perversion becomes apparent. Such an unidimensional system could provide a very "groupy group" but one without direction and with a control over members that would result in stultifying conformity rather than self growth.

Multi-Functional Approach to Changing Behavior

We have looked at three dimensions that are crucial influences on the behavior of people in organizations. We have explained how an organizational model could be set up that would be ideally functional in achieving the end values that each of these dimensions represent. And, while the human values that are represented in each dimension are very real and important, we saw that the extreme one-dimensional striving for these values can result in a perversion. The perversion is created because any one-dimensional effort leads to the atrophy of the others. To a group of management people the perversion of a sole focus on group satisfactions or self growth may seem the most real. But a sole focus on organizational purpose can be at least as stultifying. It could lead to a pattern of extreme organizational conformity that would not only atrophy other growth tendencies, but would, in time, be self-defeating in achieving purpose. The available research studies and our own observations indicate that this is true, without in the least denying the importance of the achievement of organizational purpose.

These observations lead us quite naturally to exploring the possibilities of taking a multi-functional approach to the creation of new behavior patterns in organizations. Is it possible to construct an explicit model for the behavior of people in an organization that would be functional in all three of the dimensions at the same time? The Food World effort at changing behavior provides an example we can use to test out this idea.

At the beginning of this study we stated that we would use management's reorganizational objectives as our temporary criterion against which to measure and judge what happened. We took their statements and, without changing them appreciably in objective, translated them into operational terms, the required interactions, activities, and sentiments, that could be observed and measured by the researcher. We are now in a position to go one step further; to supply a criterion of our own independent formulation. Was the desired change multi-functional? To what degree? How could it have been improved?

Food World's reorganizational plans were not multi-functional by conscious design. When the top management people worked out their reorganizational plans, they were talking primarily in terms of making the organization more functional in achieving purpose. They did make occasional references to developing individuals and making the company a better place to work, but this was not the focus of their conscious attention. This, of course, is not surprising.

CONCLUSIONS 217

It is customary for business management in our culture to plan consciously to achieve purpose and to leave the steps necessary for the achievement of self growth and group satisfactions to intuitive modifications of the explicit plans. Later we shall raise some questions about the utility of this planning method, but for now we shall proceed to look at the final test for multi-functionality, the results. While this study was not designed to test the over-all results of top management's reorganizational plans (for the simple reason that the final test of the plans must be the test of considerable time), nevertheless a quick review of the trends of the results after two years is in order. Was it possible for the organization to provide the conditions that would promote a somewhat better functioning in all three dimensions at the same time? Was the organization, in fact, moving in the direction of becoming more multi-functional? As of 1957 the answer to both questions is a qualified yes.

The company had by 1957 succeeded in providing to a limited extent the conditions called for by our model of an organization ideally designed to achieve purpose. We saw that they had changed to some degree the workings of their communication-decision procedures to make them more functional. They had begun the job of codifying these new requirements and getting them generally understood in the organization. It was not a picture of perfection but of limited progress toward reaching our model for the conditions that would help achieve purpose. And did these new conditions contribute to achieving purpose?

In terms of the generally accepted test of the market place, the organization was improving in its achievement of purpose. Over the two-year period (fiscal 1955–1957) its sales had increased 50% and its net profit, 75%. It had been improving its competitive standing in the industry. These results cannot, of course, be attributed directly or exclusively to the reorganization, but at least it evidenced that the company was not falling apart competitively in the course of the reorganization. In fact, every available indication was that the organization was moving forward in becoming more functional in achieving its organizational purpose.

As regards the second dimension, we have seen evidence that the organization did succeed to a limited extent in providing conditions that better fostered self growth. We saw several ways in which these conditions were provided, in the behavior of the store operations manager toward his subordinates, in the formal training programs, and in the district managers' meetings. These are merely examples. They, of course, did not provide ideal conditions for self growth but they were improvements. Did growth follow?

Again the evidence shows that the organization was getting a limited success in achieving self growth among the management people being studied. This affirmative answer is based on the assumption that movement toward a balanced problem-solving type of interaction pattern, and toward a greater awareness of self–environment, conflict, and choice, constituted individual growth. The progress of DM2 and DM3 along these lines has been presented. The researcher's observations of store managers showed that some but not all of them were moving in this direction. The researcher observed only one man whose behavior suggested he was moving in the opposite direction, toward greater dependence and rote conformity. There were probably others who were so influenced but there is no reason to think they were not far outnumbered by the ones who were growing. Again the organization seemed to be inching forward in providing a climate that really fostered individual growth at the middle management level.

The evidence of achievement of social satisfactions was not so clear. While this study has not focused on group phenomena, there were signs that the "old timers" among the district managers and others at a comparable level in middle management shared a feeling of camaraderie that had grown out of sharing the struggles of operating the small stores of the thirties. The younger men in these positions were kidded about being "neophytes" and had to wait in line to express their views in group meetings. This group value of seniority and the social satisfactions of membership in such an old timers' group were somewhat weakened by the formal recognition that went to the younger men promoted to be district and store managers and the demotion of a few old timers. These group values were, as we have seen, not completely ignored by top management nor was the old timers' group completely broken up. There were also signs that new membership criteria and new group routines were beginning to emerge that could replace the lost social satisfactions. It was too early to be sure but the possibility existed of the new middle management group forming that derived its social satisfactions as a sort of by-product of its group efforts to solve the problems of the business and its individual members—in other words, solving the problems of purpose and self growth. Certainly by his own behavior the store operations manager was trying to foster such a development. Such a development would be most desirable in making the organization more functional along all three dimensions. Whether this happens is still to be seen.

Our over-all look at the initial results of the Food World organization's efforts to reorganize shows considerable evidence that the organization was becoming more multifunctional. The progress along any one dimension was by no means ideal, but by our criteria a balanced movement along all three dimensions is more desirable than a lopsided development of one while others tend to atrophy. Not perfection but the process of inching along on all fronts is our objective, and Food World seemed to be doing just that, in spite of the fact that in many specific instances simultaneous achievement along all three dimensions was impossible because of conflicting interests. Our Food World example does demonstrate that an organization can draw up a model for becoming more multi-functional and can make over-all headway on all three dimensions of achievement at the same time. In fact, this study suggests that the simultaneous improvement of function in all three dimensions is not only possible but is a *prerequisite* for sustained improvement along any single dimension. This idea has profound implications but it needs much further testing in different settings.

In 1957 there were still influences at work in Food World that could reverse the encouraging trends summarized above. Certain individuals and groups were still in an intuitive way trying to restore the old familiar behavior patterns. They could still succeed. One of the best protections against these efforts was the ability of the leaders of the reorganization to be explicit and clear about what they were striving to achieve in all three dimensions. This brings us to the point where we can address the question: how, on the basis of hindsight, could the reorganizational efforts of the company have been improved?

The researcher was personally impressed with the degree of success the company achieved in its reorganization and the wisdom and skill its top management used in pursuing its objectives. The single suggestion the researcher can offer for improving on the record is in the area of explicit advance planning. We saw throughout this study that, while top management struggled to be explicit about its plans and objectives, it had difficulty in conceptualizing its plans. The researcher believes that the planning models that have been presented so far in this chapter would have helped clarify management's thinking.

By making their models more explicit, management people could have consciously acknowledged their interest in becoming more functional in all three dimensions. This is not a suggestion that they should have given more speeches about developing people and providing social satisfactions. There is probably too much public talking on this subject already. It does mean that the development of plans that took explicit cognizance of their objectives in all three dimensions would have provided them with a firmer guide to their own daily behavior.

With clearer plans they would have felt more comfortable about making the "detours" from a sole striving for purpose that their intuitions told them to take. They could have seen that these "detours" were not really diversions from their objectives but necessary steps to achievement in other dimensions. It would help them to maintain a sense of consistency in their behavior and prepare them to deal with the many sources of resistance.

Clearer planning would provide the top executives with a way of dealing with questions about their motives. They knew that they were not purely money hungry materialists, but they also knew that it was important to achieve organizational purpose. They were interested in making achievements along the lines of self growth and social satisfactions, but they did not want to be accused of being sappy sentimentalists. The idea of stating their objectives as being a balanced multi-functional effort would take them off these hooks. It would give them an assurance in performing their role as leaders of an evolving organization, taking justifiable pride in balanced progress. It would not, we trust, lead to smug self-righteousness. It is the researcher's belief that, with clearer advanced planning, the company could have somewhat improved its remarkable record of achievement along all three dimensions.

There are those, however, who, out of concern for our entire society, voice grave doubts about the wisdom of increasing our conscious planning in all these dimensions. Let us look at these considerations.

Ethical and Societal Considerations

Many writers have recently expressed a concern about certain trends they see in our modern industrial society. Two of these writers who have received considerable attention are David Riesman [9] and William H. Whyte.[10] They are expressing fears that are widespread. The essence of their concern is that too many people are guiding their behavior by the standards of our large organizations and our mass communication media. This researcher will not attempt to judge whether these trends toward mass conformity are as real as claimed. However, one result of their writing is to cast the large-scale organization in the role of the villain that by efficient planning is pushing a conformist pattern onto those it contacts.[11] They are fearful of this power of the large organization to manipulate the lives of its employees. They feel that these trends are a threat to some of the highest ideals of our society. On this point our study can throw some light.

It is our contention that the problem of excessive conformity in our society is not fostered by organizational planning of behavior, per se, but by the kind of models constructed. A large organization could, of course, develop a precise model for the kind of behavior that would solely increase the achievement of organizational purpose. To the extent they succeeded in translating this model into actual behavior (and we have suggested that there are built-in limits to such a success), it would tend to create an "organizational man" stunted in individuality and in capacity to enjoy the homely pleasures of spontaneous conviviality. This would be the objective of the model, and undoubtedly much of this is being attempted. However, this result would be a reflection on the nature of the particular model used—not on the *process* of deliberate and conscious model building.

This study has suggested that it is possible to construct models for behavior that aspire to be multi-functional and

---

[9] David Riesman, *The Lonely Crowd* (New Haven, Yale University Press, 1950).
[10] William H. Whyte, Jr., *op. cit.*
[11] For a further documentation of such attacks see J. D. Glover, *The Attack on Big Business* (Boston, Harvard Business School, Division of Research, 1954).

that take advantage of the best available knowledge about each dimension. The striving to translate such models into actual behavior need not lead to rote conformity to either the dictates of organizational purpose or small group values. When the model has built into it the necessity of increasing the individual's awareness of self–environment and the necessity for personal choice, such a model is asking for the opposite of conformist behavior. It is asking the individual for a thinking, choosing, adaptive response to his environment. It is not a deterministic model that can be pressured into existence. Self growth and social satisfactions can be fostered but not forced.

It is our further contention that developing more explicit multi-dimensional models for the desired behavior in organizations will tend to lead to less selfish manipulation of others and more ethical behavior. All of us are engaged in the process of trying to influence those around us whether we admit it or not. As long as we keep our efforts to manipulate others below the level of conscious attention, we do not have to try and reconcile them with our ideals. As soon as we start being explicit about the kind of behavior we want from others, we have to live with a gnawing inconsistency or try and reconcile our desires with our ideals. In fact, we have here a fourth dimension that is a profound influence on behavior, our shared ideals for achieving a good society.

We express our ideals differently but at certain times everyone seems to feel an identification with our entire society and our noblest hopes for achieving a healthy, open, pluralistic community of men. If our models for the behavior we want in an organization, when made explicit, turn out to be narrowly centered on one dimension, the influence of our ideals comes to bear to change the model. If, on the other hand, our explicit model for behavior is a concerted effort at being functional in all three dimensions discussed above, it will emerge as a model that will meet the test of our social and ethical ideals. This statement will strike some as heretical so it best be restated. If behavior patterns pass the test of being simultaneously functional in achieving organizational purpose, self growth, and social satisfactions, that behavior will contribute to (or at least not be in conflict with) attaining the ethical ideals of our society—and hence be functional along our fourth dimension of contributing to the achievement of a good society.

People bring to their life in an organization not only the influence of the ideals but also the beliefs of our society. They bring with them status beliefs drawn from the larger reference groups they and their fellow employees are identified with. This can be an identification with an ethnic or race group, an educational grouping (grammar, high school, or college level of education), an age category (old men vs. young men), an experience classification, (journeyman, machinist, etc.), a social class, or a combination of these and other status groupings. Some recent studies [12] indicate that in many organizational settings these different status classifications may be the major determinates of group membership—instead of personal capacity to contribute to sociability, development of others, or organizational purpose. Since these classifications are largely predetermined and fixed, to the extent they control behavior in an organization they block achievement along the other three dimensions. And since these classifications are rooted in persistent and widespread beliefs in our society, they can be most stubborn resistants to the changing of behavior patterns in a significant and lasting way. Perhaps the best way of overcoming these freezing influences is that used by the Food World organization, by putting emphasis on achievement in the first three dimensions, while avoiding behavior that would do gross violence to the prevailing status beliefs.

We have now quickly explored four dimensions that are

[12] A study by A. Zaleznik, C. R. Christensen, and F. J. Roethlisberger, *The Motivation, Productivity, and Satisfaction of Workers: A Prediction Study*, to be published in the fall of 1958 by the Division of Research, Harvard Business School, provides, among other things, an intensive study of external status factors as determinants of organizational behavior.

basic influences on the concrete behavior of people in organizations. We have seen the important values inherent in each of these dimensions and the hazard of perversion in each dimension. We have considered the possibility of constructing a model for behavior in an organization that would be functional in all these dimensions. We saw that the Food World effort at reorganization, while inevitably less than perfect in any one dimension, was making headway on all these fronts. In total this has been a rather abstract consideration of the whole problem of changing basic behavior. We have ranged far beyond the evidence of this one study, and many more studies are needed to add to our knowledge of the whole problem. But for now, what can be said to bring our conclusions to bear on the behavior of the individual administrator who is trying to deal with his constant and central problem of introducing behavior changes in his organization? What does all this mean for his behavior?

The Administrator's Role in Changing Organizational Behavior

Our late colleague at the Harvard Business School, Charles I. Gragg, often remarked that the behavior of the administrator would always be an enigma. This study points up some of the reasons. The administrator has to live in a multi-dimensional world with a responsibility for taking action in leading people and in dealing with concrete problems. He must constantly seek multi-functional solutions. This forces him into many paradoxical situations.

The administrator must constantly strive to maintain a consistency in his own behavior while accepting the fact that his behavior will always appear inconsistent from any simple, one-dimensional frame of reference.

The administrator must constantly seek for solutions that resolve conflicts between the interests of the several dimensions, but accept the fact that such conflicts are inevitable and never ending.

The administrator must constantly seek to change behavior in the social system he is a part of but never break up or destroy the system as a viable entity.

The administrator must seek a perfection of balanced development but accept the inevitability of imperfection. Or to state it the other way around, he must be pleased with signs of progress but never be satisfied with them.

The administrator must, by the very nature of his job, put a heavy emphasis on achieving organizational purpose, but he must also seek balanced progress along other dimensions and not expect all others in the organization to give primacy to the achievement of purpose.

The administrator must maintain the perspective of an outside observer on the organization he leads but not lose his impassioned involvement with the results of the system. Or in the words of F. J. Roethlisberger, he must maintain a "disinvolved-involvement."

It is no wonder then that the behavior of the administrator is an enigma. It is one of the most complex and exacting jobs that man can aspire to fill. One of the problems that arose in the Food World situation provides a classic example of this complexity.

Top management was concerned with whether to leave a certain district manager on that job at the time of the initial reorganization. This district manager's daily behavior followed the traditional pattern of the company. He had a demonstrated ability to get profitable results for the short run, but his behavior did not foster self growth or social satisfactions for his subordinates. However, management recognized his right to the chance to grow as a person and perhaps by giving him the proper working climate he could become more self-aware and choose to bring his behavior into line with management's multi-functional objectives. But would he learn? Could the time be spared considering the blocking he was doing to his subordinates? On the other hand, what would be the effect on others of demoting a man who more than met the existing status expectations for the rank of district manager? This was the conflict of interests as seen by an outsider, but the man who had to make the decision was also involved as a feeling, flesh and blood person who was influenced by the ties of friendship, and subject to the disappointments and irritations of trying to help the man work out a changed behavior pattern. It is not easy to say what a consistent multi-functional course of action would be in such a situation. Our concepts are useful to help us describe the problem clearly but they do not provide any automatic answer.

The administrator can be helped by clearer ways of thinking about the problems of changing behavior in an organization, and by increased knowledge from research studies, but these helps can never remove from him the most difficult process of weighing the factors in a given situation, searching creatively for the solution that is as functional as possible along as many dimensions as possible, and energetically and feelingly committing himself to a decision. This will never be easy. But the challenge to the administrator remains. It is the great abiding challenge of seeking his own self-fulfillment by leading in the creation of new and better institutions for achieving human values.

APPENDIX

Methodology of the Measurement of Interaction Patterns

THE SYSTEMATIC observational method used in the study was specifically designed to measure certain aspects of the interactions between an organizational superior and his subordinate. For the purposes of this study the researcher was interested in measuring changes in the behavior patterns of management people. The one element of behavior that was "supposed" to change and that was also directly observable was the element of interactions. The aspects of interactions that were "supposed" to change were not the more commonly measured aspects of frequency of interaction and direction of initiation, however, but rather more subtle matters of content and control. In other words, the measuring device needed to throw light on such matters as degree of delegation vs. domination, the problem-solving qualities of the interaction, and the degree of balance in the flow of information, opinion, and directions. These objectives governed the design of the method. They created a need to devise a system to record the duration and content category of each separate comment made by the participants. This called for a relatively complex recording system.

The researcher found, however, that it was possible to record such detailed aspects of interactions in the field by using a small lined notebook and a simple system of recording symbols. Exhibit 17 presents a sample page of the notebook that records about fifteen minutes of interaction. This field system evolved on a trial-and-error basis, and in the form shown in the exhibit it proved to be entirely practical. While actually scoring a conversation, the researcher frequently checked the time by wrist watch. Later the time totals for the interaction were added up by using a ruler to measure the vertical length of the lines in each category. The total number of comments could be secured by simply counting up the different marks. As is apparent in the exhibit, it was also possible to readily keep a record of new topics as they were initiated. In addition, the researcher found it useful to record on this sheet additional details of any conversation he wanted to recall for subsequent dictation on an approximate verbatim basis.

In several ways the characteristics of the Food World organization facilitated making systematic interaction observations. The superior-subordinate interactions of special interest were, of course, those between the district manager and the store manager. The geographical dispersion of the stores made it usually necessary for the district manager to take the initiative in interacting with his subordinates, to interact with one subordinate at a time, and to take an appreciable amount of time for each interaction. This meant that the researcher, simply by traveling with the district manager, could conserve his own time in observing interactions in a concentrated form, and not have too many other things getting into the act. Each "call" by a district manager on a store was also a distinct and complete episode that could be compared with other such "calls." All these conditions for observation at Food World facilitated the systematic observation of interactions but they were not essential to it.

In selecting the categories of speech (questions, information, opinions, suggestions or directions) the researcher was guided by the earlier work of Robert Bales.[1] These categories proved to be practical in use in the sense that two observers, with practice, could secure a high degree of agreement on how to categorize different comments. In categorizing comments, the researcher followed the manifest intent of the speaker rather than either the literal interpretation of his

[1] *Interaction Process Analysis.*

EXHIBIT 17
Sample Interaction Scoring Sheet

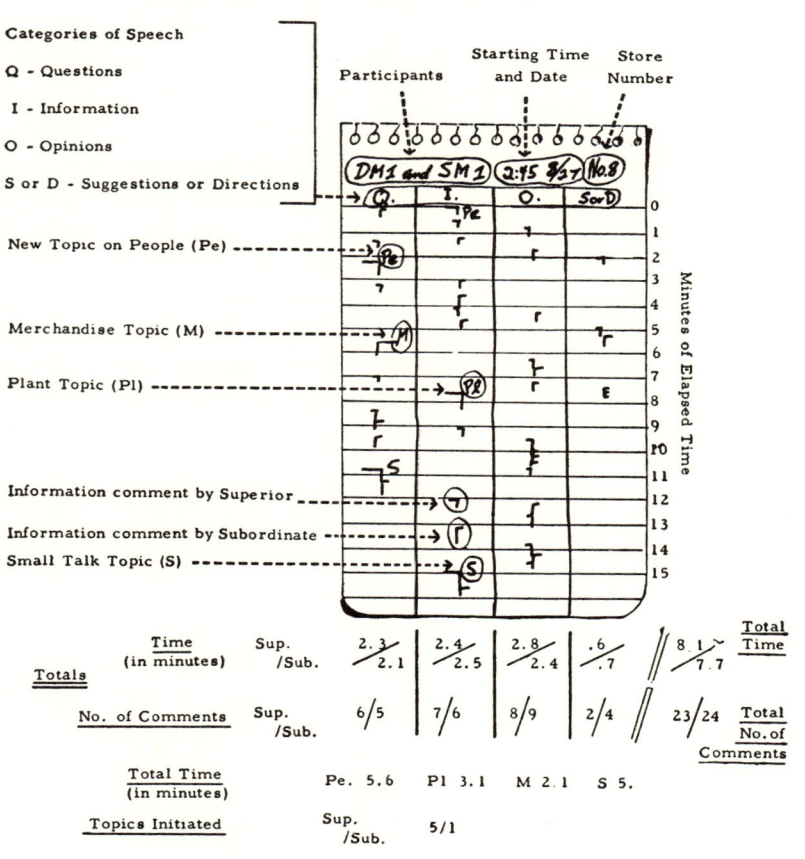

Categories of Speech
- Q - Questions
- I - Information
- O - Opinions
- S or D - Suggestions or Directions

New Topic on People (Pe)

Merchandise Topic (M)

Plant Topic (Pl)

Information comment by Superior

Information comment by Subordinate

Small Talk Topic (S)

Totals

Time (in minutes)	Sup./Sub.	2.3/2.1	2.4/2.5	2.8/2.4	.6/.7	8.1/7.7	Total Time
No. of Comments	Sup./Sub.	6/5	7/6	8/9	2/4	23/24	Total No. of Comments

Total Time (in minutes)   Pe. 5.6   Pl 3.1   M 2.1   S 5.

Topics Initiated   Sup./Sub.   5/1

words or the way they were perceived by the hearer. For example, a comment such as, "In my opinion, you should do so and so about that display" would be scored as a *suggestion or direction* rather than an *opinion*. On the other hand, a comment, "I don't like the appearance of that display," would usually be scored as an *opinion* even though the person spoken to might perceive it as a *suggestion or direc-*

tion. To take another example, a comment from a superior such as, "Why don't you rearrange that display?" would usually be scored as a *suggestion or direction* in spite of the question mark. It is conceivable, of course, that in a different verbal context or with a different inflection it would be properly scored as a request for information, a *question.*

The above examples indicate the rather obvious fact that the researcher had to make on-the-spot judgments in scoring comments and this could contribute to confused scoring. However, these problems proved to be fairly manageable in practice. The two men who did field scoring on this project practiced independently scoring the same conversations and comparing results until very nearly identical scoring results were achieved. The amount of remaining scoring error could, of course, be measured even though it was not done in this study. The problem of consistent scoring proved more difficult in the categorization of topics.

The topic categories (people, records, merchandise, plant, and small talk) were selected on a rather arbitrary basis after the researcher had acquired considerable familiarity with the business. Later experience did not reveal any other topical categories that would have had greater research utility. However, some difficulty was experienced in categorizing the various conversations by these topics. This arose because frequently conversations were about compound topics. For example, a discussion of an individual's pay rate might be scored either as a *people* topic or a *record* topic. In practice on-the-spot judgment had to be used as to whether the major focus of attention was on the individual, per se, or on the wage regulations, payroll procedures, etc. The topic was then scored according to this major focus. The two field men were less confident of their consistency in making these scoring discriminations.

Another minor difficulty that arose in using this research method was in scoring the parts of any conversation that the researcher became a participant in. After the researcher had

APPENDIX 233

spent considerable time traveling with district managers, his role as a silent observer became well accepted so that there were relatively few times when there was any need to enter the conversation. On these few occasions that portion of the conversation was eliminated for purposes of scoring interaction patterns.

This study was, clearly, not focused on the development and refinement of the field quantification of interaction patterns as a research tool. But in spite of its lack of refinement, this research method proved to be highly useful for this study and could well prove useful in other studies of organizational behavior. Certainly it opens up many possibilities of relating interaction profiles to data on satisfaction, productivity, social structure, etc.

BIBLIOGRAPHY

Bales, Robert Freed. *Interaction Process Analysis; A Method for the Study of Small Groups.* Cambridge: Addison-Wesley Press, 1950.

Barnard, C. I. *The Functions of the Executive.* Cambridge: Harvard University Press, 1947.

Blake, Robert R., and Ramsey, Glenn V. *Perception: Approach to Personality.* New York: Ronald Press, 1951.

Blau, Peter M. *The Dynamics of Bureaucracy: A Study of Interpersonal Relations in Two Government Agencies.* Chicago: University of Chicago Press, 1955.

Cantril, Hadley. *The "Why" of Man's Experience.* New York: The Macmillan Company, 1950.

Glover, J. D. *The Attack on Big Business.* Boston: Division of Research, Harvard Business School, 1954.

Gouldner, Alvin W. *Patterns of Industrial Bureaucracy.* Glencoe, Ill.: Free Press, 1954.

Gouldner, Alvin W. *Wildcat Strike.* Yellow Springs, Ohio: Antioch Press, 1954.

Homans, George C. *The Human Group.* New York: Harcourt, Brace and Company, 1950.

Jacques, Elliott. *The Changing Culture of a Factory.* London: Tavistock Publications, Ltd., 1951.

Kaye, Carol, "The Effects on Organizational Goal Achievement of a Change in the Structure of Roles," paper presented at the American Psychological Association as part of the Symposium on *Change in Control Processes in Social Organization: A Field Experiment,* New York, September 4, 1954.

Lecky, Prescott. *Self-Consistency.* New York: Island Press, 1945.

Lombard, George F. F. *Behavior in a Selling Group: A Case*

Study of Interpersonal Relations in a Department Store. Boston: Division of Research, Harvard Business School, 1955.

Lombard, George F. F., "Self-Awareness and Scientific Method," *Science,* Vol. 117, No. 2907, 1950.

Mann, Floyd, "Changing Superior-Subordinate Relationships," *The Journal of Social Issues,* Vol. VII, No. 3, 1951.

Maslow, A. H. *Motivation and Personality.* New York: Harper & Brothers, 1954.

Mayo, Elton. *The Social Problems of an Industrial Civilization.* Boston: Division of Research, Harvard Business School, 1945.

Morse, Nancy. *Satisfactions in the White Collar Job.* Ann Arbor: Survey Research Center, Institute for Social Research, University of Michigan, 1953.

Morse, Nancy C., and Reimer, Everett, "The Experimental Change of a Major Organizational Variable," *The Journal of Abnormal and Social Psychology,* Vol. 52, No. 1, 1956.

Reimer, Everett, "Creating Experimental Social Change in an Ongoing Organization," paper presented at the American Psychological Association as part of the Symposium on *Change in Control Processes in Social Organization: A Field Experiment,* New York, September 4, 1954.

Riesman, David. *The Lonely Crowd: A Study of Changing American Character.* New Haven: Yale University Press, 1950.

Roethlisberger, F. J., and Dickson, William J. *Management and the Worker.* Cambridge: Harvard University Press, 1939.

Roethlisberger, F. J., Lombard, George F. F., Ronken, Harriet O., and others. *Training for Human Relations: An Interim Report of a Program for Advanced Training and Research in Human Relations, 1951–1954.* Boston: Division of Research, Harvard Business School, 1954.

Rogers, Carl R. *Client-Centered Therapy.* Boston: Houghton Mifflin Company, 1951.

Rogers, Carl R., "Toward a Theory of Creativity, *ETC.*, Vol. XI, II–III, 1954.

Ronken, Harriet O., and Lawrence, Paul R. *Administering Changes: A Case Study of Human Relations in a Factory.* Boston: Division of Research, Harvard Business School, 1952.

Snygg, Donald, and Combs, A. W. *Individual Behavior.* New York: Harper & Brothers, 1949.

Tannenbaum, Arnold W., and Allport, Floyd H., "Personality Structure and Group Structure: An Interpretative Study of Their Relation Through an Event-Structure Hypothesis," *The Journal of Abnormal and Social Psychology,* Vol. 53, No. 3, 1956.

White, William H. *The Organization Man.* New York: Simon and Schuster, 1956.

Whyte, William F. *Leadership and Group Participation.* Ithaca, New York: State School of Industrial and Labor Relations, Cornell University. Bulletin No. 24, May 1953.

Whyte, William F. *Pattern for Industrial Peace.* New York: Harper & Brothers, 1951.

Zaleznik, A., *Worker Satisfaction and Development: A Case Study of Work and Social Behavior in a Factory Group.* Boston: Division of Research, Harvard Business School, 1956.

Zaleznik, A., Christensen, C. R., and Roethlisberger, F. J. *The Motivation, Productivity, and Satisfaction of Workers: A Prediction Study.* Boston: Division of Research, Harvard Business School, 1958.

92009362

```
HD          Lawrence, Paul R.
58          The Changing of
.8          organizational
.L38        behavior patterns
   1991
```

DATE DUE			